The Eclipse

of the Demos

THE ECLIPSE

OF THE

DEMOS

The Cold War

and the Crisis of

Democracy before

Neoliberalism

Kyong-Min Son

University Press of Kansas

© 2020 by the University Press of Kansas

Permission from *American Political Thought* for an earlier version of chapter 4: © 2018 by The Jack Miller Center.

Published by the University Press of Kansas (Lawrence, Kansas 66045), which was organized by the Kansas Board of Regents and is operated and funded by Emporia State University, Fort Hays State University, Kansas State University, Pittsburg State University, the University of Kansas, and Wichita State University.

Library of Congress Cataloging-in-Publication Data
Names: Son, Kyong-Min, author.
Title: The eclipse of the demos : the Cold War and the crisis of democracy before neoliberalism / Kyong-Min Son.
Description: Lawrence, Kansas : University Press of Kansas, [2020] | Includes bibliographical references and index.
Identifiers: LCCN 2019042726
    ISBN 9780700629190 (cloth)
    ISBN 9780700629206 (paperback)
    ISBN 9780700629213 (epub)
Subjects: LCSH: Democracy. | Cold War. | Neoliberalism. | Political culture.
Classification: LCC JC423 .S685 2020 | DDC 306.209/045—dc23
LC record available at https://lccn.loc.gov/2019042726.

British Library Cataloguing-in-Publication Data is available.

Printed in the United States of America

10 9 8 7 6 5 4 3 2 1

The paper used in this publication is recycled and contains 30 percent postconsumer waste. It is acid free and meets the minimum requirements of the American National Standard for Permanence of Paper for Printed Library Materials Z39.48–1992.

To Namkyeong

CONTENTS

ACKNOWLEDGMENTS

This book began its life as my doctoral dissertation, and I owe a debt of gratitude first of all to my wonderful committee. Susan Buck-Morss introduced me to the world of critical theory and encouraged me to find my own perspectives with patience and enthusiasm. Isaac Kramnick guided me with his erudition, matched only by his kindness. Jason Frank inspired me with his insightful approach to democratic theory, as well as through many conversations. And Richard Bensel read everything I wrote with superhuman dedication, pushing me to make my arguments clearer and more rigorous. I was also fortunate to meet Aziz Rana, who generously served as my external reader, and whose interest in my project and thoughtful comments were indispensable. Even though I did not realize at the time how far I would have to travel to get to this book, what I learned from them and, perhaps most important, their example have been a continuing source of inspiration.

Many friends and colleagues read drafts, talked things over with me, and offered advice and encouragement at various points in writing the book. I am especially grateful to Sonja Amadae, David Ciepley, Emily Hauptman, Bonnie Honig, Sharon Krause, and Marc Stears for their exemplary work and the conservations we had. I was privileged to complete this book at the University of Delaware, surrounded by great colleagues and friends. I wish to thank Wayne Batchis, Gretchen Bauer, Daniel Green, Kara Ellerby, Phil Jones, Daniel Kinderman, Dave Redlawsk, Matt Weinert, and especially Alice Ba and Claire Rasmussen for their support and friendship. Earlier versions of various parts of the book were presented at Seoul National University's Institute for Political Studies, and at the annual meetings of the American Political Science Association, the Western Political Science Association, and the Association for Political Theory. I am thankful to discussants, panelists, and audiences whose feedback was invaluable to refining and augmenting my arguments.

My research for chapter 4 was generously funded by the University of Delaware's General University Research Grant.

An earlier, shorter version of chapter 4 was previously published as "Cybernetic Freedom: David Easton, Systems Thinking, and the Search for Dynamic Stability," *American Political Thought* 7, no. 4 (2018): 614–645. Earlier versions of parts of chapters 3 and 5 appeared in "The Cold War Origins of the 'Crisis of Democracy,'" *Democratic Theory* 5, no. 1 (2018): 39–63. And small portions of chapters 3 and 5 were published, respectively, in "A Discordant Universe of Pluralisms: Response to Wenman," *Political Theory* 43, no. 4 (2015): 533–540 and "The Making of the Neoliberal Subject: Response to Whyte," *Political Theory* 47, no. 2 (2019): 185–193. I thank these journals for allowing me to reprint parts of these essays here.

I am deeply grateful to David Congdon, my editor at the University Press of Kansas, who believed in this project and offered key editorial suggestions, as well as to the two anonymous reviewers whose truly helpful feedback allowed me to significantly improve the book. Needless to say, I alone am responsible for all remaining errors and flaws.

No words can fully express my gratitude to my family. My parents' unconditional faith in me sustained me through the long process of writing. My brother Sungmin, also in the profession of pursuing those everelusive bits of knowledge, understood my struggles and humbled me with his devotion and hard work. Taein, my sister-in-law, created the images used in this book with an expert's hands. Sojin and Soyun endured Dad's perpetual retreat to the office. Finally, I owe an immeasurable debt of gratitude to Namkyeong. Without her wisdom, love, patience, and tireless optimism, I could not have finished this process, which felt, at times, as if it was determined not to end. This book is dedicated to her.

CHAPTER ONE

Democratic Theory and
the Crisis of Democracy

> The old saying that the cure for the ills of democracy is more
> democracy is not apt if it means that the evils may be remedied by
> introducing more machinery of the same kind as that which already
> exists, or by refining and perfecting that machinery. But the phrase
> may also indicate the need of returning to the idea itself, of clarifying
> and deepening our apprehension of it, and of employing our sense of
> its meaning to criticize and re-make its political manifestations.
>
> —John Dewey (1927)

One of the most remarkable phenomena after the end of World War II is the
global spread of democracy. In 1941 there were only eleven democracies in
the entire world. By the end of the twentieth century, however, 119 out of
192 countries could be described as electoral democracies. The worldwide
trend in favor of democracy had been so striking that a recent Freedom
House report announced that the twentieth century was "democracy's
century."[1] Not surprisingly, the extraordinary ascendance of democracy
has invited a number of celebratory accounts. Francis Fukuyama declared
as early as 1989 that liberal democracy marks "the end point of mankind's
ideological evolution" and "the final form of human government."[2] While
acknowledging the presence of serious social ills in old democracies and
the precariousness of new democracies, Fukuyama nonetheless insisted
that "these problems were ones of incomplete implementation of the

twin principles of liberty and equality on which modern democracy is founded, rather than of flaws in the principles themselves."[3] For him, liberal economics and liberal politics constitute a virtuous circle. Capitalist industrialization, especially when accompanied by universal education, spurs popular demands for equal recognition, which Hegel identified as a distinctly human quality and the primary driving force of human history. Liberal politics, in turn, provide the only mechanism that can channel the struggle for recognition into a peaceful competition by "replac[ing] the irrational desire to be recognized as greater than others with a rational desire to be recognized as equal."[4]

Historical prognostication is a risky thing to do. Euphoria had barely run its course before democracies began to show signs of trouble. According to Freedom House, the spread of electoral democracy stalled around 2000 and was reversed in the mid-2000s. Observing this trend, its most recent report now speaks of a "decade of decline."[5] Even in countries that are still considered democracies, substantive features of democracy, such as political participation, the rule of law, and the representativeness of political institutions, show signs of sharp deterioration[6]—so much so that scholarly attention has shifted from democratization and democratic consolidation to "defective democracies,"[7] "democratic backsliding,"[8] and "de-democratization."[9] Nor are symptoms of crisis observed solely in new democracies. In the United States and Europe, signals abound that both people's electoral participation and their trust in established democratic institutions are declining,[10] leading prominent observers to identify "democratic disaffection" as a major challenge facing advanced democracies in the twenty-first century.[11] Democratic theorists have been preoccupied with a "crisis of democracy" for some time now;[12] the recent surge of populism is only putting it on dramatic display.

In late Middle English, to which we can trace the current use of the term "crisis," crisis meant the turning point of a disease that might lead to death or recovery.[13] The current crisis-of-democracy debate reflects this ambivalence and uncertainty. Some scholars stress the existing democratic institutions' less-than-optimal performance[14] and propose various ways to make those institutions more responsive and participatory.[15] Others advance a more fundamental critique, pointing to the detrimental impact of neoliberalism, which dismantles citizens' entitlements, undermines government's capabilities and authority while empowering corporations,[16] and displaces citizens' commitment to social cooperation and the responsible collective use of power.[17] Still others contend that what we are witnessing is not so much a crisis as a transition to a different type of democracy. According to these thinkers, broad social changes such as globalization and the rise of new communication technologies like the internet are eroding the efficacy of conventional models of political participation and representation and facilitating the ascendance of alternative modes of democratic action.[18] From this perspective, pervasive distrust may actually be a sign of democracy's health that demonstrates individual citizens' political sophistication and increased capabilities for critical thinking.[19]

The current debate on the crisis of democracy, I suggest, can benefit from a closer look at the development of democratic theory in the post–World War II era. In particular, this approach helps us address two related lacunae in some of the most prevailing diagnoses of democracy's ailment today. First, the current debate is implicitly framed by a binary between institutions and citizens, as scholars point either to the institutional decay or to citizens' unconventional activism in their interpretation of signs such as low turnout and declining institutional trust. But I argue that this disagreement elides a crucial condition of democracy's health. Responding to its members' demands is surely one of democracy's main functions, but that is true of other political systems as well, if in varying degrees. What makes democracy distinct is the premise that power must be shared and exercised by citizens so as to ensure that their demands continue to shape the direction and contours of their community. In other words, democracy is a public institution that organizes power in a particular way—and not just an instrument that individuals already possessing different levels of power use to advance their private interests—and partaking in it entails accepting certain constraints on individual freedom. (As I will elaborate in chapter 2, it is the same with all other principles of social coordination, including the "free market.") Citizens' commitment to this premise is what sustains democracy, but this vital condition is obscured when we only ask how freely people make their demands or how efficiently institutions satisfy the electorate's wants.

Second, we need to expand the purview of our inquiry beyond neoliberalism. Recent years have seen numerous accounts of how neoliberalism penetrates into and undermines democracy. While these accounts are compelling, their exclusive focus on neoliberalism as the culprit of the erosion of democracy risks portraying it as a more coherent and powerful force than it actually is, and turning attention away from democracy's internal problems that might make it vulnerable to neoliberalism. Also, as critics foreground neoliberalism, they end up establishing the late 1970s as the starting point of the crisis of democracy, and describing the postwar period preceding neo-liberalism's visible ascendance as the golden age of democracy. I challenge this view and suggest that neoliberalism did not simply attack democracy from without but seized on and exploited tendencies within democracy that had already been formed in the postwar era. In the following sections I examine these two problems limiting the current debate on the crisis of democracy and make the case that a fresh look at the reconstruction of democratic theory during the Cold War can help address them.

Beyond the Activist Conception of the Demos

As I noted at the outset, scholars disagree about whether the current moment marks a decline of democracy or its transition to a less mediated form of popular sovereignty. Despite evident differences, however, they operate within the same theoretical framework predicated on a particular conception of "the people," or the demos. The assumption here is that the demos consists of those who *make* certain political claims directed at institutions, and democracy is a matter of whose claims are heard and addressed by institutions. We might call this an activist conception of the demos, since it foregrounds people's action or inaction. The activist conception leads us to conclude that democracy is in crisis when not enough people get to make their claims, or when institutions fail to satisfy all constituents' expressed claims as fully as possible. In this respect, the crisis-of-democracy debate reflects the broader trend in contemporary democratic theory, in which theorists are divided between those who focus on enhancing the legitimacy of representative institutions,[20] and those who try to make democracy more participatory,[21] inclusive,[22] or "fugitive."[23] Here, too, the focus is squarely on people's claims-making activities. Some theorists try to regulate how those claims are made, whereas others resist those regulations as another way of perpetuating institutional exclusion and marginalization, pushing instead to get more people recognized as claimants. But they both define the demos in opposition to institutions, either as a source of their legitimacy or as a disruptive force that exposes their failings and animates their alterations.

The activist conception of the demos illuminates an intuitive and indispensable dimension of democratic politics. Certainly, a society's institutional response to people's demands must be one of the main yardsticks by which we judge its democratic credentials. However, the activist conception also constrains our view, not least because it lands us in a binary conception of democracy that pits people against institutions. For some, the demos as a claims-making entity poses a potential threat to democratic institutions. No matter how democratic, political institutions can accommodate only so much; if too many people make too many demands at once, institutions become "overloaded" and unsustainable.[24] For others, the demos is indeed positioned against institutions, but that is not a threat but a boon to democracy; institutions become sterile and oppressive as they inevitably contain people's claims making within preset parameters.[25]

This binary can be blinding in a number of ways. For one, it can make us too quickly accept the notion—which I will dispute shortly—that the demos is always at odds with institutional stability. Also, it can lead us to overstate the significance of constant and direct popular participation while dismissing the democratic potential of institutions in too categorical a manner. As Bernard Manin reminds us, the principal feature of direct democracy, for which Greek democracy often serves as the archetype, was not everyone's constant participation but the institutional assurance that everyone gets to experience—on a rotating basis—the power, and the burden, of managing public affairs.[26] On the other hand, representative mechanisms do not always render citizens passive political subjects. When major issues or events occur, for example, elections can be a powerful occasion in which previously passive or indifferent individuals develop an enduring sense of political agency. Likewise, as a number of theorists have recently argued, representation and leadership are not invariably elitist but can empower citizens by bringing them together and exposing them to issues and perspectives transcending their immediate concerns, creating a symbiotic rather than antagonistic relationship with participation.[27]

We can identify another equally essential aspect of the demos: a distinct kind of *responsiveness*. A full theoretical account is offered in chapter 6, but I conceptualize this responsiveness as attunement to public claims appealing to the common good and political equality. Democratic attunement is not a cognitive skill—like cost-benefit analysis—that one chooses to deploy in each instance of judgment. Rather, it is an embodied disposition that precedes that choice; it is what activates our attention and orients our response. We do not make a deliberate choice every time we are faced with various issues competing for our attention; we simply take certain matters more seriously than others. Likewise, we rarely engage in a full-blown evaluation of all the skills in our possession before using some of them to respond to the issue at hand; we just rely on them, whether it be cost-benefit analysis, moral reasoning, or heuristics such as ideological judgment. Put differently, democratic attunement is one possible con-figuration of subjectivity, a relatively settled way of being, thinking, and judging. (I elaborate my approach to the problem of subjectivity in chapter 2 through an engagement with the contemporary literature on affect.)

In developing the conception of democratic attunement, I build on a growing literature in contemporary political theory that stresses respon-siveness and attentiveness as a crucial civic and democratic virtue.[28] This so-called ethical turn is animated by the awareness that democracy can-not be reduced to institutions, as well as by the dissatisfaction with the elevation of reason as the primary quality of the democratic citizen, and I share these concerns. But as critics have pointed out, this literature has (so far) focused almost solely on ontology, without linking individual ethics to democracy as a collective organizing principle, especially in relation to historical, structural, and ideological factors that shape and constrain the cultivation of an ethic at the individual level.[29] I take a different approach in this book and treat democratic attunement less as an ethical goal than as a discursively and socially conditioned entity. Democratic attunement belongs, along with other subjectivities, to a distinct political economy, meaning that it is produced, circulated, and "consumed" (embodied by individuals) in patterned rather than random ways. As such, it can become dominant or marginal depending on how democracy is conceptualized, organized, and practiced. This book, then, examines how the transforma-tion of democratic theory during the Cold War created a discursive political economy that eclipses democratic subjectivity.

The concept of democratic attunement as an essential trait of the demos opens up avenues of inquiry otherwise unavailable when we are beholden to the activist conception. For example, the activist conception focuses our attention on the *distribution* of decision-making power, that is, on the question of how much power one possesses to influence institutional decisions. In doing so, it elides an entire domain of issues concerning the *nature* and *organization* of power. Insofar as decision-making does not take place in a vacuum, determining the normative criteria by which specific decisions are guided, creating and maintaining sites in which decision-making is undertaken, and responding to the decisions made—all of which are not overt claims-making activities—are to be viewed as equally crucial elements of popular sovereignty. To account for these concerns, we need to expand our understanding of the demos.

Though perhaps not readily tangible or measurable, democratic attunement is neither a utopian luxury nor an expendable supplement. Democracy cannot sustain itself without citizens committed to the primacy of the (contested) notion of the common good and political equality in their collective life. It is that commitment that secures their allegiance to democracy even when they are inevitably disappointed by specific political outcomes. As Danielle Allen puts it, "The hard truth of democracy is that some citizens are always giving things up for others. Only vigorous forms of citizenship can give a polity the resources to deal with the inevitable problem of sacrifice."[30] Nor is civic forbearance the only issue at stake. When citizens do not recognize the primacy of democratic claims, responding to those claims is a costly, and thus rarely justifiable, endeavor. Freed from the public's vigilance, democratic institutions succumb to the rivalry or alliance of competing private interests and thus deepen the public's apathy and cynicism even further. This goes on, until democracy, hollowed out, systematically works in favor of powerful minorities at the expense of the majority—a situation that most people resent but are too powerless to correct. When the gap between a society's professed dedication to democratic principles and its autocratic reality becomes too glaring to conceal, democracy finds itself in an extremely volatile situation, which is often exploited by demagoguery.

The activist conception of the demos, and the accompanying blindness to the problem of democratic responsiveness, was reified in the postwar era. The encounter with totalitarianism brought to the very forefront of intellectual consciousness the notion that the majority of people were unfit or even dangerous to be directly involved in political matters. Put differently, in the postwar era "the masses" as the lethal threat to democracy overshadowed "the people" as the legitimate foundation of popular sovereignty. As a result, Cold War democratic theorists juxtaposed people's political activities with the stability of existing democratic institutions, arguing in favor of the latter. Critics vigorously contested this stance, to be sure, but typically by valorizing political participation while failing to challenge both the binary framework in which popular political participation always stands opposed to institutional stability and the one-dimensional conception of power that links it exclusively to decision-making. While largely bypassing the problem of democratic subjectivity, critics simply complained that elites were granted too much decision-making power and citizens too little.

Some of the familiar labels of Cold War democratic theory—such as "elitist," "procedural," "minimalist," or "competitive"[31]—are, while certainly illuminating, the products of a critique that falls short of fully confronting some of its target's central presuppositions and most troubling implications. At stake are not simply a quantitative diminishment of democracy (as indicated by minimalist democracy), disproportionate attention to representative institutions at the expense of the distribution of power in the society at large (as implied by procedural democracy), or an overblown faith in elites (as signaled by elitist or competitive democracy). Rather, what is really distinct about postwar democratic theory is that it abandoned the conception of democracy as a public institution organizing collective life and redefined it exclusively as an instrument that individuals use only to advance their private interests. In other words, the midcentury iteration of democracy naturalized *instrumental democracy*.

Instrumental democracy does not simply reduce room for citizens' political activity. Rather, by turning democracy into an instrument for private gains, it induces generalized indifference to democratic claims—claims that do not affect individual citizens' immediate interests. Put differently, it is a type of democracy that systematically marginalizes and displaces democratic subjectivity. While critics did note Cold War democratic theory's embrace of political apathy, they did not always explore its meaning in depth, treating it merely as a barrier to political participation, sometimes collapsing apathy and inactivity into a single category contrasted to participation. Because they did not specify what democratic subjectivity is and how it connects to democratic institutions, critics were not equipped to directly challenge the claim that a certain level of apathy helps maintain the stability of the existing form of democracy—one of the main reasons why many Cold War democratic theorists advocated instrumental democracy. This is partly why the debate about postwar democratic theory often resulted in a stalemate: critics complained that their opponents placed too much emphasis on stability while understating or ignoring the value of participation, and proponents simply reversed the complaint and returned it.

In this book, I recast this binary and reinterpret the development of democratic theory during the Cold War as the consolidation of instrumental

democracy that systematically thwarts and displaces democratic attunement as a key quality of the demos. My primary aim is to examine how
various intellectual trends gained ground against a particular historical
backdrop to find their way into an instrumental conception of democracy,
and to show how instrumental democracy's internal logics deflect citizens'
attention and commitment away from democratic claims. I will elaborate
my argument over the course of the book, but it is striking that a conception of democracy with such a deep apprehension toward the demos was
embraced so wholeheartedly as a democratic ideal in the postwar era.
To be sure, distrust of the demos is hardly unprecedented in the history
of political thought. Plato likened the masses to a lawless and easily manipulated beast whose endless desire for freedom drags democracy into
tyranny. James Madison wrote that the first task in founding a government was to "enable the government to control the governed."[32] But they
rejected democracy for that reason, endorsing instead rule by philosopher
kings and a republic. Postwar democratic theorists, on the contrary, incorporated biases against the demos into the very theory of democracy. In
this respect, instrumental democracy represents a peculiar mutation of
the democratic ideal through which elements undermining it from within
have become its integral part. The origins, nature, and implications of that
mutation are the major themes of this book.

The Cold War Origins of
Instrumental Democracy

In addition to identifying the decline of democratic attunement as a distinct
yet neglected conceptual issue of democratic theory, a close consideration
of the development of democratic theory during the Cold War can put the
current debate about neoliberalism in broader perspective. As neoliberalism
widens its influence, critics charge, the principle of quid pro quo market
exchange distorts the functioning of the state; the imperative of competition
undermines social trust and stability; and the ideas of personal responsibility,
human capital, and entrepreneurialism cultivate an economically aggressive
yet politically disengaged subjectivity—all to the effect of fundamentally
dismantling the ideal of democratic self-government.[33]

    These are crucial criticisms. But a singular focus on neoliberalism can
limit our understanding of the present crisis of democracy and debilitate

our efforts to address it. Neoliberalism—which is a somewhat imprecise label for various, though not entirely incoherent, trends—does operate on premises at odds with the ideal of democracy. But there is an important line, both analytical and empirical, between this observation and the claim that neoliberalism is single-handedly remaking democracy, a line that contemporary critics sometimes cross too readily. One of the unfortunate consequences of this tendency is that neoliberalism appears as a monolithic juggernaut. Many compelling critiques of neoliberalism tend to foreground its relentless and almost intractably multifaceted and surreptitious antidemocratic operation, rarely investigating the volatilities within it and the supplemental forces it latches onto. In doing so, those critiques land us in a curious state in which analytical acuity and moral urgency are beset, as Wendy Brown admits in her recent book, by a deep sense of "exhaustion and despair."[34] In a similar vein, critiques of neoliberalism effectively externalize the cause of the crisis of democracy, finding fault only with ideological and social trends supposedly outside of democracy. This approach is troubling not only because it bypasses democracy's internal problems but also because it has the effect of idolizing democracy before neoliberalism as democracy proper, a state to which our crisis-ridden democracy should return. As the critics mark the late 1970s and the disintegration of the postwar welfare state as the starting point of the crisis of democracy, many of them look back on postwar democracy with nostalgia, treating it as a platform on which to construct an alternative to neoliberalism. But a close look at the development of postwar democracy produces a more complex picture, one that admonishes against the simple juxtaposition of neoliberal and postwar iterations of democracy. To put it provocatively, I contend that a crucial part of the groundwork for neoliberalism's ascendance had already been laid in the postwar era through a transformation within democratic theory. The crisis of democracy began well before neoliberalism's arrival.

I highlight various ideological motifs—including elitist critiques of the masses, the image of democracy as a self-regulating system at once dynamic and stable, and the embrace of the capitalist economy as a correlate of democracy—as constitutive elements of instrumental democracy. To be clear, none of them was newly invented during the Cold War. But before the middle of the twentieth century, their democratic credentials, as well as their mutual compatibility, were sufficiently contested that they did not make up a coherent meaning of democracy. That contestation was suspended to a great extent, and the meaning of democracy streamlined, under the pressures of the Cold War.

As I develop my argument, I offer a close examination of some of the most influential political and social scientists' work, building on the scholarship on the postwar social sciences. A number of historians have examined how the Cold War shaped the construction of the social sciences,[35] with some of them paying particular attention to the linkage between patronage, by the government as well as private foundations, and the institutionalization of various academic disciplines.[36] I rely on these vital studies to situate particular figures and arguments I examine, but they are part of the broader story I wish to tell: how the idea of democracy underwent a general shift in the postwar era. I discuss a select group of social scientists not because they played a formative role in shaping their disciplines but because they derived a particularly coherent account of democracy from a set of assumptions that prevailed in postwar America at large. For the same reason, they appear with a wide array of other figures, including philosophers, social critics, mathematicians, economists, and even policy makers. In this respect, the parameters of my discussion are wider than those of the typical history of political science, which tends to highlight intradisciplinary issues such as the rise and fall of different approaches and methodologies (political theory, behavioralism, or rational choice theory)[37] or to trace permutations of certain key concepts within the discipline (the state or pluralism).[38] So as I examine why many postwar democratic theorists were more alert to certain problems and indifferent to others, why they were tackling those problems through a similar framework, and, most important, why they converged on an instrumental conception of democracy, I do not try to find out whether they were staging a methodological revolt within their discipline or responding to lucrative funding opportunities on the horizon. Rather, I analyze their theories as a symptomatic articulation of the intellectual presuppositions and thrusts widely circulating in the Cold War intellectual universe.[39] Drawing on intellectual history and more specialized accounts of other branches of science, I attempt to describe and assess the many-sided construction of instrumental democracy.[40]

Historians usually stress totalitarianism as a singular factor that shaped the contours of democracy as postwar America's identity. In one of the most impressive recent efforts to assess the Cold War's legacy on democracy, for example, David Ciepley discusses the encounter with totalitarianism as a singular driving force behind the reconstruction of democracy during that period.[41] In Ciepley's account, antitotalitarianism is responsible for some of the most momentous changes of American democracy: it effected a rightward turn in economic thought and policy; it established interest group pluralism as the only viable modus operandi of democracy; and it entrenched the doctrine of state neutrality and the emphasis on civil liberties in America's legal thinking and practice.

I, too, highlight totalitarianism, but less as a direct or coherent cause of democratic theory's transformation than as a trigger that accentuated and inflected various old themes, which then made their way into an instrumental conception of democracy. The fear that totalitarianism stoked about the all-powerful state controlling the economy, social relations, individual liberties, and independent thinking itself—which is at the center of Ciepley's account—was undoubtedly crucial, but it was still one among numerous specters it awakened. It also aroused anxiety about ordinary citizens as ignorant and irresponsible "masses," which had been a common theme in antidemocratic political thought, and helped establish it as a staple of democratic thought. Likewise, the encounter with totalitarianism did not simply bring about changes *within* economic thought and practice. Equally important, it effected a repositioning of free-market capitalism vis-à-vis democratic politics. Moreover, the worry about the ideologically driven nature of totalitarianism, along with the remarkable technological apparatuses produced for war, gave new form to American democracy's old fascination with science, importantly including scientific management of human affairs. The intellectual universe created by the Cold War was an internally heterogeneous space fraught with tension, and as one of its products, instrumental democracy, too, was far less congealed or stable than suggested by the changes in postwar institutions that Ciepley compellingly tracks. Taking into account instrumental democracy's internal multiplicity is crucial to understanding its resilience.

This book combines the history of ideas and normative political theory. My primary goal is to put together a composite picture of instrumental democracy as a theoretical construct, and to analyze its systematic tendencies and contradictions. This requires a careful tracing, because elements of instrumental democracy germinated in different corners of the postwar intellectual universe and fused together in defiance of conventional ideological divides. The widespread embrace of the autocratic Joseph Schumpeter's arguments by (mostly) liberal postwar thinkers is probably the best-known instance of such a peculiar hybrid, but other affinities, crossbreeds, and transplants also need to be interrogated closely. Also, some elements of instrumental democracy were not as equally established or dominant as others, even in the realm of ideas. Therefore I not only revisit some of the well-known themes of Cold War democratic theory but also introduce less well-known or obscure intellectual trends that are not typically examined in the history of postwar democratic theory.

Throughout the book, I use the terms "Cold War" and "postwar" somewhat interchangeably as a temporal marker. Historians often note that the Cold War as a political event began in 1947, symbolized by the announcement of the Truman Doctrine. But the intellectual underpinnings of the Cold War were already well in the making in the mid-1930s and congealed during World War II. In examining the Cold War as an intellectual event, therefore, I take a slightly longer view and trace the construction of its constitutive elements before they were fully codified into an official doctrine. And since part of my intent is to write a "prehistory," as it were, of the crisis of democracy, my discussion ends in the late 1970s, before neoliberalism took off in earnest. Historically, then, my account of Cold War democracy actually spans the period from the mid-1930s to the 1970s.

While I certainly do not intend this book to offer a comprehensive history of postwar democratic thought, because the construction of instrumental democracy happened across conventional ideological and disciplinary lines, my discussion admittedly ranges widely. The well-known debate between Cold War liberals, such as Daniel Bell and Arthur Schlesinger Jr., and their critics, such as C. Wright Mills, and the equally well-known (at least to political scientists) debate about methodological behavioralism constitute the backdrop of my discussion. But I refocus the often dichotomous terms of those overlapping debates by examining how both proponents and opponents of instrumental democracy shared implicit assumptions about democratic subjectivity, despite their otherwise diverging arguments. Further, I interweave my reinterpretation of this familiar debate with a scrutiny of figures whose ideas are not typically examined in the history of postwar democratic theory, including the political theorist Hannah Arendt, the mathematician Norbert Wiener, and the proto-neoliberal economist Friedrich Hayek. My eclectic choice of thinkers is driven mostly by the clarity that, in my estimation, they bring to the conception of instrumental democracy, but I focus mostly on intellectuals and social scientists who wrote in midcentury America, including many émigré scholars who deeply shaped the intellectual debates in their new, sometimes temporary, home. Cordoning off the world of ideas by geographical lines is inevitably arbitrary, and even more so in the case of the Cold War era, when ideas, as much as persons, traveled across national borders so frequently. But in a postwar America that was preoccupied with presenting itself as an example of democracy and protecting it around the globe, the task of conceptualizing democracy took on particular significance and generated debates with such focus and intensity that it provides a sufficiently rich intellectual setting in its own right.[42] I do sparingly make exceptions to this rule, however, when I analyze the implications—rather than the construction—of instrumental democracy.

As I have noted, instrumental democracy is a composite of various motifs, not all of which attained prominence in the postwar period, and even those that did were still *a* component of postwar political thought. Thus the thematic scope of the book is also limited. Some intellectual trends scarcely appear. Conservatism, for example, developed as a highly sophisticated and potent intellectual tradition in the postwar era, but I do not discuss it extensively, except when it exerted pressure on the formation of instrumental democracy.[43] Even the themes I do explore are treated selectively, to the extent that they enhance our understanding of instrumental democracy. The implications of the national security state, systems thinking, and Cold War neoliberalism, among others, are hardly limited to democratic thought and warrant full-scale studies devoted solely to them. Likewise, I engage with critiques of Cold War democratic theory only selectively. I acknowledge the voluminous existing literature mostly in notes and focus on revisiting and developing less discussed aspects of their arguments to bring into focus its particular perils that I think have so far escaped a thorough interrogation.

Organization of the Book

In what follows, I trace the historical construction of instrumental democracy, identifying its principal components and analyzing its implications. Chapter 2 lays out the basic concepts that guide my analysis of Cold War democratic theory in the subsequent chapters. I theorize democracy as a principle of social coordination competing with other such principles, and I explain why it rests on a particular subjectivity. I suggest subjectivity is not a radically subjective or random collection of free-floating affective energy but formed in a particular discursive economy that distributes affects in patterned ways. Building on this theoretical discussion, I discuss how concerns about democratic subjectivity were central to the democratic theorizing of progressive thinkers in the early twentieth century—concerns that would be decidedly marginalized in the postwar era.

Chapters 3 through 5 examine the formation of Cold War democratic theory qua instrumental democracy. Chapter 3 traces how assumptions about political subjectivity drove postwar democratic theorists to redefine democracy as an instrument for the pursuit of individuals' private interests rather than a public institution organizing collective life. Challenging the conventional critique of postwar democratic theory, I suggest that its most distinct aspect is not the suppression of political participation as such but its redescription of what counts as legitimate political claims and its alteration of the broader environment in which those claims circulate. The instrumentalization of democracy was occasioned by the encounter with totalitarianism, which blurred the line between "the people" as the legitimate foundation of popular sovereignty and "the masses" as the lethal threat to democracy. Under the spell of totalitarianism's powerful imageries, postwar democratic theorists incorporated the critique of the masses—a long-standing theme of the antidemocratic tradition—into democratic theorizing. The typical criticism that faults postwar democratic theorists for reducing room for popular political participation is, while correct as far as it goes, a limited one. Rather than simply suppressing popular political activities, postwar democratic theory recognizes all democratic claims exclusively as an expression of private interests. Within that framework, all political claims become morally equivalent, and the idea of a public that discriminates and weighs competing claims according to the principles of the common good and political equality is tarnished as a perilous flirtation with totalitarianism.

Chapter 4 explores the idea of dynamic stability as one of the major challenges of instrumental democracy. Postwar democratic theorists' embrace of pluralism as a principal feature of democracy created a delicate problem. To claim its fundamental difference from totalitarianism, democracy needed to tolerate, if not promote, diverse ideologies and political groupings; but in the face of perceived totalitarian threats, it could not let its commitment to pluralism strain its stability too much. Many postwar democratic theorists resorted to the idea that multiplication of interest groups and dispersion of power among them would help accomplish that two-pronged task, but less by substantiating it than by implicitly assuming that democracy is a self-regulating system. One of the rare attempts to directly confront this problem was made by David Easton, and I examine his theory of political systems as one of the most comprehensive and sophisticated theoretical accounts of how democracy might accommodate pluralism and stability. Recognizing the limits of the biological and economic perspectives that have often been used to analyze Easton's theory, I navigate some of the conceptual ambiguities and tensions in his account by turning to two related branches of Cold War science: systems science and cybernetics. While Easton highlights the democratic system's diffused political structure and its responsiveness to its members' spontaneously formed inputs, my investigation suggests that conceiving politics as an adaptive system generates and conceals tendencies toward centralized decision-making and the regimentation of inputs. In postwar democratic theorists' glorious vision of democracy as a self-regulating system, its normalizing and disciplinary mechanisms were obscured, and democratic subjectivity rendered superfluous.

Chapter 5 takes up Cold War neoliberalism as one of instrumental democracy's crucial blind spots. Cold War neoliberalism has rarely been treated as an important part of Cold War democratic theory, in part because its favored economic policies were not embraced by most postwar democratic theorists. But Cold War neoliberalism was not a purely economic doctrine. Through an analysis of Friedrich Hayek's wide-ranging works, I suggest that it is a distinctly political project that seeks to fundamentally reorganize social relations. Hayek identified people's commitment to the common good and equality as a major hurdle that obstructs the establishment of the neoliberal order, and predicted with trepidation that the surge of such democratic subjectivity would lead to the *decline* of instrumental democracy. Despite his worries, however, Hayek's theory illustrates, more than it protests, the relationship between democracy and capitalism forged in the postwar era. In the fraught intellectual and political climate wrought by antitotalitarianism, capitalism became a correlate of democracy and market prices a dominant social signal. While many postwar intellectuals critically analyzed cultural ramifications of capitalism and economic abundance, they rarely interrogated the ways in which democracy and capitalism merged in the dominant political-economic framework with equal keenness. Ironically, it was Hayek who was far more sensitive to the tension between capitalism and democracy. Rather than assuming that democracy and capitalism are harmlessly reconcilable, Hayek recognized that they are fundamentally different principles of social organization and insisted that the neoliberal order can take hold only when democratic subjectivity is supplanted by capitalist subjectivity, so that people view democracy as but another instrument they use to advance their private welfare. In this respect, postwar democratic theory's instrumentalizing tendencies may have unwittingly helped clear the most daunting obstacle to neoliberalism's ascendance.

Chapter 6 brings my analysis of Cold War democratic theory into focus by developing a fuller theoretical critique of instrumental democracy through a reinterpretation of Hannah Arendt's political theory. Although her thinking, like that of many other postwar democratic theorists, was indelibly shaped by the experience of totalitarianism, Arendt arrived at conclusions strikingly opposed to the prevailing outlook of the time. I reread her account of totalitarianism with a focus on her critique of liberalism, where she diagnoses it as a perilously volatile form of politics that is ultimately consumed by its tendency to instrumentalize politics. For Arendt, the so-called masses, which other postwar theorists viewed as a mortal threat to liberal democracy, were a perverse manifestation of antipolitical subjectivity nurtured by instrumental politics, characterized by the exclusive concern with private economic interests and political submissiveness. I track how her critique of instrumental politics recurs in her later works, and extrapolate a particular type of responsiveness or attunement, not as a private feeling but as a public force that animates and orients individuals, as a crucial element of her political theory. Thus reconstructed, the Arendtian perspective enables us to discern the seeds of a crisis planted by Cold War democracy beyond the issue of political participation. Also, it helps counter one of the central claims of Cold War democratic theory more directly than its critics did. Advocates of Cold War democratic theory contended that some level of apathy was conducive to the integrity of a democratic system, but the case may actually be precisely the opposite: the apathy produced by instrumental democracy jeopardizes its stability in the long run.

Chapter 7 returns to the debate about the crisis of democracy and neoliberalism discussed in the opening pages of this first chapter. The present crisis is not merely a birth pang signaling the emergence of a more direct democracy, but its roots may go deeper than existing representative institutions' defects. We need to scrutinize the underlying conception of democracy and the dominant political subjectivity, both of which shape and animate those institutions. In this respect, critics are correct to call attention to the ways in which neoliberalism has transformed politics, social relations, and subjectivity since the 1980s. But I suggest that neoliberalism ascended not on the virtue of its intrinsic strength or appeal but by exploiting the postwar regime's weaknesses and contradictions stemming from its instrumental character. To truly overcome neoliberalism's threats to democracy, therefore, we need to resist the temptation to view postwar democracy as an alternative and move beyond it, making efforts to deinstrumentalize democracy.

Writing in the early twentieth century, another turbulent time for democracy, John Dewey stressed the need "of returning to the idea [of democracy] itself, of clarifying and deepening our apprehension of it, and of employing our sense of its meaning to criticize and re-make its political manifestations."[44] Only a clearer and deeper understanding of that fundamental idea, he urged, could turn a crisis of democracy into an opportunity for its renewal. Perhaps our own crisis demands the pursuit of such an understanding.

CHAPTER TWO

Locating the Demos

In this chapter, I first clarify the main concepts I will be deploying through-out the book, and then analyze the democratic theorizing of progressive thinkers in the early twentieth century through the lens of those concepts. As I discussed in chapter 1, understanding the demos simply in terms of claims-making activities is limited unless we pay equal attention to the problem of democratic subjectivity—which I define as responsiveness to public claims appealing to the common good and political equality. Democratic subjectivity is an essential condition for democracy's opera-tion, and its cultivation cannot be reduced to day-to-day decisions that tend to dominate our perception of democracy. For that reason, democ-racy cannot and should not be viewed exclusively as an instrument of attaining a particular goal. Rather, one of its main features is to reproduce democratic people who are committed to a particular organization of power independent of the immediate benefits it may generate in a given instance. Proceeding from this preliminary discussion, I consider how these concerns were central to some of the progressive thinkers' attempt to reimagine democracy in the age of mass industrial society. To be clear, my intent is not to articulate a coherent democratic theory out of the ca-cophonous world of ideas at the beginning of the twentieth century.[1] My aim is more modest: to show that an underlying motif animated demo-cratic theory during the period. Despite their evident differences, many progressive thinkers sought, variously and inconclusively, to substitute a democratic subjectivity for the prevailing subjectivity forged by economic liberalism and political hierarchy. In their concern about the formation of democratic subjectivity, progressive thinkers were continuing the tradition of democratic theory; classical theorists such as Rousseau and John Stuart Mill, too, grappled with the idea in different contexts. In but a few decades, however, that concern would largely disappear from democratic theorizing, and its disappearance was one of the most important aspects of democratic theory's deep transformation during the Cold War.

Terms of the Argument

Democracy can be understood most fundamentally as a principle of social coordination, and as such, it competes with other such principles, most notably bureaucracy and the capitalist market. Insofar as coercion without consent is illegitimate in modern democracies, those principles require affected individuals' voluntary adoption—or, more often, unthinking and habitual compliance—to gain and retain influence over social and political institutions and practices. If people constantly refuse to report their personal information according to the twenty-seven categories designated by a bureaucratic agency, bureaucracy becomes costly and ineffective, if not altogether dysfunctional. If people do not address their needs through a chain of profit-seeking activities and monetary exchanges, the capitalist market would be severely limited in its reach.

Unlike bureaucracy or the capitalist market, democracy requires a subjectivity that is attuned to public claims appealing to the common good and political equality. This does not mean that democracy is predicated on a permanently fixed and universally agreed-on concept of the common good—an almost farcically simplistic proposition that Cold War democratic theorists ascribed to classical democratic theory in their attempt to discredit it (more on this subject in chapter 3). Rather, it simply means that, like agents of other principles of social coordination, democratic citizens recognize some claims as more relevant than others. As administrators in bureaucratic organizations register information insofar as it is amenable to streamlined management of mass subjects, and as sellers and buyers in the capitalist market exclusively speak the language of profit, so democratic citizens prioritize claims bearing on the common good and political equality.

The common good as democracy's master reference point is important not because it guarantees morally or epistemologically best decisions or the most efficient allocation of existing resources in the narrowly economic sense. The common good is important because it helps promote political equality, which liberalism in principle guarantees but threatens to undermine by privatizing essential resources. Put differently, the common good helps ensure that democratic contestation occurs, not just once but continually, on equal terms. It does so partly by safeguarding citizens' access to certain basic goods regardless of their particular traits and situations, thereby reducing the extent to which private resources determine one's political capabilities. Equal distribution of basic goods is not enough, however. Political equality is unlike private property, which is owned and used by each individual. Political equality can take effect only when individuals transcend, never fully and always temporarily, their private selves, either by aligning themselves with public claims or by eliciting responses from their peers. And therein lies another crucial function of the common good: it connects otherwise isolated individuals. The common good serves as a site where citizens recognize one another's presence and diverse needs, experience shared conditions, and learn to deal with collective problems as equals. What the common good does, then, is not so much dictating a particular outcome as creating an environment in which citizens negotiate disagreements and reach temporary decisions. Many Cold War democratic theorists decided that the concept of the common good was antithetical to pluralism and should thus be banished from democratic theory—a fateful decision that eventually resulted in a deep transformation of democratic theory. It was a misguided decision, however, insofar as midcentury democratic theorists saw the common good exclusively as a goal of democracy while failing to recognize it as a basis of democracy's fundamental condition: democratic people who are disposed to address their collective problems through mutual engagement.

By democratic subjectivity, I mean this orientation toward the twin principles of the common good and political equality. To function as a principle of social coordination, democracy must continually cultivate democratic subjectivity, just as bureaucracy and capitalism need to reproduce subjects who internalize certain collective rhythms and requirements, as well as the constraints on their individual freedom that such internalization entails. While claims *making* is perhaps a more readily visible part of democratic politics, democratic subjectivity is arguably even more important when people *respond* to public claims.[2] When people make claims, they typically do so for personal reasons, and that is how it should be. The burden of public claims making requires a level of passion that is often possible only when things are personal on some level. But because of this inevitably personal dimension, no public claim can be given the presumption of moral superiority. Instead, various claimants' proposed contributions to the common good and political equality are assessed by those who respond to those claims. Citizens are in a better position to make that assessment when they respond, not only because they are less attached to the claims made, but also because their decision's impact on their personal interest is smaller (to the extent that associated benefits and costs are widely shared and dispersed), and thus the price of winning or losing is morally more surmountable. In this respect, what democracy requires is not simply or even necessarily constant or large-scale participation, if participation is understood solely as claims making. Rather, it needs citizens to pay attention to public issues that do not immediately affect their private welfare, and to judge competing public claims by the criteria of the common good and political equality.

The significance of democratic subjectivity, especially with regard to people's response to public claims, means that we cannot reduce democracy to decisions being made here and now. Democratic interactions always produce residues, as it were, that go beyond the issues immediately at stake: which candidates are elected, which laws are passed, or which policies are adopted. Each of those interactions also serves as an occasion on which people realize their interconnectedness, develop their capabilities and dispositions for handling their collective problems through debates and cooperation among equals, and test their understanding of the common good and political equality—an occasion, that is, through which the demos as a responsive public is re-formed, bucking the inexorable trend toward dissolution. To put it another way, democratic subjectivity is formed out of democratic residues, and for that reason, democratic politics cannot and should not be completely instrumental.

Democracy's noninstrumental nature, however, raises a difficulty. In the cases of bureaucracy and the capitalist market, our compliance typically yields immediate and tangible benefits. (If I fill out a form as instructed, then I leave the DMV with a driver's license.) In democracy, however, the benefits of responding to public claims are often uncertain or intangible; indeed, it is precisely for that reason that the public can better judge political claims than the claimants themselves. Still, from the perspective of each individual, democratic responsiveness often does not produce easily discernible benefits. This is compounded by the fact that the cost of exit in democracy is far lower, at least in the short term, than in bureaucracy and the capitalist market. (Tuning out politics is significantly easier than trying to get a loaf of bread outside the commercial chain.) Lacking natural mechanisms of compulsion or inducement, democracy requires a higher level of moral commitment than other principles of social coordination.

Seen in this light, the hardest and most important question of democracy might not be *how* to carry out democratic debates. It might be *whether* people are disposed to engage in those debates in the first place. The former question has been the focus of deliberative democracy, arguably one of the most influential strands of contemporary democratic theory. John Rawls, for example, has famously suggested that citizens can find "fair terms of social cooperation" by assuming that they are "free and equal" and ignoring any natural abilities or economic and social position that may give them unfair bargaining advantages.[3] Calling this imaginary state the "original position," Rawls insists that it is simply a cognitive tool that citizens can freely use to temporarily distance themselves from their particularities and come to an agreement on the basic structure of society that would be fair to everyone.[4] As he states, anyone can "enter the original position at any time simply by reasoning in accordance with the enumerated restrictions on information."[5]

It is not clear, however, why individuals would prioritize determining the basic structure of society as a whole over their particular private goals, and why they would do so from the perspective of free and equal citizens, as Rawls asks of them.[6] Rawls himself recognized this problem and modified his theory to address it. When he first introduced the concept of the original position in *A Theory of Justice* (1971), Rawls insisted that it could serve as the basis of social cooperation purely on rationalist grounds, independent of concerns about subjectivity—people's orientations, sentiments, and dispositions, which motivate and condition their engagement with the external world. He assumed that individuals using the original position are "rational and mutually disinterested," in the sense that they are "concerned to advance their interests" and "take no interest in one another's interests."[7] Following mainstream economic theory, he also adopted an instrumental conception of rationality, which is concerned exclusively with finding "the most effective means to given ends."[8] Rawls relied on these assumptions to clear the original position of affective states such as impartiality, sympathy, and benevolence, because they are "so complex that no definite theory at all can be worked out."[9] To attain "a kind of moral geometry with all the rigor," he wrote, we must "assume as little as possible" and "not presuppose ... extensive ties of natural sentiments."[10]

Rawls later admitted, however, that placing instrumental rationality at the center of his account of moral psychology was a "very misleading" error.[11] And he tried to address that error, in *Political Liberalism* (1993), by adding the concept of "the reasonable" to his account of the individual's moral psychology. If the individual is rational in the sense that she pursues her private life goals, then she is also reasonable insofar as she is "ready to propose principles and standards as fair terms of cooperation and to abide by them willingly, given the assurance that others will likewise do so."[12] The reasonable and the rational "work in tandem,"[13] Rawls asserted, but "the reasonable has priority over the rational and subordinates it absolutely."[14] This psychological makeup is a crucial condition for the working of his deliberative democracy, but it is a condition that cannot be reduced to cognition. As Rawls himself noted, what sets apart reasonable agents from rational ones is "the particular form of *moral sensibility* that underlies the *desire* to engage in fair cooperation as such."[15] Despite this admission, however, his pursuit of this matter remains speculative and highly controversial.[16]

Deliberative democracy is an important corrective to Cold War democratic theory, especially its tendency to indiscriminately aggregate individual preferences and to uncritically approve the outcome as the public good.[17] Keen to devise normative principles by which citizens may conduct democratic deliberation, however, deliberative democrats often overlook the problem of moral sensibility—subjectivity, more generally—which may well be a condition of possibility for democracy, deliberative or otherwise.

Recognizing the limitations of the narrow focus on reason, numerous scholars have recently turned their attention to affect. It is difficult to summarize the sprawling and quickly proliferating literature on this subject,[18] but many political theorists are drawn to affect by their dissatisfaction with prevailing political theories' apparent inability to account for the recalcitrant persistence of political injustice, which defies reason-centered perspectives' implicit presumption that the only cure for biases is rational persuasion.[19] Biases become politically potent, it seems, not despite their lack of validity but because of their irrationality. Those who mobilize biases tap and intensify the emotional undercurrents of fear, anxiety, and anger precisely to bypass and undercut reason giving as a legitimate mode of public discourse. So it is naive to believe that they can be confronted, let alone defeated, by the force of better argument. To move beyond this na-ïveté, affect theorists suggest, we need to revise the very understanding of thinking and judgment at the base of rationalist or intellectualist political theories, such as deliberative democracy. Deliberative democrats assume that thinking is governed by conceptual consistency, logical reasoning, and the strengths of evidence, affect theorists complain, when in fact it is more embodied, visceral, and affective. People feel, without fully understanding why, before they think. The fear and disgust that are entangled with racial prejudice, for example, kick in before people think rationally about criminal justice or immigration policies. In fact, what people say are their reasons are often merely rationalizations of how they feel.

This insight is important, and I draw on it. But as they stress how our beliefs and decisions are often driven by affective processes beyond the grasp of conscious reasoning, contemporary affect theorists do not always offer a clear account of our freedom and agency. If our political behavior is governed by ideas deeply lodged in the region of our identity that is hard to reach by consciousness and reason, then there is little we can do to confront, let alone correct, them. This curious conclusion, then, misses arguably one of the most important contributions of affect theory in psychology, pioneered by Silvan S. Tomkins. Tomkins developed his theory as a challenge to Freud's then dominant theory of the drives as an account of human nature.[20] Tomkins posited that affect exists as a primary motivational system in addition to, and independent of, biological drives.[21] Babies cry for attention, for example, not simply because they are hungry but because they wish to form a communion. Thus understood, the concept of affect constitutes a breakthrough in our understanding of human freedom. If we can only accept or reject the drives, human existence is either completely bound by natural needs (radically determined) or totally free from such needs (radically subjective). In comparison, affects permit far more freedom than the drives do (e.g., we cannot stay long without food, but we can withstand, say, the absence of excitement for quite some time) while still alerting us that we never exercise our freedom simply by rationally forming our will, free from emotions, as the Cartesian or Kantian view would have it. Shame, for example, surely inflects our thinking, but because we can typically live with shame for a while, it is also an occasion for thinking about ourselves and sometimes also about broader social relations (why do *I* feel ashamed about my poverty? I work as many hours as my boss. Shouldn't *he* feel ashamed to pay me so little?).

We are not blindly beholden to affects also because our affective response to sensorial stimuli is inflected by discursive and social constructions, which can be subjected to critical interrogation and conscious alteration.[22] Suppose that a driver sees a policeman and is frightened. Her heart starts beating fast and her palms sweating, even though she knows she has nothing to worry about. While fear may be one of the intrinsic affects we all have, the driver experiences it only in relation to a particular situation, when, in this case, she encounters a policeman. And this encounter is socially structured. For example, the driver must have an intuitive understanding of what the policeman is and how to tell if someone is a policeman, as well as when one is supposed to be fearful of the policeman. If she grew up in a neighborhood where crimes were rampant and the police presence constant, she would be more likely to be readily fearful. In other words, the driver's fear shows that she has internalized, among other things, legal institutions, social norms, and her past experiences. What this means is that affects—and subjectivity as a congealed configuration of affects vis-à-vis objects—exist in a particular political economy that attaches affects to different things and amplifies certain affects while subduing others. A politically significant quest for a new subjectivity, then, requires in the first place attention to that political economy.

Approaching subjectivity through these lenses, I investigate how some of democracy's conceptual pillars, as well as its relation to other principles of social coordination, were reimagined in the post–World War II era. One distinct effect of these discursive formations, I suggest, was the displacement of a distinctly democratic subjectivity attuned to public claims appealing to the common good and political equality.[23] This was a striking break. As I briefly show in the rest of the chapter, the problem of democratic subjectivity has long been a chief concern of democratic theory, and it was central to the democratic theorizing of many progressive thinkers at the beginning of the twentieth century. Despite their many differences, the progressives agreed that the age of mass industrial society required a new democracy, and such a democracy could exist only when there was a demos radically different in its orientation from its earlier iterations. This overriding concern served as a vantage point from which progressive thinkers scrutinized prevailing institutions and practices and conceived alternatives. That vantage point would largely vanish in a matter of a few decades, however. Postwar democratic theorists would pose different questions (or not ask certain questions), make different assumptions, and ultimately put together a markedly different democratic theory.

The Search for the Demos in Progressive Political Thought

The intertwinement of the common good and democratic subjectivity has been one of the running threads of classical democratic theory. Rousseau, for example, conceptualized his social contract not simply as a mechanical instrument for generating the determinate general will but as a process through which individuals, who have been swindled into forsaking their freedom to create a government that only serves the interest of the rich, are transformed into citizens. When an individual engages in the "act of association," Rousseau famously wrote, "his faculties are so stimulated and developed, his ideas so extended, his feelings so ennobled, and his whole soul so uplifted."[24] A similar concern also informs John Stuart Mill's resolute, if sometimes theoretically awkward, attempt to combine utilitarianism and democratic theory. Mill favored utility over abstract right as the basis of liberal democracy, partly because he regarded people's feeling of happiness as the indispensable animating force for individual as well as social progress. In an unorthodox move, he then labored to link the subjective feeling of happiness to the common good, insisting that "the happiness which forms the utilitarian standard of what is right in conduct, is not the agent's own happiness, but that of all concerned."[25] Believing that one could discern a more desirable and valuable pleasure only through actual experience, Mill hoped that active political participation would cultivate such a "utilitarian" character.

In the early twentieth century, many progressive thinkers continued to wrestle with the question of democratic subjectivity, responding to the momentous historical changes that were unfolding.[26] What loomed large in their thought, of course, was the formation of mass industrial society. Against the backdrop of economic industrialization, the rise of new transportation and communication technologies that helped form the mass market and the mass public, and deepening economic inequality and social unrest, the progressives tried to reimagine democracy by rethinking its foundational premises and prevailing institutions. Many progressive thinkers believed that the then reigning principle of social coordination—free-market capitalism—was disorderly, unjust, and wasteful. The trouble was that democracy, which could and should serve as the alternative, remained beholden to preindustrial notions that had become obsolete. Based on this judgment, the progressives critically interrogated the prevailing building blocks of democracy: the image of the isolated and independent self and the single-minded focus on individual rights as its corollary, political parties that made vote gathering the only relevant mode of political organization, the institutional arrangements set by the Constitution that forced political fragmentation and compromise while suppressing popular mobilization, and the courts as the final arbiter of democratic interaction.

The "Social Self": Democratic Subjectivity in the Age of Mass Industrial Society

The progressives believed that the image of the sovereign individual that had formed the foundation of liberal democracy became utterly obsolete in the age of mass industrial society and needed to be replaced by a different understanding that foregrounded the socially constructed, interdependent, and evolving nature of the self. As Wilfred McClay has eloquently put it, they "came to regard the self not as a hard, well-defined object endowed with objective rational capabilities and imprescriptible natural rights, but as a more or less plastic expression of intersecting social and cultural forces, a permeable entity with indistinct boundaries and a fundamentally adaptive nature."[27] It is not an exaggeration to say that the idea of the "social self" was an anchor for all the major thinkers of the period—William James, George Herbert Mead, Thorstein Veblen, Mary Parker Follet, Albion Small, Charlotte Perkins Gilman, Jane Addams, Charles Horton Cooley, Charles A. Beard, Herbert Croly, and John Dewey—and shaped their otherwise different ideas.

Among progressive thinkers, John Dewey provided the most sustained theoretical account of the social self and its political implications. Dewey challenged the individual-society dualism, placing both in the fluid (re)-construction of culture. According to him, we are evolved organisms who use intelligence to address problems conveyed to (felt by) us in the form of stimuli. Crucially, we are *social* organisms because, as he suggested in his innovative claim, even what seems like a purely physical stimulus must first be interpreted to prompt the working of our intelligence. "The stimulus must be constituted for the response to occur," he wrote.[28] And our interpretation of stimuli rests on social conditions, including a society's institutional structure and other people's judgment, that shape our experience. (Hunger, for example, can trigger shame, despair, or outrage, depending on our interpretation.) The individual is necessarily social, in other words, because without social interaction she cannot even determine what the problem is and thus is unable to employ, let alone develop, her intelligence. Dewey called these acquired dispositions to certain modes of intelligent responses "habits." Importantly, in emphasizing habits, he did not make the individual a passive being. He stressed that habits are "adjustments *of* the environment, not merely *to* it."[29] Far from designating routinized and unreflective behaviors, habits are for Dewey the object of study and alteration that aims to better address changing human needs and aspirations. A "demand for a changed environment," he observed, would emerge from the gap between people's aspirations and the current environment, and since the environment is but a collection of settled habits, social change can be "achieved only by some modification and rearrangement of old habits."[30]

From this standpoint, Dewey, and other progressives, challenged almost all the major doctrinal pillars of American democracy, whether philosophical, moral, social, economic, legal, or political, as old habits that needed to be discarded. For example, Dewey rejected metaphysics on the grounds that it was practiced to justify "power over other men in the interest of some class or sect or person" instead of giving individuals "power over natural forces in the common interest of all."[31] And he viewed traditional liberalism and its foundational concept of the isolated self as an expression of the metaphysical worldview that suppresses human freedom. Taking particular aim at traditional liberalism's tendency to glorify "freedom in general at the expense of positive abilities,"[32] Dewey complained that nineteenth-century liberal individualism was not based on an insight into the nature of the individual but premised on "a metaphysics which held that harmony between man and nature can be taken for granted, if once certain artificial restrictions upon man are removed."[33] Under the spell of this metaphysics, traditional liberalism "neglected the necessity of studying and regulating industrial conditions so that a nominal freedom can be made an actuality."[34] And no doctrine manifested this negligence more clearly than the theory of negative liberty. "Find a man who believes that all men need is freedom *from* oppressive legal and political measures, and you have found a man who, unless he is merely obstinately maintaining his own private privileges, carries at the back of his head some heritage of the metaphysical doctrine of free-will."[35] To find a conception of freedom more congruent with the plural and interdependent world that industrialization thrust into being, Dewey suggested, one needed to "turn from moral theories to the general human struggle for political, economic, and religious liberty, for freedom of thought, speech, assemblage and creed."[36]

The idea of the social self raised fundamental questions about the prevailing modes of social coordination, namely, laissez-faire capitalism and electoral democracy. Observing capitalism, Dewey lamented that it was characterized by a fundamental "split": "The results of industry as the determining force in life are corporate and collective while its animating motives and compensations are so unmitigatedly private."[37] He found this social chasm—which was reinforced by the mythical glorification of individual freedom so deeply entrenched in classical liberalism and the narratives about American identity—profoundly alarming. When people are caught in a bifurcated social order that relies on social cooperation but only prizes private endeavors, *no one*—not simply those marginalized by capitalism but even its ostensible beneficiaries—can attain "assured and integrated individuality [which] is the product of definite social relationships and publicly acknowledged functions."[38] At stake is not just a stunted prospect for self-development; the disjuncture between the fact of deepening interdependence and the veneration of individual freedom poses a real danger to society. If capitalism continues to operate on the principle of economic individualism while ignoring its collective conditions and ramifications, it will put people in a state of confusion and insecurity, which is likely to find an outlet in pathological forms of collectivism such as militaristic nationalism. "If the simple duties of peace do not establish a common life," Dewey ominously predicted, "the emotions are mobilized in the service of a war that will supply its temporary stimulation."[39]

Dewey, along with other progressive thinkers, believed that we could overcome the dangerous split in the capitalist order only through a reimagined democracy—reimagined, because the prevailing form of democracy as mere majority rule, run by party machines and bosses, was "as foolish as its critics charge it with being."[40] In Dewey's view, the categorical dismissal of democracy by critics like Walter Lippmann was misguided insofar as it confounds democracy as it is and democracy as it could be. While readily agreeing with Lippmann that traditional democratic theory was mistaken in assuming that "each individual is of himself equipped with the intelligence needed, under the operation of self-interest, to engage in political affairs,"[41] Dewey pointed out that Lippmann repeated traditional theorists' mistake in believing that intelligence is a matter of individual capability. Intelligence, Dewey countered, is in fact "a function of association and communication,"[42] a set of habits formed not in isolation but through social interaction. The trouble was that American democracy had yet to catch up with the new mode of social interaction generated by the mass industrial society. While material conditions were bringing together individuals and deepening their connections ("the Great Society"), those consequences were merely suffered rather than clearly understood and consciously lived ("the Great Community"). No matter how numerous de facto interactions and transactions are, those activities cannot "constitute a community" unless "the consequences of combined action are perceived and become an object of desire and effort."[43] Democracy, now merely electoral, can become a superior alternative to capitalism only when the people form a new set of collective habits—that is, only when a mere majority become a public disposed and able to evaluate competing political claims in light of common interests.

Taking Stock of Progressive Democratic Theory

What makes assessing progressive democratic theory difficult is not simply the variety of the progressives' ideas and reform efforts but, more importantly, the weight of history. Our understanding of twentieth-century political thought, including the demise of progressive democratic theory and the rise of Cold War democratic theory, is indelibly inflected by the overpowering image of totalitarianism. A set of dichotomies overlaid with one another—authoritarian government versus individual autonomy and rights, epistemological and moral absolutism versus relativism, and the rational elite versus the irrational masses susceptible to manipulation—structures our theoretical imagination and shapes our reception of progressivism's legacy. Elements fitting that binary framework loom large, and those lying outside it are underestimated, if not ignored.

In a classic (and still the best) book on the subject, Edward A. Purcell Jr. frames the formation of twentieth-century democratic theory as a clash of epistemological and political absolutism versus relativism, tracing it to the rise of pragmatism in the late nineteenth century and the early twentieth.[44] Dewey appears as a particularly important figure in Purcell's narrative. It was Dewey, Purcell declares, who "left American social theory with one controlling dichotomy: absolutism and authoritarianism versus experimentalism and democracy."[45] Although Purcell acknowledges that this dichotomy did not achieve intellectual dominance and political power until the late 1930s, and Dewey himself was not consistent in his use of the idea until then, Purcell nonetheless insists that it had been at the center of Dewey's thought from the beginning. When Purcell notes the differences between Dewey's democratic theory and postwar democratic theory, especially the latter's politically conservative orientation, what explains this shift for Purcell is not a theoretical transformation but the introduction of new political content, such as the Cold War. "The aggressive, confident, and reform-oriented pragmatism that John Dewey had so long symbolized thus declined, but the major epistemological assumptions behind his pragmatism remained vividly alive," Purcell writes. "Pragmatism had not been rejected, but superseded."[46]

This reading severely constrains our understanding of the transition from progressive to postwar democratic theory. Dewey's and other progressives' embrace of pragmatism as an epistemological principle was inextricably tied to their search for a new democratic subjectivity, whereas, as I will show throughout the book, one of the most distinct features of postwar democratic theory was the suspension of that search. Focusing on the apparent similarities between the progressive and postwar iterations of democratic theory without considering this key difference obscures more than it reveals.

As discussed earlier, Dewey's pragmatism is animated by his judgment that metaphysics' assumptions about higher universal truths justify the power of a small class of people supposed to have special access to those truths. When Dewey insisted that the validity of knowledge lies in its usefulness in addressing people's concrete problems, therefore, he was expressing a democratic impulse to dismantle the ruling class and empower the common people.[47] A similar impulse underlay the progressives' challenge to the Constitution, which, in their view, posed obstacles to reform not simply by dividing legislative authority and empowering the judiciary in a way that favored the concentrated power of business, but more fundamentally by "promoting a public discourse that often depicted necessary reform as disloyal for violating a unique national heritage of individualism and market self-regulation."[48] For progressives such as Herbert Croly and

Charles Beard, the Constitution was a living manifestation of the kind of metaphysics that Dewey excoriated. So they refuted the tendency to treat the Constitution as a foundational text whose literal meaning and doctrinal consistency wield the ultimate authority to shape government structure and dictate legal decisions. They demystified the Constitution as an institutional tool designed by the Founders, who were little more than an American aristocracy united by a similar socioeconomic background and a shared hostility to the poorer majority.[49] In both cases, the progressives' critique was oriented toward the formation of a new demos by empowering the people through structural and institutional reform and by cultivating a disposition that engages with, rather than blindly accepts, prevailing doctrines. For progressive thinkers, the two issues—empowerment and education—were one and the same.[50]

While conceding that the observed state of ordinary people was currently at odds with the ideal conception of the democratic citizen, progressive thinkers saw it not as an unalterable ontological condition but as a product of the institutional failure to bridge the gap between culture and the conditions of mass industrial society. As a result, the progressives did not take at face value the disparaging image of the masses propagated by the theory of mass psychology—the image that would thoroughly permeate postwar democratic theory. The enterprise of mass psychology was pioneered by Gustave Le Bon's pseudoscientific yet hugely influential tract *The Crowd* (1895; the original French title was *Psychologie des foules,* "The Psychology of Crowds"),[51] and it received a great deal of attention in America at the turn of the century. But the progressives' reception could not be farther from that of the postwar intellectuals. Leading progressive psychologists such as William James and Charles Cooley found Le Bon's claims, heavily reliant on his observations about the Paris Commune, to be a reductive and ideologically driven defense of laissez-faire. Eminent sociologists such as Edward Ross and Robert Park distinguished the crowd and the public, insisting that increased social interaction, made conscious by means of newspapers, would usher in the "rule of public opinion" rather than "the government by the mob."[52] And Dewey, again, drew out the implications of mass psychology most fully. He charged that in "assimilating the psychology of democracy with that of the masses, dissolving thus individual judgment," Le Bon demonstrated "a lack of psychological intuition."[53] By blinding us to the pernicious effects of institutions, Dewey wrote, crowd psychology effectively served to justify and perpetuate the same institutions: "Servility, ignorance, craftiness and obsequiousness are not innate qualities, but are the fruits of a system which forces men into subservience. Evil institutions bear bitter fruit, and this bitter fruit is then used to justify the institutions which produced it."[54]

One of the major impulses of progressive democratic thought was to help ordinary citizens combat "evil institutions" on their own. In Dewey's view, the most fundamental obstacle to this goal was the dominant culture, which combined preoccupation with private profit and a political fatalism that regarded the prevailing institutions with either reverence or resignation. (It is important to recall that Dewey's understanding of culture, centered as it is on the concept of habit, is not rationalistic but encompasses both reason and emotion. He defined culture as "the type of emotion and thought that is characteristic of a people and epoch as a whole."[55] In that sense, his concept of culture is consistent with my term *subjectivity*.) Unless people challenged this culture, Dewey believed, reform could be neither thoroughgoing nor enduring. If citizens continue to take private profit as the first and last principle of their judgment and action, for example, the redistribution of material benefits would address the problem of inequality only after the fact, without tackling its root cause: the profit-driven economic system's tendency to create and deepen inequality. In fact, spreading wealth without challenging the prevailing subjectivity might *strengthen* such a structure, insofar as redistributed wealth is funneled back into wasteful consumption, used to purchase privatized and often more expensive basic goods such as health care and education, or diverted to deal with adverse social consequences created by business activities (say, to buy bottled water in an area where residents are concerned about the quality of drinking water owing to lax regulation of chemical waste disposal). The first task in creating a new democracy, therefore, was to sever one's ties to existing frames of thought such as economic individualism and constitutional veneration. It is in this sense that Dewey insisted that democracy's chief challenge was "in the first instance an intellectual problem."[56]

Dewey often invoked science when he discussed the formation of democratic subjectivity. Writing that science is "capable of developing a distinctive type of disposition and purpose," he went so far as to proclaim that "the future of democracy is allied with the spread of the scientific attitude."[57] Dewey's appeal to science provoked now well-known criticisms,[58] one of which was that he naively treated politics as an intellectual problem, assuming that social harmony would naturally emerge once ignorance is removed—the charge Reinhold Niebuhr famously advanced in *Moral Man and Immoral Society* (1932).[59] I will not delve into this debate here, but recognizing Dewey's concern with subjectivity ("a distinctive type of disposition and purpose") suggests that the kind of radical political action on behalf of marginalized minorities that Niebuhr advocated and the formation of the public that Dewey tended to emphasize are not opposed but mutually constitutive.

A defense of political agitation must go hand in hand with long-term efforts to nurture the public that are attuned to the common good and political equality and vigilant to the deleterious effects of private power. When particular struggles are not linked to the (re)production of democratic subjectivity that can undergird broader institutional and structural changes, local successes—such as wage increases—can easily be co-opted so as to perpetuate and further entrench the prevailing structure. Consider the Pullman Strike, for example. As Jane Addams observed at the time, the Pullman Strike was not simply a clash of competing private interests but a contention between two worldviews. On the one hand, the "*commercial viewpoint*" was embodied by George Pullman, who asserted that only he had a right to determine employment policies because the company was his private property, and that the workers should in fact be grateful to him because he had provided, at his discretion, better accommodations than other employers did. On the other hand, the workers spoke from the "*social viewpoint*" that recognized the ways in which industrialism was fundamentally altering the meaning of private property and demanded that the conditions of work be subject to deliberation among a wider set of stakeholders and, indeed, citizens at large.[60] At stake, then, was not just which side "won." At least equally important, the Pullman Strike represented a struggle for social change as Dewey understood it—a transformation of old habits that, in this case, were founded on economic individualism that fueled Pullman's indignant claims. Put differently, it was a struggle for a new frame of thinking and feeling, or, simply, what passes for common sense.

Conclusion

Like other principles of social coordination, democracy requires people to be committed to its unique requirements—organization of collective life around the principles of the common good and political equality—and respond to competing political claims accordingly. Democracy, in short, requires people to embody democratic subjectivity. The significance of democratic subjectivity was recognized by classical democratic theorists and, closer to the historical period at the center of this study, by progressive political thinkers in the early twentieth century.[61] In sharp contrast, postwar democratic theorists shifted the focus of democratic theory to democracy's instrumental functions, especially the selection of representatives, interest group activities, and technocratic policy making. What animated this redirection is a complex story to be told in the following chapters, but postwar democratic theorists' claim that they were demystifying the metaphysical theory of democracy that is oblivious to the real empirical conditions of democracy (seemingly a Deweyan claim) does not withstand scrutiny. The postwar thinkers' theorizing was not so much driven by their professedly neutral observations about empirical facts as it was shaped by their acceptance of the intellectual assumptions and doctrines the progressives were keen to challenge—including theories of mass psychology, the sanctity of the Constitution and American political tradition, the supposed superiority of legalistic and elite-driven mechanisms of democracy, a secluded view of science, and a validation of free-market capitalism. In doing so, postwar democratic theorists occasioned an intellectual retreat to the subjectivity of old, which progressive thinkers perceived as a grave threat to democracy in the age of mass industrial society.

CHAPTER THREE

Democracy against the Demos

Specters of Totalitarianism and the Construction of Instrumental Democracy

When World War II was drawing to an end, President Harry Truman celebrated the impending victory. "It was a victory of one way of life over another. It was a victory of an ideal founded on the rights of the common man, on the dignity of the human being, on the conception of the State as the servant—and not the master—of its people."[1] Less than two years later, however, his exuberance was gone. He now cautioned that the victory was fragile, referring to the threat posed by the "aggressive movements to impose on [free peoples] totalitarian regimes." The world had ended one war, Truman observed, only to enter another, no less urgent conflict.

> At the present moment in world history nearly every nation must choose between alternative ways of life. The choice is too often not a free one.
>
> One way of life is based upon the will of the majority, and is distinguished by free institutions, representative government, free elections, guarantees of individual liberty, freedom of speech and religion, and freedom from political oppression.
>
> The second way of life is based upon the will of a minority forcibly imposed upon the majority. It relies upon terror and oppression, a controlled press and radio, fixed elections, and the suppression of personal freedoms.[2]

The starkly dichotomous worldview Truman outlined in this speech captures the fundamental frame of thought that profoundly shaped postwar democratic theory. No serious student of democracy in the postwar era thought about democracy without first wanting to protect it from the dangers of totalitarianism. The overwhelming desire to fend off totalitarianism predisposed postwar attempts to conceive what democracy is and should be.[3] Some of the things that Truman foregrounded, as well as those he did not mention (such as freedom from want, which his predecessor stressed but a few years ago), were as much a redefinition of America's identity as they were an attack on the Soviet Union.

Truman's speech shows the acute significance of distinguishing totalitarianism as sharply as possible from the liberal democracy that postwar America was supposed to embody and safeguard. Indeed, concerted efforts were made to identify totalitarianism's unique attributes and to define it as a "novel form of government."[4] The pursuit of a clean break, however, was persistently bedeviled by a troubling fact: that totalitarianism emerged from a broadly democratic setting.[5] Even as they contended that totalitarianism was "unique and *sui generis*," Carl Friedrich and Zbigniew Brzezinski admitted that totalitarianism "could have arisen only within the context of mass democracy and modern technology."[6] In this sense, they stated, totalitarianism was less the antithesis than "the perversion of democracy."[7] Similarly, despite their widely diverging views, most scholars who traced the origins of totalitarianism, apart from those who highlighted the allegedly authoritarian German "national character,"[8] debated the dynamics of capitalism,[9] the decline of Christianity,[10] and the pathologies of liberalism and the Enlightenment[11]—conditions undeniably shared by liberal democracy. Thus totalitarianism was not just an external threat, although combating the perceived worldwide "contagion" of communism was an important part of it.[12] The struggle against totalitarianism also meant preventing democracy's perversion, keeping it from falling into the traps of modernization.

This struggle to eradicate totalitarian seeds within democracy animated the reconstruction of democratic theory in the early years of the Cold War.[13] The gist of that reconstruction is often discussed with reference to Joseph Schumpeter, who, in *Capitalism, Socialism, and Democracy* (1942), proposed to supplant "classical democratic theory," alleged to be erroneously beholden to the ideal of popular sovereignty, with a new theory that defined democracy as a "method" or an "institutional arrangement" for "arriving at political decisions in which individuals acquire the power to decide by means of a competitive struggle for the people's vote."[14] An otherwise diverse group of democratic theorists, such as Robert Dahl, Bernard Berelson, Seymour Martin Lipset, Gabriel Almond and Sidney Verba, and Henry Mayo, worked within the framework that pitted the people against the "institutional arrangement," even as they expanded and modified Schumpeter's prototypical formulation.[15]

The ensuing debate was a fraught one. Advocates of Schumpeterian democracy defended their position in the name of science and realism, portraying classical democratic theory, pejoratively, as metaphysics and idealism. Opponents vigorously contested this charge, protesting what they viewed as the inaccurate and reductive description of classical democratic theory and disputing the claim to scientific neutrality as untenable, if not disingenuous. The disagreement was not simply an academic one, a fight for the definition of "social science" and the legitimacy of different methodologies. It reflected broader political concerns about the state of American democracy and the desirable direction and process of reform. Here the intradisciplinary debate in political science intersected with a more overtly political debate between leading postwar intellectuals who approved the general contours of American democracy while trying to chart a modest path for reform, such as Arthur Schlesinger Jr. and Daniel Bell, and their radical critics, such as C. Wright Mills and Herbert Marcuse. Intellectual and political allegiances that were almost indistinguishably melded together polarized the debate over postwar democratic theory, which hardened into a set of conceptual binaries: the empirical versus the normative, the elite versus the popular, stability versus participation. We still remember that debate through those binaries.

My aim in this chapter is to recast these familiar binaries with a focus on the problem of democratic subjectivity. Although it rarely rose to the surface, a concern about political subjectivity was a key factor in Cold War democratic theory's formation. While Cold War democratic theory is typically known for its formalism and strictly institutional focus, its construction was actually guided by value-laden presuppositions about "the masses," which postwar social scientists converted into professedly value-free theses. In doing so, they effectively incorporated the negative images of the masses created by antidemocratic thinkers into their democratic theory, blurring the line between the demos as the foundation of democracy and the masses as a fatal threat to it. This peculiar intellectual hybridization shaped postwar democratic theory's tendency to orient people's attention and commitment away from public claims appealing to the common good and political equality. The shifting line between the masses and the demos was a reigning concern for different iterations of Cold War democratic theory, advanced most notably by Schumpeter and Dahl, which redefined democracy so as to safeguard and manage that line.

This is not to say that the attempt to cultivate democratic citizenship disappeared altogether in the postwar period. Rather, what I suggest is that what it means to be a democratic citizen underwent a significant change. If progressive democratic theorists stressed citizens' recognition of their interdependence and their disposition to address their shared problems through collective efforts, Cold War democratic theorists emphasized citizens' allegiance to a given ideal—postwar America as an embodiment of individual liberty, toleration, pluralism, and free-market capitalism. And they placed democracy outside that sacrosanct realm of loyalty, redescribing it as an instrument that individuals and groups use only to advance their private goals. In reifying this instrumental conception of democracy, its advocates did not confront the readiness with which they adopted stock assumptions about mass subjectivity and the extent to which those assumptions colored their analysis of democracy. However, critics often passed over the question of political subjectivity too quickly as well. They faulted their opponents for reducing room for popular political activity, while tending to treat generalized political indifference as a derivative matter, as merely blocked participation, which could be resolved as soon as barriers to participation were removed. But the problem of postwar democratic theory is not simply the degree to which it encourages or discourages political participation. Nor is it just a matter of how many actors it gets involved in decision-making. The real issue, I contend, is what kind of participation it authorizes, and what kind of environment it constructs in which participation would take place.

Behind "Realistic" Democratic Theory

Many postwar intellectuals claimed to inherit pragmatism. Seizing on the dichotomy of moral and political absolutism and authoritarianism versus empirical science and democracy, they rejected "ideology" in favor of scientific pragmatism. Sidney Hook, a self-appointed disciple of Deweyan pragmatism and one of the staunchest cold warriors, put the matter in characteristically stark terms. Maintaining that "the Communist crusade against the Western democracies" required an understanding of the respective political system's philosophical and cultural basis, Hook identified the "experimental, empirical attitude" that "assesses the truth of assertions and claims ... in terms of relevant results and consequences" as the most important element of democracy, contrasting it to the "fanaticisms of political and social creeds emotionally based on *Weltanschauungen.*"[16] Similarly, Daniel Boorstin, one of the most exuberant celebrants of American democracy, argued that Americans' lack of interest in a metaphysical political philosophy protected them from the "idolatry" that plagued the "characteristic tyrranies [*sic*] of our time—naziism, fascism, and communism," going so far as to reinterpret American history (the struggles of the Puritans, the American Revolution, and the Civil War) as the unfolding of the "pragmatic spirit."[17] But even more cautious thinkers employed the same binary. Calling ideology "a secular religion," Daniel Bell argued that postwar liberalism's vision must be an "empirical one."[18] Arthur Schlesinger mocked the "sentimentalists, the utopians, wailers," who, in his view, seek in politics an "emotional orgasm," failing to recognize that "the great decisions of public policy are not actors' poses, struck with gestures for purpose of dramatic effect [but] made in practical circumstances with real consequences."[19]

Although much of the conceptual framework for the postwar studies of democracy was already prepared during the interwar period,[20] it is hard to make sense of the stranglehold that the stark divide between "unrealistic" political theory and "empirical" science held over postwar democratic theory without taking into account this broader, explicitly political, debate. Almost all the political scientists relied on that divide to stake out their position. Henry Mayo stated that the classical ideal of the "rule by the people" was plainly obsolete, announcing that "it makes almost no sense to say that the people rule in any modern state, in any ordinary sense of the word."[21] In an influential study on voting behavior, Bernard Berelson and his colleagues argued that "realistic research" about voter ignorance and apathy pointed to the need to "correct the empirical presuppositions of normative theory."[22] Asserting that the conventional view of democratic citizenship stressed "activity, involvement, rationality," Gabriel Almond and Sidney Verba observed that such a norm was inconsistent with the empirical fact that citizens in real democracies were "not well informed, not deeply involved, not particularly active."[23]

In their attempt to build a "realistic" theory of democracy, many postwar democratic theorists relied on what Robert Dahl called the "descriptive method" or what came to be known as methodological behavioralism. In contrast to the "method of maximization," which specifies a set of goals to be maximized in a democracy, the descriptive method would consider "as a single class of phenomena all those nations states and social organizations that are commonly called democratic by political scientists," and extrapolate a theory of democracy from the distinguishing features of those so-called democracies.[24] Critics countered that this purportedly descriptive method was already normative, since it reified the existing conditions of postwar America—which was used as a primary case for the purpose of "describing" democracy—as the definition of democracy. This conceptualization, critics complained, severely distorts political observation and analysis, as it makes what might otherwise be perceived as a problem, such as low levels of participation, a "normal" state consistent with the definition of democracy.[25] In turn, practitioners of behavioralism insisted that they were not justifying the status quo and professed their commitment to reform. At this point, the debate reached a stalemate, as behavioralists and their critics were now apparently arguing over how quickly reform should proceed, rather than its nature and direction.

We can approach the normative implications of "realistic" democratic theory from a different vantage point. As discussed in chapter 2, the apparent continuation of pragmatist epistemology in the postwar period can be deceptive, insofar as it conceals that postwar democratic theorists detached pragmatism from its central concern: the formation of democratic subjectivity. From this perspective, the real problem with postwar democratic theory is not just that it constrains popular political activity. Rather, the trouble is that it recognizes and thereby authorizes only a particular kind of political claim as befitting democracy: that is, claims based on private interests. When one conceives of democratic claims in this way, one has no basis for discriminating competing claims; they are all merely an expression of private interests, so they are not—should not be—subject to a moral and political judgment of anyone other than the claimants themselves. The notion of a responsive public attuned to the common good and political equality, then, is but a justification for moral imposition and political oppression. In instrumental democracy, citizens either make their own political claims about their private concerns or, when their private concerns are not at stake, do not engage at all. Instrumental democracy is organized by a binary code: it is either participation or nonparticipation, with the former indicating demand and the latter contentment. Prevailing critiques of postwar democratic theory stop short of challenging that binary code.

The instrumentalization of democracy and the eclipse of the demos qua a responsive public in postwar democratic theory cannot be explained by its practitioners' professed commitment to science. As noted earlier, in postwar America, pronouncing one's commitment to science was already a political act. I suggest that the formation of instrumental democracy was driven by concerns about "the masses."[26] While the critique of the masses is a long-standing theme in political theory, it remained outside democratic theory in that it justified rejecting or curbing democracy rather than calling for a reimagination of the democratic ideal itself.[27] Only under the pressure of totalitarianism did the hostility to the masses become an integral component of democratic theory. Showing this, however, requires some excavation, as it is buried in abstract and deliberately value-neutral language. I first examine how Joseph Schumpeter's democratic theory, *the* point of reference for postwar democratic theorists, is premised specifically on worries about the masses. Then I discuss how antimass presuppositions found their way into the postwar intellectual universe to shape the reconstruction of democratic theory. Finally, I analyze Robert Dahl's theory of polyarchy—perhaps the most sophisticated iteration of instrumental democracy—through the lens of democratic subjectivity.

Schumpeter's Democratic Theory

In *Capitalism, Socialism, and Democracy,* Joseph Schumpeter advances a number of key claims that frame postwar democratic theory. Anticipating a widespread trend, Schumpeter presents his democratic theory as a realistic one, contrasting it to the "classical doctrine of democracy," which is allegedly premised on logically unsustainable assumptions. Particularly untenable for him are the foundational concepts of the common good and the will of the people. Schumpeter claims that classical democratic theory presupposes that "there exists a Common Good . . . which is always simple to define and which every normal person can be made to see by means of rational argument," and "there is also a Common Will of the people

... that is exactly coterminous with the common good."[28] On the surface, his charge seems to be that classical democratic theory rises and falls on the metaphysically predetermined concept of the common good and the common will. If that were the case, then it would be easy to reject his claim because, although it appealed to many postwar democratic theorists who were eager to reject metaphysics in favor of more scientific studies of democracy, it is patently false.[29] One can simply point out that both Rousseau and J. S. Mill, whom Schumpeter groups together, along with Bentham, as proponents of classical theory,[30] make the opposite argument and treat a common good as an outcome of, not a precondition for, political participation and discussion.[31]

But there is something odd about Schumpeter's dismissal of classical democratic theory. He is no political theorist, to be sure, but throughout *Capitalism, Socialism, and Democracy* he shows a remarkable historical sensitivity. He develops his well-known thesis about the demise of capitalism by engaging with Max Weber's theory of rationalization, emphasizing long-term historical trends that he predicts would ultimately undermine the major engine of capitalist development: seemingly irrational innovative entrepreneurial activities.[32] In this light, we might more plausibly view Schumpeter's attack on the common good not as a critique of any value-laden metaphysics but as a refutation of a particular kind of democracy that he thought, as did many others in the early twentieth century, was emerging as a historical reality. What he describes, in other words, may not be a set of philosophical premises but his perception of what would happen in mass democracy.[33]

For Schumpeter, rationalization paves the ground for capitalism's supersession by socialism, not simply by marginalizing the entrepreneurial spirit but also by spreading hostility to capitalism itself. Although entrepreneurs lead capitalist development, he contends, they need docile workers to carry out that function. In other words, the success of capitalism requires a hierarchy in the labor force as much as it relies on entrepreneurial leadership. But the progress of capitalism threatens this condition. According to Schumpeter, workers' voluntary subordination rests on "traditional" sources such as their unquestioning acquiescence and customary deference to their superiors, but capitalism dismantles these very sources by cultivating the calculating mind-set and tearing down the feudal institutions. The "rationalization of the soul," he writes, "rubs off all the glamour of super-empirical sanction from every species of classwise rights."[34] Schumpeter also rebukes the bourgeoisie for their shortsighted destruction of all the "fetters" of feudalism: "Those fetters not only hampered, they also sheltered [the interest of the bourgeoisie]."[35] Worse, the breakdown of labor discipline in the factory does not remain an isolated phenomenon; it eventually overflows into government. It is here that the expansion of democracy, promoting the belief to "the laborers that they were just as valuable citizens as anyone else," is so dangerous. Schumpeter laments that as feudalism gives way to mass democracy, government's attitude experiences a shift from "backing the master" to "backing the workingmen's right to being considered an equal partner in a bargain, and from this to backing the trade union against both employers and individual workingmen."[36] The democratic inclusion of new constituents, many of them embodying anticapitalist values, would turn the historical tendencies that were eroding capitalism into irreversible facts by entrenching those values in the political and legal structure. And they would do so by usurping political symbols such as the "common good" or the "will of the people." *That* is what worries Schumpeter.[37]

Schumpeter's historical account of modernization is largely invisible in his discussion of democracy. As he propounds his new conception of democracy, Schumpeter shrouds his disapproval of workers' demands and dispositions, which may be considered quite rational in light of the historical processes he charts, and transhistoricizes the matter, portraying ordinary citizens as irrational in their psychological makeup. Relying heavily on Gustave Le Bon's concept of the "psychological crowd," Schumpeter asserts that people suffer from "a reduced sense of responsibility, a lower level of energy of thought and greater sensitiveness to non-logical influences," and not only when they are physically copresent.[38] "Newspaper readers, radio audiences, members of a party even if not physically gathered together are terribly easy to work up into a psychological crowd and into a state of frenzy in which attempt at rational argument only spurs the animal spirits."[39] As we will see, Cold War democratic theorists paid exclusive attention to this part of Schumpeter's book, in complete disregard of his far lengthier discussion of modernity that precedes and shapes it, as they preoccupied themselves with studying the correlation between certain psychological traits and antidemocratic attitudes and behavior.

Schumpeter does qualify his application of Le Bon's crowd psychology. He points out that there are areas in which individuals are not subject to the crowd mentality and are able to make rational decisions. We see this ability, for example, in consumers' behavior ("It is simply not true that housewives are easily fooled"), but the same holds true more generally when an individual is engaged in activities that "directly concern himself, his family, his business dealings, his hobbies, his friends and enemies, his township or ward, his class, church, trade union or any other social group of which he is an active member."[40] Even in politics, chances are diminished but do not disappear altogether. When it comes to local affairs or certain national issues that concern people "so directly and unmistakably," such as taxes or economic policies, individuals are capable of forming relatively rational opinions.[41] These qualifications, then, would seem to buttress the case for classical democratic theory, at least in those areas where rationality prevails, but Schumpeter dismisses that inference. Even when circumstances are such that we can believe individual opinions to be rational, he writes, those opinions may "often strike us as unintelligent, narrow, egotistical." Thus "it may not be obvious to everyone why, when it comes to political decisions, we should worship at their shrine, still less why we should feel bound to count each of them for one and none of them for more than one." Again, classical democratic theory "evidently stands to gain little" from people's rationality exhibited in certain political issues, because people are "bad and indeed corrupt judges" of their long-term interests.[42]

In a strange turn of reasoning, Schumpeter partially acknowledges ordinary citizens' rational capacity, only to contradict it by reiterating his point about their lowly and corrupt nature, questioning even the minimal condition of democracy—the one-person, one-vote principle—that his realistic theory of democracy apparently embraces. And not surprisingly, his commitment to democracy only becomes shakier as he moves to consider political issues supposedly more distant from people's concern and knowledge. Here he adopts a full-blown version of Le Bon's crowd psychology, announcing, in an oft-quoted passage, that "the typical citizen drops down to a lower level of mental performance as soon as he enters the political field. He argues and analyzes in a way which he would readily recognize as infantile within the sphere of his real interests. He becomes a primitive again. His thinking becomes associative and affective."[43] "The electoral mass," Schumpeter quips, "is incapable of action other than a stampede."[44]

Once we see Schumpeter's critique of the common good not as an abstract theoretical argument but as a historically specific warning against the destruction of the bourgeois order, we can make better sense of some of the puzzling aspects of his democratic theory. Schumpeter's theory was widely embraced by postwar political scientists as a democratic one, for the reason that it foregrounds competition between elites, which supposedly grants citizens the power to produce and evict the government. But he conceptualizes electoral competition in such a way that elite circulation becomes a remote possibility, and the idea of popular selection is rendered virtually meaningless. To begin with, Schumpeter's concept of competition is extremely forgiving. Though democratic competition rules out the use of military force, he muses, it "does not exclude 'unfair' or 'fraudulent' competition or restraint of competition." Although there are various ways in which "the democratic method of government shades off into the autocratic one by imperceptible steps," it is, for realistic democrats, "as it should be."[45] Likewise, Schumpeter is remarkably cavalier about freedom of the press, which is essential for political competition to be democratic in the minimal sense. If not everyone is given the equal chance of running for office, then citizens should at least have access to information and a variety of opinions to confirm that the elites they are electing are indeed the ones they actually want. Schumpeter notes that elite competition is often conducive to freedom of the press, but only to say that "this relation between democracy and freedom is not absolutely stringent and can be tampered with."[46] This is especially troubling, since Schumpeter argues that the "will of the people" is often "manufactured" by influential political and social groups in a manner "analogous to the ways of commercial advertising."[47] Without freedom of the press and robust deliberation, people are constantly cajoled and manipulated into artificial political preferences, and minimal democracy morphs into a propaganda war. At that point, citizens' political role, already reduced to occasional voting, becomes nothing but redundant and, purportedly, democratic elitism turns into full-fledged autocracy. Even if people's opinions are somehow formed despite all of this, it is unclear when, if ever, the elite would respond to them. As he observes, "even if strong and definite," people's opinions "remain latent, *often for decades,* until they are called to life by some political leader."[48]

Embracing Schumpeter: Postwar Democratic Theory Meets the Masses

Unlike Schumpeter, postwar democratic theorists did not blatantly approve fraudulent electoral competition and the overt manipulation of public opinion. Nonetheless, the same anxiety about the irrationality of the demos qua the masses deeply inflected their ideas about democracy, bringing them strikingly close to his basic propositions about democracy. In the postwar era, studies of the irrationality, prejudice, and ignorance of people poured forth, and many democratic theorists believed that those findings revealed not just the implausibility but the danger of the ideal of popular sovereignty. Influential research on voting behavior, such as *Voting* (1954) and *The American Voter* (1960), offered apparent evidence that the average voter was neither informed nor consistent in his or her preferences.[49] And such findings greatly impressed postwar democratic theorists. Robert Dahl and Charles Lindblom stated that "the greater number of people often do not have definite preferences on a given issue ... or their preferences are often so ambiguous or conflicting."[50] Henry Mayo announced that "the bulk of the voters are quite incompetent to judge complex details of public policy."[51] A similar verdict was issued by Gabriel Almond and Sidney Verba, who argued that "it is becoming clear" that "the process by which they [citizens] come to their voting decision is anything but a process of rational calculation."[52]

Still, if the concern is simply a matter of people's ignorance or inconsistency, it is difficult to understand why so many democratic theorists were so adamant that the very ideal of democracy must be revised. Why did they not study how to help citizens become better informed? Why did they not rail against manipulative campaign practices that tried only to sway citizens' emotions while obscuring substantive issues? Why did they not call for more robust civic education? That was exactly how some political scientists reacted to similar findings about voting behavior only a few decades earlier.[53]

Postwar democratic theorists took the apparently deplorable state of the citizens they observed as a premise rather than a challenge because, like Schumpeter, they believed that the masses are not just ignorant but irrational—and destructively so. Theories of mass society gave that assumption intellectual currency and credibility and put it at the center of postwar intellectual consciousness. Postwar social scientists were deeply affected by that discursive milieu, but rather than directly importing European-born psychological theories whose philosophical-historical approach was unfamiliar and seemed unscientific to them, they detached mass psychology from its historical context, fashioned some of its findings into variables amenable to "scientific" tests, and looked for correlations between psychological traits allegedly engrained in certain groups of people and more overtly political tendencies that they exhibited, such as susceptibility to antidemocratic propaganda.

The Specter of the Masses

The tide of mass society theory began to rise well before the Cold War commenced in earnest. By the late 1930s, the concept of totalitarianism almost completely dominated the intellectual discourse as Nazism and Soviet communism merged in intellectual as well as popular discourse (more on this in chapter 5). And it sharply focused attention on the image of the masses, who, driven by their deep-seated frustration and mystified by ideology, are supposedly eager to reduce themselves to an unthinking and violent cog of a collectivity, renouncing their individual autonomy and destroying that of others. Already in the 1940s, influential accounts, both scholarly and fictional, analyzed and portrayed threats of totalitarianism in these terms, including Erich Fromm's *Escape from Freedom* (1941), Arthur Koestler's *Darkness at Noon* (1941), and George Orwell's *1984* (1949). There were also accounts of the concentration camps and the complete destruction of individuality there, as in Bruno Bettelheim's "Individual and Mass Behavior in Extreme Situations" (1943) and Leo Lowenthal's "Terror's Atomization of Man" (1946).[54] But it was Hannah Arendt's *The Origins of Totalitarianism* (1951) that put the experience of totalitarianism in a broader philosophical and historical perspective, leaving, it seemed, no doubt about the indissoluble connection between the masses, ideology, and the destruction of individuality. The disintegration of traditional social ties such as nation-states and hierarchically organized classes, Arendt wrote, produced "one great unorganized, structureless mass of furious individuals" who had nothing in common except for their vague but intense hostility to the status quo.[55] Thoroughly deprived, those individuals were drawn to an ideology that promised a complete overthrow of the existing social structure, and unsure of their place in the world, they developed a strong yearning to belong to something larger, paying absolute obedience, trusting propaganda even when it was at odds with the "reality" of their own experience, and, finally, willingly sacrificing themselves for a destructive cause.[56] Thus fueled, totalitarianism culminated in the concentration camps as its "laboratories" where individuality was obliterated so completely that "nothing ... remains but ghastly marionettes with human faces, which all behave like the dog in Pavlov's experiments, which all react with perfect reliability even when going to one's own death, and which do nothing but react."[57]

Many intellectuals saw in postwar America a society in which individuality was besieged by mass conformity. If their pragmatism was defensive in its political orientation, it was not simply because they believed the Soviet Union was waging a particularly effective campaign for absolutism, but because they worried that many of their own people were already susceptible to it. While this worry was sometimes expressed as a general concern about ineradicable human depravity, as in Reinhold Niebuhr's account of original sin,[58] what gave it shape was the so-called theory of mass society, which Daniel Bell proclaimed to be "Marxism apart ... probably the most influential social theory in the world today."[59] Mass society theory stems from modernization theory, advanced most notably by Emile Durkheim and Max Weber, which highlights how major features of modernization, such as secularization, industrial capitalism, and technologies of mass communication and transportation, cause social and psychological disarray by depriving the masses of traditional social bonds and communal ties. This broad motif developed in many directions, but against the backdrop of totalitarianism, the alleged connection between the masses' psychological dispositions and political authoritarianism became the focus of intense interest.

Mass society theory helps explain why postwar intellectuals were so preoccupied with the danger of the masses in America, even though their mobilization in totalitarian regimes occurred under remarkably different circumstances. Whereas the group of furious individuals that Arendt described came into being in the midst of a deep economic depression and a disintegrating social order, America had just emerged victorious and relatively unscathed from a war and was beginning to experience a tremendously prosperous economy. Postwar intellectuals were duly impressed by America's economic abundance as well as its drift toward welfare capitalism, and they hoped those trends would expand a middle class and strengthen democracy.[60] So why were they worried that the masses, who, by their own account, were beneficiaries of triumphant liberalism, would subvert it?

Because the masses are afflicted with deep-seated psychological tendencies drawing them toward ideology and totalitarianism. Erich Fromm's widely read *Escape from Freedom* was one of the influential sources of this presupposition, though the conclusion Fromm derived from his analysis was nearly opposed to the one drawn by most postwar intellectuals. Fromm identifies as one of the most important aspects of modernity "individuation," the growth of individual independence resulting from the decline of traditional ties maintained by collective, authoritarian institutions such as the church, state, or community.[61] Individuation is an ambivalent process because, with the dissolution of traditional ties that used to give people security and a sense of belonging, individuals feel isolated, lost, and powerless even as they gain more independence. Freedom becomes an "unbearable burden," and "powerful tendencies arise to escape from this kind of freedom into submission."[62] Fromm discusses various "mechanisms" of escape from freedom, including authoritarianism, destructiveness, and cultural conformity, but what is most pertinent to our discussion here is his discussion of sadomasochism in relation to political authoritarianism. Fromm theorizes that, though seemingly opposite, masochism and sadism are derived from the same psychological tendency to "give up the independence of one's own individual self and to fuse one's self with somebody or something outside of oneself in order to acquire the strength which the individual self is lacking."[63] In its attitude toward authority, the sadomasochistic character is one and the same with the "authoritarian character" in that the sadomasochistic person simultaneously submits to authority and wants submission from others, and it constitutes the psychological basis of fascism and Nazism.[64]

In *The Vital Center* (1949), an authoritative statement of Cold War liberalism, Arthur Schlesinger explained the threat of totalitarianism precisely in these psychoanalytical terms. Relying on Fromm's "remarkable analysis," Schlesinger asserts that totalitarianism appeals to those nominally free yet anxious individuals who have developed "the strivings for submission and for domination, the losing of self in masochism or sadism."[65] In his Niebuhrian twist, however, Schlesinger turns this into a "consistent pessimism about man," which, he insists, "alone can inoculate the democratic faith" against authoritarianism.[66] Schlesinger does not mention that his inspiration, Fromm, draws conclusions quite opposed to his. Fromm sees the modern individual's higher risk of developing sadomasochistic tendencies not as a premise of politics to be accepted but as an outcome of inadequate political, economic, and social conditions. Nor does Fromm believe that only authoritarian regimes represent those inadequate conditions. He warns that the current form of democracy imposes conformity and offers only bogus ways of expressing individuality, such as "personalized" commodities. To counter these trends, Fromm calls for an expansion of democratic principles—both old ("government elected by the people and responsible to people") and new ("that no one shall be allowed to starve, that society is responsible for all its members, that no one shall be frightened into submission and lose his human pride through fear of unemployment and starvation")—to establish a more participatory politics, a planned economy that reflects its members' concerted efforts and serves their needs, and a vibrant culture that encourages and celebrates genuinely individual spontaneity and difference.[67] Fromm's radical agenda is nowhere to be seen in Schlesinger's "new radicalism." Schlesinger notes with trepidation that "the 'anxious man' ... is the characteristic inhabitant of free society in the twentieth century," who is constantly tempted by totalitarianism's promise of existence without anxiety—the promise that liberalism cannot make.[68] All liberal democracy can do, in his view, is guard itself against its characteristic inhabitants.

As Fromm's defense of social democracy indicates, the insights into the modern individual's psychological precariousness were open to widely different approaches to democracy. While Schlesinger's generalized pessimism goes some way toward explaining the motivation behind the instrumentalization of democracy, it does not fully account for postwar democratic theorists' discriminating attitude toward different subjectivities. For this we need to consider another strand of mass society theory that explicitly implicates democracy in the supposedly irrational psychology of the masses. This viewpoint, articulated most clearly by the Spanish philosopher José Ortega y Gasset, depicts the masses not as a victim of modernity but as its ungrateful beneficiary and, in a darker departure from Fromm's analysis, indicts democracy for intensifying the masses' psychological propensities. According to Ortega, totalitarianism is not a conspiracy of some sinister outside force; the *internal* dynamics of mass democracy are responsible for it.[69] This argument, although it first appeared in the 1930s, provided a key inspiration for postwar political thought. As the intellectual historian Jan-Werner Müller reports, Ortega's *The Revolt of the Masses,* published in 1932, "remained *the* philosophical bestseller in a number of West European countries from the early 1930s to the late 1950s."[70] Contemporaneous sources confirm Ortega's influence. In his critical survey of mass society theory written in 1956, Daniel Bell treats Ortega as one of its major representatives.[71] In her account of postwar political thought published in 1957, Judith Shklar went further and placed

Ortega squarely at the center of the shift from the "dramatic efforts of many intellectuals during the Thirties to join the masses" to "fear of the masses" in the postwar era, noting that "Ortega y Gasset speaks for more intellectuals now than ever."[72]

In *The Revolt of the Masses,* Ortega announces that the political ascendance of the mass, as a "psychological fact," is the "greatest crisis that can afflict peoples, nations, and civilization."[73] For Ortega, the mass man is characterized not by intellectual inferiority but by a specific moral disposition. The mass man's defining characteristic, Ortega writes, is an unwillingness to evaluate his own worth by independent standards and to strive to better himself. The mass man is "satisfied with himself exactly as he is" and "affirm[s] as good everything he finds in himself: opinions, appetites, preferences, tastes."[74] Like Fromm, Ortega analyzes this mass subjectivity as an outcome of a broad historical process. Specifically, Ortega maintains that the mass man was "produced and prepared" by conditions formed in the nineteenth century.[75] The nineteenth century witnessed the fruition of all the groundbreaking trends initiated centuries earlier, including industrialism, the formation of a strong and effective administrative state, and the ideal of liberal democracy. As a result, an unprecedented number of people had come to enjoy vastly improved economic conditions, physical comfort, public order, and political and social freedom. What these changes amount to, Ortega declares, is nothing short of a "radical innovation in human destiny."[76] For a long time, the life of the common person had been defined by "limitation, obligation, dependence ... oppression ... in the cosmic [sense]."[77] In the nineteenth century, in contrast, the world "does not compel him to limit in any fashion, it sets up no veto [but] incites his appetite, which in principle can increase indefinitely."[78] What once had to be acquired through great effort is now simply given to the masses, and they take those privileges for granted, claiming them as their natural rights. Worse, as Ortega's last remark suggests, what the masses feel they can rightfully demand tends only to increase, as progress appears to them almost automatic. They fail to realize that the civilization they enjoy is built by the self-sacrificing efforts of a few "highly-endowed individuals" who, unlike them, always strive for excellence and lead a disciplined life with a deep sense of obligation.[79] Invisible and unappreciated, these select individuals face extinction in the age of the masses.

Ortega does not believe that the masses could be tamed, must less superseded via participatory social democracy. For him, the masses are a permanent feature of modern society, and what they are doing is far worse than causing occasional disorder; they are bringing a whole new kind of politics into existence: a monstrous species of democracy entirely antithetical to liberal democracy. In Ortega's narrative, liberal democracy is the epitome of civilization, the culmination of the efforts to secure a common life among different people by negotiating their disagreements through discussion governed by independent norms and standards. It is by internalizing this highly unnatural practice that individuals are able to minimize the role of force in their relations and become civilized. What liberal democracy manifests, Ortega proclaims, is the "radical progressive desire on the part of each individual to take others into consideration." By guaranteeing minorities their rights, the majority effectively "announces the determination to share existence with the enemy; more than that, with an enemy which is weak."[80] The masses reverse all of this. Since the mass man is so used to being free of external restraints, he is not in the habit of controlling his impulses in consideration of others. Nor is he amenable to discussion, as he loathes any standard that transcends him. The "most palpable manifestation of the new mentality of the masses," displayed in political movements such as syndicalism and fascism, is the utter lack of care to "give reasons or to be right" and a blind resolution to impose one's opinions.[81] Thus discussion is replaced by violent "direct action." With the rise of the mass, Ortega famously declares, the "old democracy ... tempered by a generous dose of liberalism and of enthusiasm for law" degenerates into a "hyperdemocracy in which the mass acts directly, outside the law, imposing its aspirations and its desires by means of material pressure."[82]

When we focus on the allegiance to pragmatism that postwar liberals apparently shared with progressives, we lose sight of a deep chasm separating them. A crucial link in postwar intellectuals' turn away from their forebears' radical politics was their embrace of mass society theory, which focused attention on conformity as a manifestation of mass subjectivity that could prevail and usher in totalitarianism in any modern society. As postwar intellectuals were trying to draw the lesson of totalitarianism by relying on the theories of mass psychology, a number of slippages occurred. If Fromm portrayed mass subjectivity as a product of a series of historically specific events and political failures, postwar intellectuals interpreted it as an already existing, unalterable condition that liberal democracy must manage. And Fromm's defense of participatory social democracy was inverted into an indictment against it in favor of constrained liberal democracy. Soon after Ortega introduced the distinction between liberal democracy and hyperdemocracy, the notion that there are fundamentally different kinds of democracy—one inundated by the masses and the other keeping them in check—began to take root. In his 1933 essay, Karl Mannheim contrasted a "democracy of reason" led by elites to a "democracy of Impulse" defined by the masses' "uninhibited expression of momentary emotional impulses," warning that the democracy of impulse would give rise to dictatorship.[83] Likewise, Karl Loewenstein characterized authoritarian government as "a supersession of constitutional government with emotional government."[84] It was this binary framework that postwar social scientists codified to fashion a new conception of democracy that contained and managed, if not explicitly antagonized, the demos. But first they had to translate mass society theory into familiar terms.

Operationalizing the Masses

The Authoritarian Personality (1950), a massive multiauthor study sponsored by the American Jewish Committee, heralded the positivist codification of mass society theory. The authors put forth a bold thesis: "The rise of an 'anthropological' species we call the authoritarian type of man," they declared, was "threaten[ing] to replace the individualistic and democratic type prevalent in the past century and a half of our civilization."[85] Led by the critical theorist Theodor Adorno, the authors of *The Authoritarian Personality* were aware of the danger of psychological reductionism their study might reinforce.[86] They ended their study by warning against the idea that fascism could be combated by "psychological means alone" and calling attention to "the total organization of society."[87] Despite this acknowledgment, however, their main claim was that they could identify distinct personality types made of "the political, economic, and social convictions of an individual."[88] Most chapters were devoted to establishing, primarily through the coding of the data gleaned from surveys and interviews, a correlation between an individual's protofascist tendencies and her alleged psychological structure. For instance, the authors would link prejudiced (e.g., anti-Semitic or ethnocentric) opinions that respondents expressed in their questionnaire to certain character traits such as submissiveness, aggressiveness, or the tendency to project unconscious emotional impulses onto the outside world.[89] In one sense, this was a truly damning indictment of prejudices, as it portrayed them not just as reprehensible opinions but as a manifestation of psychological and even cognitive deficiencies. (One of the claims made in *The Authoritarian Personality* is that the authoritarians are more likely to distort reality to fit their preconceptions or to project their repressive needs.[90]) But this framing of the issue has clear limits and dangers. It brushes aside a variety of prejudices as "irrational," putting an end to serious social analysis. Politically, too, it can become a powerful tool for self-justification, when people's support for what is considered an "extremist" position from the observer's viewpoint is ascribed to their internal psychological flaws rather than to legitimate grievances or broader socioeconomic processes.[91]

Seymour Martin Lipset's *The Political Man* (1960)—one of the major texts of Cold War democratic theory—displays some of those limits and dangers. While drawing on findings like the ones in *The Authoritarian Personality* that affinities exist between certain psychological tendencies and support for extremist movements, Lipset goes further in aligning the authoritarian personality with a particular class. The result is his notorious thesis of "working-class authoritarianism." (It is also significant that Lipset redirects the focus of the authoritarian-personality debate from fascism and anti-Semitism to communism. Edward Shils, who, along with Lipset, was one of the major proponents of the end-of-ideology doctrine, criticized *The Authoritarian Personality* for neglecting the apparent fact that communists displayed the same authoritarian psychological traits.[92] Lipset cites Shils's article.[93]) As Lipset puts it, "The lower-class individual is likely to have been exposed to punishment, lack of love, and a general atmosphere of tension and aggression since early childhood—all experiences which tend to produce deep-rooted hostilities expressed by ethnic prejudice, political authoritarianism, and chiliastic transvaluational religion."[94] According to Lipset, these propensities are amplified by lower-class individuals' limited education, their cultural milieu characterized by homogeneity and low intellectual stimulation, and their allegedly habituated pursuit of short-term gratification in disregard of long-term rewards. The outcome is truly frightening: "All of these characteristics produce a tendency to view politics and personal relationships in black-and-white terms, a desire for immediate action, an impatience with talk and discussion, a lack of interest in organizations which have a long-range perspective, and a readiness to follow leaders who offer a demonological interpretation of the evil forces (either religious or political) which are conspiring against them."[95]

To be sure, Lipset resists a deterministic account, pointing out that these predispositions could lead to multiple political outcomes. But the possibility of workers' "normal" political activities is already ruled out; the other outcomes he enumerates are political withdrawal and apathy, which "can be activated by a crisis."[96] Moreover, he does not argue that workers are the only social group that is attracted to extremist movements. He writes that each ideological grouping (left, center, and right)—which is loosely associated with a class position—can develop into either a democratic or an extremist movement, characterizing fascism, in particular, as the extremism of the middle classes comprising "small businessmen, white-collar workers, and the anti-clerical sections of the professional classes."[97] But in Lipset's analysis, the extremism of nonworkers is presented as far more interest based. Small businessmen's opposition to large corporations or labor unions is "irrational" and "reactionary" insofar as they try to reverse some of the inevitable trends of modernization, but Lipset describes this opposition as stemming from their concern about "economic security and high standing in society."[98] He briefly mentions the idea of the authoritarian personality, but mostly as an additional factor that affects a small segment of the fascism-supporting middle class, such as "the small entrepreneurs who live in small communities or on farms" or "the self-employed" as compared to "white-collar workers, executives, and professionals."[99]

Like Schumpeter's account of mass psychology, Lipset's working-class authoritarianism masks his substantive normative concern: his opposition to challenges to the basic organization of the mature industrial society that was exemplified, in his view, by postwar America: "The fundamental political problems of the industrial revolution have been solved: the workers have achieved industrial and political citizenship; the conservatives have accepted the welfare state; and the democratic left has recognized that an increase in over-all state power carries with it more dangers to freedom than solutions for economic problems."[100] As in Schumpeter's case, moreover, Lipset's argument turns into a policing of the legitimate boundaries of democratic politics. Although he does not quite endorse Schumpeter's semiautocratic democracy, Lipset effectively makes democratic politics trivial, redundant, and indeed "boring," as he says when recalling his conversation with the editor of a leading Swedish newspaper. "Now the only issues are whether the metal workers should get a nickel more an hour, the price of milk should be raised, or old-age pensions extended," the editor apparently told him. And those issues, for Lipset, are now the "very stuff of the internal struggle within stable democracies."[101] Class politics are not irrelevant, he notes, but they will become democratic, meaning they will remain within the prevailing consensus of postwar America, as well as within the bounds of electoral politics. "The democratic class struggle will continue," Lipset pronounces, carefully planting the word "democratic" where it simultaneously delimits and subsumes the class struggle, "but it will be a fight without ideologies, without red flags, without May Day parades."[102]

While postwar democratic theorists' concern about the masses was triggered by the specific historical experiences of fascism and especially Nazism, it was soon transhistoricized as they constructed positivistic links between political behavior and the psychological structure. Believing that they could isolate universally valid variables from long, complex, and contingent historical processes, postwar democratic theorists took a snapshot of history and reified the relationship between a particular personality structure and the activation of totalitarianism. Assured by supposedly scientific models, they drew a sweepingly general lesson from traumatic but hardly generalizable cases, such as the breakdown of the Weimar Republic: the danger of any and all political involvement of the masses. Thus Henry Mayo confidently speculated: "It is not an established truth that democracy suffers from voting apathy, or that any democracy has fallen because of it. . . . My own impression is that the evidence points overwhelmingly the other way, that there has always been wide, almost feverish public interest in politics and voting in countries where democracy has collapsed, e.g., in the Weimar republic."[103] Similarly, Lipset contended that "the events of the 1930s in Germany" show that "the belief that a very high level of participation is always good for democracy is not valid."[104] Robert Dahl, while professing his eagerness to see higher levels of participation from marginalized groups, cautioned that participation must not come at the expense of stability, invoking "the possibility of democratic failures eventuating in brutal dictatorships."[105] This is why the evidently different conditions of postwar America did not do much to assuage these theorists' fear of the masses. They were sure of it: a large group of people, especially those who were poor, not highly educated, and socially alienated, posed a mortal threat to democracy not because they benefited least from the regime but because their mind was wired differently. Thus their dissatisfaction with the present construction of democracy was cause for alarm, not an occasion for citizens' attention and response.

The Cycle of Apathy: The Pluralist
Iteration of Instrumental Democracy

Considering their deep wariness about the masses, it is not entirely surprising that postwar democratic theorists met their empirical findings about widespread apathy with a measure of relief. In one of the most influential postwar studies on voting behavior, Bernard Berelson and his colleagues suggested that "low affect toward the election—not caring much—underlies the resolution of many political problems," arguing that "lack of interest by some people" prevents political fragmentation, provides maneuvering room for political shifts, and facilitates compromise.[106] "It is (perhaps fortunately) true that not everyone is actively interested in politics," Mayo stated, conveying a similar sentiment. "Instead ... of preaching the duty to act as a political animal to those who have no inclination that way, and would do it badly if compelled, it may well be wiser to leave them to cultivate their private gardens, and to rely merely upon the experience of democracies that there is always in fact a wide enough interest in politics and voting to work the political machinery."[107] Herbert McClosky, reporting that many ordinary citizens neither understood nor supported not just particular issues but basic principles of American democracy, put the matter even more bluntly: "Democratic viability is ... saved by the fact that those who are most confused about democratic ideas are also likely to be politically apathetic and without significant influence.... Apathy ... keep[s] doubters from acting upon their differences."[108]

For critics, postwar democratic theorists' blithe embrace of apathy was one of the most glaring pieces of evidence that revealed the elitist character of instrumental democracy. But Robert Dahl would have none of it. Thoroughly rankled by the charge of elitism, Dahl complained that the critics failed to recognize the distinction between empirical description and normative prescription.[109] As a general point, this argument is not persuasive, not only because it is hard not to read some of the foregoing remarks as a judgment on the desirability of apathy but, as Quentin Skinner has pointed out, also because the very use of the term "democracy" has, then as now, the ideological effect of commending a political system thus labeled. In that context, empirically describing a political system characterized by widespread apathy as democracy effectively constitutes the speech act of normatively endorsing it.[110] Still, Dahl was adamant that, if not others, then he for one was committed to the ideal of popular sovereignty and supported citizens' vibrant political activity, and he was troubled by the existing level of political participation. As evidence of his commitment, he pointed to the theory of polyarchy he developed in *A Preface to Democratic Theory* (1956).[111]

Thus Dahl's theory of polyarchy or political pluralism presents itself as a particularly tough test case for my analysis of postwar democratic theory. Dahl specifically claimed that the typical criticism did not apply to his theory, and critics, too, were generally appreciative of its intellectual rigor and sophistication and tended to exempt it from their criticism.[112] Moreover, Dahl's theory of polyarchy may be considered not just the most sophisticated but the most democratic iteration of instrumental democracy. Unlike Schumpeter's leadership democracy, which erects a dividing wall between the world of elites and that of citizens and nonchalantly permits a one-way manipulation by the former of the latter, Dahl's polyarchy is genuinely committed to basic political rights, stresses the importance of citizens' control over elites, and places far more emphasis on political participation. Highlighting these aspects, some later observers went so far as to suggest that Dahl's theory anticipates more radical strands of pluralist democracy.[113] In light of all of this, we might expect polyarchy to be free from instrumental democracy's distinct characteristics and perilous tendencies. To test this expectation, in what follows I examine Dahl's theory of polyarchy, first by outlining its conceptual architecture, and then by analyzing its implications.

Robert Dahl's Theory of Polyarchy

Dahl accepts the basic precepts of instrumental democracy proposed by Schumpeter—that democracy is an instrument standing apart from the formation of the demos and used differently by elites and ordinary citizens but commonly to advance their private goals—but refines those precepts in three important ways. First of all, unlike Schumpeter, who limits democracy to the mere existence of elections or citizens' nominal right to select their leaders, Dahl stresses that democracy involves "processes by which ordinary citizens exert a relatively high degree of control over leaders."[114] Second, while Dahl rejects the idea of "the people," he does so neither by caricaturing them as the embodiment of a singular will nor by dismissing citizens as irrational and irresponsible masses, as does Schumpeter. Instead, Dahl debunks the notion of the people through a brilliant discussion of intensity. Traditional democratic theory has paid most attention to *what* people decide, Dahl reasons, but in a pluralist society where people are faced with multiple issues, what is equally important is *how much* they care about a particular issue relative to others.[115] The concept of intensity makes clear that the election of a particular candidate could rarely, if ever, be interpreted as an expression of support, on voters' part, for all the policy positions of that candidate. Voters often select a particular candidate if her position on one policy they care intensely about accords with theirs, even if they disagree with her on all the other issues about which they care only mildly or not at all. Candidates are elected, therefore, not because they reflect the preferences of a monolithic majority, but because they have managed to gather enough policy positions, each of which strongly appeals to some people—typically a minority, since the majority of people usually do not have strong feelings about most policies. In this respect, what is realized in democracy most of the time is neither majority rule nor minority rule but *"minorities* rule."[116]

Finally, this insight leads Dahl to place far more emphasis on citizens' political activity, not just voting but also participation through interest groups. If elites are controlled not by the "will of the people" but by intense preferences held by various minorities, then the distinguishing mark of democracy is not consensus formation but citizens forming or lending support to minorities, "all seeking in various ways to advance their goals, usually at the expense, at least in part, of others."[117] Indeed, that is what two major mechanisms of democracy—recurrent elections and continuous political competition—promote. "Elections and political competition do not make for government by majorities in any significant way, but they vastly increase the size, number, and variety of minorities whose preferences must be taken into account by leaders in making policy choices."[118] For Dahl, therein lies the normative appeal of American democracy. Observing that "perhaps in no other national political system in the world is bargaining [between minorities] so basic a component of the political process," he insists that, despite "all its defects," this feature is what allows American democracy to provide a "high probability that an active and legitimate group in the population can make itself heard effectively at some crucial stage in the process of decision." "This," he declares, is "no mean thing in a political system" and "no negligible contribution ... Americans have made to the arts of government."[119]

The attraction of Dahl's theory is clear. It addresses the concerns about the degeneration of the demos into the masses, not by excluding them outright from the decision-making process but by diffusing their influence by assigning them to various groups. So Dahl's theory is in a better position to claim democratic credentials without endangering stability. Dahl's argument also accorded well with the dominant intellectual tenor of the time. If one political virtue was universally recommended by postwar liberals, it was compromise. Edward Shils argued that "compromise and reasonableness, and prudent self-restraint," are a major requirement of "civil politics" as opposed to "ideological politics."[120] Arthur Schlesinger, while calling for a "revival of American radicalism," insisted that this new radicalism should not "disrupt the fabric of custom, law and mutual confidence," and he declared that "compromise is the strategy of democracy."[121] Daniel Bell praised the political system that forces its participants to make the "deal" as the "pragmatic counterpart of the philosophic principle of toleration" and the "saving grace" of American politics.[122] Even Reinhold Niebuhr, who just a few years earlier had championed open social conflict in the struggle for justice and repudiated precisely the counsel of accommodation and moderation as a justification for the status quo at the expense of marginalized groups, veered toward this trend.[123] In an assessment that would have shocked his former self, Niebuhr declared that "we have managed to achieve a tolerable justice in the collective relations of industry by balancing power against power and equilibrating the various competing social forces of society."[124] Dahl's characterization of compromise and bargaining between minorities as a major dynamic of American democracy validated postwar intellectuals' value orientation.

The Displacement of Democratic Subjectivity in Polyarchy

The numerous critiques of Dahl's pluralist theory of democracy tend to take issue with its scope—how inclusive it is—rather than its framework. The well-known "faces of power" debate is a good example. Peter Bachrach and Morton Baratz object that Dahl's behavioralist approach, with its exclusive attention to readily observable claims in disregard of unarticulated or dormant ones, is blind to a "second face" of power or the problem of "non-decision"—the ways in which powerful actors set agendas so that certain issues are not even recognized.[125] Steven Lukes further suggests that power has a "third face" that molds and manipulates people's preferences so as to favor the interest of the powerful while making people believe those preferences are the outcome of their independent thinking.[126]

To be clear, I think these critics are correct. In fact, judged by the criterion of inclusion, Dahl's polyarchy is quite limited even in terms of power's "first face." Although he professes to be committed to the ideal of popular sovereignty, Dahl shares other postwar democratic theorists' deep anxiety about the masses. Citing "current evidence" that "the lower one's socioeconomic status, the more authoritarian one's predispositions and the less active politically one is likely to be," Dahl warns that "if an increase in political activity brings the authoritarian-minded [lower class] into the political arena," it could undermine polyarchy.[127] He repeats this point right after he remarks, protesting the charge of elitism, that he would like to see higher rates of participation, especially among marginalized social groups.[128] Put differently, Dahl is not opposed to increased participation only when it happens slowly and gradually as the lower class somehow change their authoritarian mind.[129] In polyarchy, the coming of participatory democracy is continually, if not infinitely, delayed.

But there is another problem. What kinds of issue come to the fore when democracy is competition between contending groups? We can begin to tackle this question by engaging with the arguments of two brilliant critics of political pluralism, Theodore Lowi and Robert Paul Wolff.[130] While their critiques are wide-ranging and have a different focus, both Lowi and Wolff find political pluralism to be contradictory and self-undermining as a theory of democracy. The crux of the problem is that political pluralism increases the expectations for government's positive role while at the same time eroding its authority and independence vis-à-vis organized interest groups. On the one hand, political pluralism justifies the enlargement of government and its delivery of the "public goods," which have long been feared in the liberal tradition, by portraying the government's increased involvement in the provision of social goods and services as a direct outgrowth of social pluralism. On the other hand, as social pluralism—the existence of competing interest groups, which is presumed to be simultaneously an expression and a condition of individual freedom—serves as the exclusive justification for government action, government loses the basis of its authority and becomes an ever-expanding treasure box to be divvied up among competing groups. The only relevant factor in public decision-making is that a political claim is made with sufficient intensity by some group that represents its members' interests. Meanwhile the question of whether that claim is consistent with the norms of justice, equality, or fairness, and the question of how different claims should be weighed and prioritized in relation to others, gets completely sidelined. No entity or process, including government, is endowed with the authority to ask that question. As long as a particular political claim survives intergroup competition and finds its place in whatever equilibrium is reached by that competition, it is presumed to be part of public interest. Political plural-ism, or "interest-group liberalism" as Lowi calls it, "defines public interest as a result of the amalgamation of various claims."[131]

At first glance, the concept of political equilibrium seems to permit a satisfactory account of how purposeless, instrumental democracy works. What generates public decision in democracy is not a preconceived notion of the common good dictated by a mythical entity supposedly represent-ing the whole, such as the demos or the state, but a compromise between rational individuals who seek their private goals. Public interest is noth-ing but a converging point of those countless self-seeking behaviors. On a closer inspection, however, equating public interest with political equilib-rium proves far more problematic. The aggregative view of public interest requires several logical leaps of faith. One must assume, for instance, that established groups' demands, taken together, approximate the composite interest of the entire citizenry. Or if one admits that the interests repre-sented by those groups are parochial, then one must assume that those groups would not press their demands so far as to endanger what may be considered public interest by many, even when most citizens remain apathetic. If all these assumptions prove to be untenable, one must then assume that when interest group competition becomes too intense or strays too far from the view of the larger public, a mechanism exists to detect and check such a deviation and restore it to its desirable state, whatever it is. Postwar democratic theorists were fuzzy on these points and invoked the notion of "overlapping memberships" to suggest that it would prevent a particular interest group from pushing its demands too far, keeping over-all competition within a range that the public would endorse.[132] But this idea remains speculative and, in any case, addresses only the problem of stability and little else.[133] Postwar democratic theorists' readiness to skip an investigation into the cogency of these assumptions stands in sharp contrast to the exacting manner in which they deconstructed the concepts of popular sovereignty and the common good. The outsize benefit of the doubt they gave to the pluralist conception of democracy is hard to under-stand except for the fact that the image of political equilibrium appealed to a broad array of motifs that permeated postwar political thought: the valorization of individual autonomy, the aversion to the idea of collective standards transcending the individual, the promotion of ideological flexibility and compromise, and the emphasis on the stability of existing democratic institutions.

Political pluralism is open-ended to the extent that it is contingent on bargaining between groups, but its openness is directed at a particular type of issues—issues surrounding the *distribution* of the existing resources. As various interest groups struggle to maximize their share of public resources, a whole dimension of democratic politics gets elided. Wolff vividly illustrates this problem: "America is growing uglier, more dangerous, and less pleasant to live in, as its citizens grow richer. The reason is that natural beauty, public order, the cultivation of the arts, are not the special interest of any identifiable social group. Consequently, evils and inadequacies in those areas cannot be remedied by shifting the distribution of wealth and power among existing social groups."[134]

It is thus entirely possible that a particular equilibrium of interest group competition jeopardizes the interest of the majority. Lax environmental regulation, to use one of Wolff's examples, may be satisfactory to various groups involved—companies that might expand their operations more quickly and enlarge their profit margins, current employees who might see salary increases, prospective employees who might benefit from more job openings, and even consumers who might enjoy a lower price—but it can so damage the quality of air and water that, even in purely monetary terms, it is far costlier for the society at large. To make matters worse, political pluralism constricts the scope of government action in favor of established interest groups, making it extremely difficult to change direction. As Lowi puts it, interest group pluralism ends in "the *state of permanent receivership*" in which organized interests collude with large state bureaucracies to entrench "a tremendous pro-organization, pro-establishment, anti-innovation bias," erecting a barrier to the entry of new groups and suppressing reform even if that is what most (unorganized) citizens want.[135]

Wolff and Lowi show the alarming narrowness, inefficiency, and unaccountability of political pluralism. To their argument, one might add that it is a type of democracy that relies for its stability less on its approximate accommodation of citizens' interests and the virtue of compromise, as suggested by its proponents, than on the refusal to address political and socioeconomic *organization* and the reinforcement of the politically apathetic public. These two conditions are closely related. I elaborate the first point in chapter 5, so a brief sketch will suffice here. As postwar democratic theorists observed and celebrated compromise between the leaders of large-scale organizations, few of them paused to consider that postwar America was an exceptionally favorable place for making compromises. As the nation experienced unprecedented economic growth, there were enough resources to satisfy contending parties' demands, albeit partially and differentially. Established political actors could put the difficult question of how to arrange the social and economic structure on hold, as long as the economy kept growing at a stupendous pace and allowed most people to gain in material terms. The distribution occurred unequally, to be sure, but any gain could not be discounted for Americans recovering from the devastating economic depression and the war. The political effect, however, was that American democracy was left without the ability to deal with the volatility of modern capitalism that the Great Depression had brought to the fore of social consciousness, and instead became wholly dependent on its success.

As for the second point, despite Dahl's protestations to the contrary, his polyarchy does not problematize, let alone help overcome, political apathy but actually induces it. Reconsider Dahl's repudiation of the concept of the demos. The flip side of his insight about minorities with intense preferences is the majority with weak ones. The concept of the demos is erroneous for him not just because individuals are not united in their opinion but also because most people are simply not interested; they have other things to care about. As he writes, "Political equality and popular sovereignty are not absolute goals; we must ask ourselves how much leisure, privacy, consensus, stability, income, security, progress, status, and probably many other goals we are prepared to forego for an additional increment of political equality."[136] This statement may seem like a plain description of the plurality of values, but its implications become clear when we consider it side by side with Dahl's peculiar formulation of political pluralism. Despite his focus on contentious bargaining between competing interest groups, Dahl also stresses, in no less strong terms, the importance of consensus on what he calls "the democratic creed." Among the components of the democratic creed are a belief in democracy as the best form of government, the desirability of basic rights and procedures, and the essential legitimacy of governmental institutions. This does not sound particularly oppressive, but as Dahl recognizes, it can easily mutate into a perilously complacent view that "our system is not only democratic but is perhaps the most perfect expression of democracy that exists anywhere; if deficiencies exist, either they can, and ultimately will, be remedied, or else they reflect the usual gap between ideal and reality that men of common sense take for granted."[137] Still, it is not the democratic creed's latent complacency that worries Dahl. On the contrary, he proposes ways to reproduce the value consensus, which "tends to be incomplete" and typically "decays," going so far as to favorably entertain the possibility that powerful social processes like formal schooling could make "rejection of [the democratic creed] almost impossible." For a pluralist, Dahl's emphasis on the democratic creed is startlingly strong. "To reject the creed is infinitely more than a simple matter of disagreement. To reject the creed is to reject one's society and one's chances of full acceptance in it—in short, to be an outcast.... To reject the democratic creed is in effect to refuse to be an American. As a nation we have taken great pains to insure that few citizens will ever want to do anything so rash, so preposterous—in fact, so wholly un-American."[138]

In a society where the democratic creed is so thoroughly instilled in people, democratic politics take on a radically different meaning. They become "merely the chaff ... the surface manifestation, representing superficial conflicts," contained within the boundaries already drawn by "the underlying consensus on policy that usually exists in the society among a predominant portion of the politically active members."[139] Combine this idea with Dahl's assumption that most people are "marginalists" who make choices among various life goals by relying on basic cost-benefit analysis. Within this framework, political equality and popular sovereignty are treated on equal terms with other private goals such as leisure, privacy, stability, income, and security that compete for people's attention with claims to higher utility or efficiency. It is a competition fundamentally skewed against democracy. Because a relatively high degree of democracy is presumed to have already been achieved in the form of liberal democracy (it is part of the democratic creed), the utility-to-effort ratio of deepening democracy any further is far lower than that of a myriad of other private goals. Consequently, people are unlikely to respond to or partake in the efforts of those who make claims about alternative possibilities of democratic life. Put differently, the combination of the entrenched democratic creed and the marginalist subjectivity lands us in a strikingly depoliticized world in which ordinary citizens have no reason to care about claims that do not affect their leisure, privacy, or income. Dahl unwittingly gives expression to this reality of polyarchy. Rejecting the concept of democracy as majority rule, Dahl insists that the central question of polyarchy is "the extent to which various minorities in a society will frustrate the ambitions of one another with the *passive acquiescence or indifference of a majority of adults or voters.*"[140] Dahl might not have personally endorsed the "passive acquiescence or indifference" of the majority, but it is nonetheless a reality that his theory systematically reinforces.

The foregoing analysis, then, reveals limitations of the conventional critique of postwar democratic theory's treatment of apathy. While critics did note postwar democratic theory's nonchalant acceptance of apathy as a telling marker of its departure from traditional democratic theory, they too equated apathy with nonparticipation. In an otherwise searching critique, for example, Graeme Duncan and Steven Lukes contrasted apathy directly to participation, without questioning their opponents' treatment of apathy as the absence of political activity: "Arguments about the necessity of apathy may always be confronted with the suggestion that any given society with democratic institutions or a democratic temper can in certain conditions tolerate an appreciably higher degree of participation than these theorists allow."[141] Rather than engaging closely with the assumptions about mass subjectivity that drove the instrumentalization of democracy, critics focused on fighting their opponents' denigrating description of participation with their own idealized vision, subsuming the question of subjectivity under it. Lane Davis, for instance, offers a typical account of this approach: "Participation in the management of public affairs would serve as a vital means of intellectual, emotional, and moral education leading toward the full development of the capacities of individual human beings."[142] In moments like these, critics' attempts to vindicate popular political participation threaten to become too categorical a defense—a claim that *more* participation in decision-making is desirable for its intrinsic value, regardless of on what terms and in what environment it occurs.

But if my analysis of Dahl holds some validity, postwar democratic theory's instrumental tendencies cannot be fully countered simply by getting more citizens to participate. Postwar democratic theory does not merely suppress participation; it creates a particular environment for participation that is characterized by the public's *generalized indifference* to claims appealing to the common good and political equality. As a result, in instrumental democracy, political contestation takes place exclusively between those with immediate material interests at stake, and political decisions are made solely by the balancing act of their relative power, divorced from public discussion and scrutiny. The terms of political participation—not its absolute amount—are the problem, and more participation alone cannot offer an adequate solution.

Conclusion

In the postwar era, a peculiar strand of democracy arose to erect a dividing wall between democratic institutions and the demos, fortifying the former against the latter and alienating the latter to protect the former. While this transformation was examined and criticized from various perspectives, the debate tended to revolve around the question of how much participation might be desirable. Opponents of the new democratic theory complained that its reduction of democracy to electoral competition and occasional voting greatly restricted the scope of participation for most citizens. Critics did recognize that an important aspect of postwar democratic theory was to suspend, if not actively thwart, the construction of democratic subjectivity that had been a crucial concern of traditional democratic theory, but they tended to conceive of democratic subjectivity too broadly in terms of the fulfillment of each individual's potential and to fold it almost entirely into the question of participation. They implicitly assumed that political participation itself would help people broaden their purview and their orbit of caring, without specifying what participation entails or considering participation in relation to other factors that might precondition people's disposition. To be sure, this somewhat generalized affirmation of participation was a response to postwar democratic theorists' categorical assault on it. Still, the critique that postwar democratic theory shrinks room for citizens' participation is a limited diagnosis of its nature and implications.

Limitations of the prevailing critiques of Cold War democratic theory are manifested most clearly by critics' acceptance of their opponents' one-dimensional reading of apathy as nonparticipation. Cold War democratic theorists' embrace of apathy indicates not simply their theory's elitist character, which assigns little value to ordinary citizens' political activities. Rather, it reveals their theory's instrumental character, which recognizes only private interest as the basis of political claims. Instrumental democracy does not simply condone people's nonparticipation, pace the typical criticism. It authorizes particular kinds of political activity and arranges democracy in such a way that citizens do not have reason to pay attention to contending political claims unless their own immediate welfare is at stake. Seen from this perspective, the distinct peril of instrumental democracy is not that it is too stable, as its critics charged, but that it weakens political relations and undermines the political basis of legitimacy, building up volatility under the guise of stability. (I develop this point in chapter 6.) So far I have sought to show that postwar democratic theorists' embrace of instrumental democracy was driven by their fear that "the people" might morph into "the masses." The explanation is not complete, however. The instrumental reconstruction of democracy was also animated by the confidence that people's massifying tendencies could be controlled and managed—that people could be made safe for democracy. To this belief we now turn.

CHAPTER FOUR

The Search for
Dynamic Stability

Democracy as a
Self-Regulating System

For advocates of instrumental democracy, the pluralist iteration of instrumental democracy successfully navigated the delicate challenge posed by the encounter with totalitarianism: it distinguished itself from totalitarianism by promoting diverse ideologies and political groupings while remaining resilient and stable enough to withstand totalitarian threats, both from without and from within. This idea, however, was met with formidable objections. To begin with, it was not clear how competition between various interest groups eager to pursue their advantages at the expense of others could help secure overall stability. As David Easton, otherwise a champion of behavioralism, noted, supporting evidence for this widely held contention was "so indecisive that as valid a case might be made for a contrary generalization."[1] History offers at least as much evidence that the existence of equally powerful groups poised against each other leads to the disintegration of a political system. From a different standpoint, critics charged that instrumental democracy attained political stability only by diluting its professed pluralism—not through truly open political contestation but by suppressing popular political participation, excluding inchoate or yet-to-be-articulated political claims, and ignoring the manipulation of people's preferences and opinions. Thus Cold War democratic theorists faced a twofold challenge: on the one hand, they needed to show that interest group competition did result in stability; on the other hand, they also needed to show that stability was achieved not by ignoring and suppressing people's demands but by accommodating them. Postwar democratic theorists needed to show, in short, that American democracy exhibited dynamic stability that fuses change and durability into a seamless whole.

The notion of dynamic stability was crucial to postwar democratic theorists' self-understanding as reformers. They believed that their focus on the elites' responsiveness, rather than the public's responsiveness, as a major feature of democracy would not compromise its ability to accommodate popular demands and, if necessary, to undergo a fundamental transformation. If constructed well, postwar democratic theorists assumed, democracy would gradually evolve through a series of disequilibriums created by people's ever-changing needs and diverse claims instead of continually reverting back to the status quo. Critics were wrong to accuse them of trying to suppress popular participation, postwar democratic theorists protested; they were championing it. But they discovered, or so they believed, that carefully designed political mechanisms and processes could find out people's opinions better than public deliberation—with the added benefit of being less burdensome and more favorable to stability. Thus the concept of dynamic stability offered a perfect solution to postwar democratic theorists' conflicting orientations: their apprehension toward the masses and their commitment to democracy, which, even according to their preferred definition, must respond to the masses' demands.

In this chapter, I analyze David Easton's theory of political systems as one of the most sophisticated attempts to theorize dynamic stability within the framework of instrumental democracy. Easton developed his systems theory as a general guide for empirical political research, so its applicability is not limited to democracy. Dictatorial regimes need information about popular demands and sentiments as much as do democracies, even though they may not respond to the same degree or in similar fashion.[2] Nor does Easton champion democracy as a normative value. In line with the prevailing doctrine of behavioralism, he took pains to separate his normative commitments from his supposedly empirical theory. ("Ethical evaluation and empirical explanation ... should be kept analytically distinct."[3]) So what I am examining here is not Easton's systems theory in general but the moments in which his theory, as an ideal type, should best explain democracy.

Easton indicated the broad parameters of his understanding of democracy in his early work. Not yet adhering fully to the norm of the fact-value distinction, Easton warned of "a glaring discrepancy between the end of self-government and the facts of the social structure" and declared that "the real problem confronting the undictatorial areas of the Western world today in their domestic affairs is how to transfer a larger share of political control to the people."[4] Some of the remarks in his later, more analytical works can be considered to specify the conditions that facilitate such a transfer of power and distinguish democratic systems from dictatorial ones. "The mark of democratic regimes ... is that their norms permit greater freedom of entry into the political market place for new organizations that seek to collect and transmit supportive sentiments. They also encourage a greater diffusion and competition among the collecting points and a greater decentralization of control over and timing of the discharge of discontent." Easton added that in democracies, members are "encouraged to communicate freely and frequently with the authorities," and in turn, the authorities pay close attention to popular sentiments.[5] In foregrounding mediating political organizations and the authorities' responsiveness rather than citizens' direct participation, Easton's definition of democracy reflects the outlook that prevailed in postwar democratic theory. But as I will elaborate, his articulation of that outlook was more capacious and sophisticated than that of most postwar pluralists: he envisioned democracy not simply as competition between political elites or between salient interest groups but as an information-processing system in which political signals (demands and articulated sentiments of support and disaffection) are generated more diffusely and flow more freely through a complex web of channels. Moreover, whereas most postwar pluralists too quickly assumed stability to be a felicitous outcome of interest group competition, Easton tried seriously to theorize how democracy can genuinely reconcile political dynamism and stability without subordinating one to the other. According to him, pluralist democracy's apparent stability reflects not stasis but dynamism—constant, if not always perceptible, movements it creates as it adjusts and even transforms itself to accommodate various political claims. Easton's theory therefore warrants a close examination as the most potent response to the charge of conservatism brought against pluralist democracy.

Easton's theory synthesizes insights from various disciplines, and critics highlighted different intellectual lineages to come to terms with his complex and sometimes ambiguous arguments. Some have identified biological or "vitalist" tendencies in his theory, pointing out that some of the progenitors of general systems theory by whom Easton was influenced, such as Ludwig von Bertalanffy and Talcott Parsons, developed their ideas through engagement with biology,[6] or that James G. Miller, a psychologist who introduced Easton to systems theory via an interdisciplinary research group at the University of Chicago, the Committee on Behavioral Sciences, was "an unabashed vitalist."[7] Others have noted affinities between Easton's theory and neoclassical economics, stressing that some of his central concepts, starting with his definition of politics as the allocation of values, resemble those of neoclassical economics.[8] These interpretations helpfully give shape to Easton's highly abstract formulations, but they are not without difficulties. For one thing, we must consider the problem of Easton's refusal to link his theory to those fields. Unlike Parsons, Easton never referred directly to biological theories, though Walter Cannon's account of homeostatic equilibrium in living organisms—which inspired Parsons—is reported to have "significantly shaped Easton's early interests."[9] In fact, Easton expressed significant reservations about applying biological knowledge to politics, warning that such an approach may overshadow distinctly political and institutional aspects of politics.[10] As for economics and functionalist sociology, he explicitly stated that "it would represent a profound misconstruction of those disciplines" if their conceptual apparatuses were to be identified with his.[11]

Perhaps more important, too much emphasis on putative affinities between Easton's theory and biology or economics can obscure his most distinct contribution: his conceptualization of a political system as distinguished from, and irreducible to, other types of systems. According to Easton, a system is political only when it involves an authoritative allocation of values. A decision made in the system is authoritative "when the people to whom it is intended to apply or who are affected by it consider that they must or ought to obey it."[12] What is also unique about the political system is that it can transform itself, not just its internal organization so as to achieve a given goal, but the very goals the system is to pursue. What distinguishes political systems from biological and mechanical ones, Easton wrote, is "the capacity to transform themselves, their goals, practices, and the very structure of their internal organization."[13] And what prompts a political system's self-transformation is the action of its members, who do not simply choose from a given set of alternatives but devise innovative systemic responses to their problems. From Easton's perspective, this is precisely what the static conception of political equilibrium fails to capture: "Unlike the implications of the equilibrium model of political processes, the members of a system need not simply absorb a disturbance and mechanically seek to re-establish some old point of stability in the political system or move on to a new one." Thus understood, a political system's "adaptation" is a "creative and constructive task, informed with goals and direction."[14] Neither biology nor economics can account for these features. To be sure, in the biological and economic spheres, too, movements of a system's parts lead to changes in the whole. The loss of a limb will probably change an animal's movement patterns; consumers' shifting tastes can lead to the demise of long-standing industries, transforming the composition of the national economy. But in those cases, it is hard to say that the limb or the individual consumer is "informed with goals and direction" concerning the whole system. (It is unlikely that the consumer changes her buying patterns because she believes that the structure of the national economy ought to be altered.) When the interrelated parts of a living body work organically to preserve the whole, or when economic actors try to maximize their material benefits, they rarely make conscious decisions about the goals that the system as a whole ought to pursue; an individual consumer generally cannot and does not question the desirability of industrial production or the commodification of certain areas. When seen through the lens of biology or economics, in other words, Easton's political system is depoliticized and loses its distinguishing character.

There is an alternative entry point. Defending the originality of his approach against the charges that his theory was essentially an offshoot of Parsonian sociology or neoclassical economics, Easton stated that he drew his "main inspiration" from "the systems sciences, at times more narrowly characterized as the communication sciences."[15] Moreover, while theorizing the concepts of response and feedback—which he considered the two pillars of his theory—Easton cited the literature on cybernetics, including W. Ross Ashby's *Design for a Brain* (1952) and *An Introduction to Cybernetics* (1956), Jay W. Forrester's *Industrial Dynamics* (1961), Norbert Wiener's two influential books *Cybernetics* (1948) and *The Human Use of Human Beings* (1954), and, separately, Karl W. Deutsch's "many articles" and *The Nerves of Government* (1963).[16] Easton's references to systems science and cybernetics are not especially idiosyncratic; in the postwar era, those two relatively new fields deeply shaped numerous branches of social science,[17] business management,[18] and policy making.[19]

Easton's appropriation of systems science and cybernetics accounts for the originality of his political theory. However, he did not pay sufficient attention to the implications of transposing those two fields to democracy, which, according to his definition, must make collective decisions in a way that satisfies not just the substantive condition (whether a decision it produces is "authoritative," that is, accepted in one way or another by its members) but also the procedural condition (whether a decision is reached through an inclusive and decentralized political process, and whether it is made as a response to its members' demands). To explore this point further than Easton did, it will be useful to examine in some detail how the conceptual apparatuses of systems science and cybernetics were developed during World War II and the Cold War to handle decision-making in a complex strategic environment. I should emphasize that, focused as it is on collective decision-making, my approach to these two fields is highly selective. As their wide application suggests, systems science and cybernetics were highly interdisciplinary fields encompassing multiple research traditions.[20] I believe that this focus, by making the dialogue between Easton's theory and systems science and cybernetics more explicit, can produce mutually illuminating insights. On the one hand, systems science and cybernetics can help illustrate the specific functioning of the feedback mechanism, enabling us to navigate some of the conceptual ambiguities and tensions in Easton's highly abstract discussion. On the other hand, Easton's theory can bring out implications of applying the frameworks of systems science and cybernetics to democratic politics. In recent years, scholars have produced a number of excellent studies on the development of systems science and cybernetics, but assessments of its political implications have tended to diverge: some criticize those fields as the progenitor of the rigid image of the rational chooser that serves to redescribe reality as a competitive or conflictual zero-sum game,[21] whereas others discover in them embryonic articulations of a situated and fluid subjectivity.[22] A close reading of Easton's theory yields a perspective that traverses these divisions. Somewhat contrary to the critique of the rational-actor model, a highly adaptive system envisioned by systems science and cybernetics was predicated on the assumption that its members are not fully rational. And partly for that reason, apparent venues for exchanges, agonistic negotiations, and transformations in a cybernetic system were organized more rigidly and hierarchically than its proponents acknowledge. Conceiving politics, as Easton does, as a highly adaptive system resting on constant communication between its elements does not alter the fact that a "higher" cybernetic entity, such as the government or corporate management, determines the goals that cybernetic subentities, such as citizens and employees, are to pursue. In certain respects, the construction of a complex organization as an integrated whole tightens the hierarchical control of subordinate units. Within the framework of systems science and cybernetics, the relationship between a democratic system and citizens is often reversed: instead of fulfilling people's demands, the system becomes an anonymous but no less real wielder of power, subjecting citizens to its requirements and dictating what is "preferable" and "rational."

Conflicting Images of Dynamic Stability

The basic outline of Easton's political system can be described in quite simple terms. He conceptualizes a political system as an informational feedback loop demarcated from, and situated in, a broader environment. It absorbs inputs (which take the form of either demands or support) from its members and delivers information about those inputs to "the authorities," who produce outputs in response (e.g., legislation, policies, rules, decrees, administrative decisions). The outputs then make changes in the environment, leading to adjustments in the existing inputs or giving rise to new ones. And the whole process is set in motion again when new inputs enter the system. From time to time, the system undergoes stress, which can be caused by the excessive volume or variety of demands ("demand-input overload") or by decline in support for the system ("a characteristic kind of stress for a system").[23] A system is equipped with various mechanisms that regulate stress, and feedback is what alerts the authorities that some of those mechanisms are in need. Alerted, the authorities typically, though not always, try to meet the demands and boost support by rearranging or adjusting certain elements in the system or, on rarer occasions, by radically transforming the system itself, so that different outputs would be produced. It is in this sense that we can view a political system as a "self-regulating, self-directing set of behaviors" (figure 1).[24]

A fundamental question guides Easton's theory: how do political systems persist? As he puts it, "How is any political system able to cope with the stresses that may threaten to destroy it?"[25] He identifies two crucial elements that secure the system's persistence—elements that he asserts "fundamentally distinguish" his systems theory from other approaches to politics: (a) variations within a system are "efforts by members of a

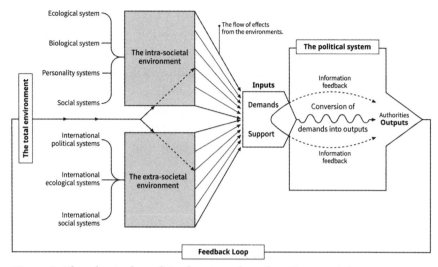

Figure 1. Flowchart of a political system, based on Easton, A Systems Analysis of Political Life, *30.*

system to regulate or cope with stress flowing from environmental as well as internal sources" (*response*); and (b) a system's capacity to persist is a "function of the presence and nature of the information and other influences that return to its actors and decision-makers" (*feedback*).[26] It is through the combination of feedback and response, Easton claims, that a system "is able to make some effort to regulate stress by modifying or redirecting its own behavior."[27]

Easton's emphasis on a system's self-transforming accommodation of diverse political claims has led some observers to discover roots of radical democracy in his thought. Henrik Bang, for example, suggests that for Easton the political signifies not a fixed entity (like the state) streamlining and integrating its components but its precise opposite: the inexorable contingency of any given decision or order and the productive force of multiple agencies.[28] While this interpretation offers a valuable counter to the views that overstate Easton's concern with stability in disregard of his equally keen attention to a system's dynamism, it risks being one-sided. Easton's theory contains elements that undercut the image of the system as "open" and "responding."[29] At times it is not clear to what extent a system's persistence actually relies on popular support. Easton theorizes that support moves along a continuum, extending from "high or positive support" to "passive acceptance, acquiescence, or indifference" to "low or negative support."[30] He does not specify how these different levels of support would impact, if at all, a system's response. But it appears that support must fall to a very low point before it threatens the system's persistence. "Decline in support will stress a system but the decline alone need not lead to its fall," he tells us.[31] Worse, Easton suggests that even when support falls below a minimum threshold, that alone may not unsettle the system. His argument here is worth quoting at length:

> Where pre-existing systems of some stability are threatened with loss of support, unless a counter-elite or organized groups are available and ready to give direction and impulse to the disaffected, the status quo can survive for long periods. Apathy, inertia or inadequate leadership have accounted for the persistence of political objects in many systems when the level of support is astonishingly low. Presumably this would be an indication that the politically relevant groups have not moved beyond the point of indifference on our support continuum.[32]

What is on display, especially in the last two sentences, is a strikingly slippery reasoning. Easton first claims that a system's persistence may rely on factors other than support, such as apathy or the absence of organized opposition, and then infers from the system's apparent persistence that support for it is not low enough. When applied to democracy, this line of thinking does not simply create inconsistencies in his theory but has dangerous implications: contrary to his earlier claims, it diminishes the significance of responsiveness as a condition for a democratic system's persistence to the point of irrelevance and bestows unwarranted legitimacy on any democracy that persists—including ones that persist without meeting their members' demands.

Elements of Easton's theory push still further in this direction. He insists that a system does not rely exclusively, even primarily, on "specific support" tied to outputs. As he puts it, "No regime or community could gain general acceptance and no set of authorities could expect to hold power if they had to depend exclusively or even largely on outputs to generate support as a return for specific and identifiable benefits."[33] Instead, crucial to the persistence of any regime is what he calls "diffuse support": a "reservoir of favorable attitude or good will" that exists "independent of the effects of daily outputs."[34] Diffuse support becomes particularly important in large, complex societies where it is nearly impossible to satisfy all the members' demands simultaneously and the challenge of "stabiliz[ing] the relationship between [the authorities] and the general membership" looms large.[35]

The introduction of diffuse support further erodes the connection between a system's responsiveness and its persistence. According to Easton, diffuse support is not a product of individuals' considered evaluation of the system's performance; rather, it is "the conviction on the part of the member that it is right and proper for him to accept and obey the authorities and to abide by the requirements of the regime"—a sentiment that is "probably instilled at an early stage in the maturation process of the individual."[36] Easton considers at length various ways in which diffuse support could be generated or reinforced. Some of them are related to the process that converts inputs into outputs,[37] but it is a marginal element, as indicated by his conceptualization of diffuse support as the often imperceptible effect of early socialization. Indeed, what prevails in his account of diffuse support is decidedly in tension with his claim that a democratic system's distinguishing mark is its openness and responsiveness to inputs. Instead of individuals' alertness to outputs that exerts pressure on the authorities to keep the system responsive, Easton now emphasizes "psychological mechanisms which justify acceptance of outputs that might otherwise lead to extreme dissatisfaction with the authorities and even the regime."[38] Rather than concrete political outcomes, he now highlights ideologies, symbols, personal charisma, and even new technologies such as railways, airplanes, and radio sets as the sources of diffuse support and system persistence.[39] All the major factors generating diffuse support, in other words, are extraneous to a system's democratic operation and allow the system to be less responsive.[40]

In Easton's account, where we might draw the line between democracy and dictatorship becomes murky, because he treats nondemocratic generators of diffuse support as but another mode of a system's response. While discussing the creation of a sense of political community as a type of diffuse support, Easton insists that systemic changes "occur[ring] less from any deliberate act on the part of relevant political leaders than as the product of many imperceptible and often relatively unconnected individual actions" could be considered "political responses."[41] As individuals behave subconsciously to alleviate their stress without fully understanding how their behavior has been triggered, he speculates, a political system may respond to a threatened decline of support "regardless of the awareness or intent on the part of the relevant political members."[42] In fact, he adds, "The response need [not] occur only when stress is present or imminent; it may simply take advantage of possibilities inherent in the situation"[43] such as the rise of mass transportation and communication technologies. In this formulation, a system's capability to perpetuate itself is separated not only from its members' demands but also from the agency of the authorities. The system, in short, runs itself.

When we apply Easton's systems theory to pluralist democracy, then, we encounter two conflicting, if not contradictory, images. Quite explicitly, he describes a system as an open and dynamic process that allows various political demands to flow freely, initiate changes in the system, and shape political outcomes. He is emphatic that the flow of demands and support is not "of a passive sort" but the driving force of changes in the system's internal composition, as well as its goals.[44] When this image prevails, Easton pays disproportionate attention to constant adaptations that the system itself undergoes ("a political system is a goal-setting, self-transforming and creatively adaptive system"),[45] by and large assuming that those adaptations are directed at satisfying the members' demands. Moreover, the members appear as emphatically autonomous agents in their relation to the system. Easton stresses that members "are not passive transmitters of things taken into the system, digesting them in some sluggish way," but "are able to regulate, control, direct, modify, and innovate with respect to all aspects and parts of the processes involved."[46] Cast thus, a system creates a symbiotic relationship between change and stability, transformation and persistence, providing a happy solution to the difficult question of dynamic stability—the question, as noted at the outset, of how to embrace a plurality of political demands while containing their potentially destabilizing effects. As Easton puts it, "The idea of systems persistence extends far beyond that of systems maintenance; it is oriented toward exploring *change as well as stability,* both of which may be interpreted as alternative avenues for coping with stress."[47]

But this image of the system competes with another. What is contained in this alternative image is a system equipped with mechanisms that delink its persistence and responsiveness: it can shape socialization processes so as to cultivate diffuse support that secures citizens' allegiance to the system despite its unresponsiveness; it can reinforce or produce political apathy and inertia, keeping dissenting groups from gaining traction; and it can delegitimize or suppress organized opposition. The system endures, not by responding to its members' demands and support but by *managing* and *controlling* those inputs. Equally important, when this alternative image of the system comes to the fore in Easton's analysis, human agency is significantly concentrated in a few hands and even disappears altogether: what maintains the system's persistence is the activity of a small group of people who suppress or displace other members' demands; sometimes it is even a felicitous outcome of "imperceptible and unconnected individual actions" rather than the members' freedom and power to mold, and remold, the system as they see fit.[48]

Easton never fully acknowledges, let alone settles, the tension between these two images of a system. The competing images thus raise fundamental questions about his conceptualization of systems and, more generally, postwar democratic theory's attempt to reconcile pluralism and stability without compromising either. Is the system's stability achieved without neutralizing the attributes Easton considers democratic? Recall that he understands democracy in terms of the members' free and frequent communication with the authorities, the multiplication of political groups, and the resulting diffusion of input sources. He assumes that these features would help decentralize a system's decision-making process and enhance its responsiveness to its members' demands. But a close look at systems science and cybernetics casts doubt on those assumptions. In fact, there is reason to believe that constructing a decision-making process as an adaptive system has requirements that at once generate and conceal contrary tendencies.

Systems Science and the Centralization of Decision-Making

Origins of Systems Science

We can begin to put pressure on Easton's implicit assumptions by examining how systems science developed the feedback mechanism as a central component of decision-making. Systems science originated in wartime operations research that used mathematical analysis to optimize the allocation of resources.[49] If operations research was concerned with the optimization of existing resources, systems science was dedicated to designing the most effective system that could help accomplish a given objective. Systems science became influential as strategic needs shifted during the Cold War. The introduction of nuclear weapons effected a transition in the military command system. The conventional army relied on the "command" model of decision-making. Despite our typical perception of the military as a quintessentially hierarchical organization, important differences distinguish hierarchy and centralization; and centralization was not the modus operandi of the conventional army. In fact, the command model was decentralized in that, once having issued a command, the chief commander left its execution largely to the discretion of field officers. As the historian Paul Edwards puts it, "Traditional military hierarchies are anything but mechanical. At every level, individuals *bear responsibilities* rather than *perform functions.*"[50] Dispersion of authority and open-ended operations, rather than concentration of authority at the upper level, were the conventional army's major characteristics.

As the Cold War unfolded, this "command" model quickly gave way to the "command-and-control" model. The gist of this transition lay in a feedback mechanism operating through the continuous flow of information: while the command model relied on a relatively linear process of decision-making, the command-and-control model was predicated on constant strategic adjustments and the micromanagement of subordinate units' activities. For its advocates, the profound change in warfare caused by the introduction of nuclear weapons made command-and-control all but inevitable. Nuclear weapons could clearly not be left to the discretion of field officers. Given the new weapons' incredible destructive power, it became essential that the deployment of nuclear arms was strictly controlled by top authorities. Initially, nuclear weapons were controlled personally by the president, but the idea of personal control soon became obsolete owing to the skyrocketing number of nuclear bombs and rapid technological advances in the delivery system, such as jet aircraft and intercontinental ballistic missiles. Various early warning mechanisms were devised to decrease response time, but they could not address the fact that, for instance, a ballistic missile launched from a Soviet submarine off America's coast could reach inland targets within a few minutes—hardly sufficient time for making reflective decisions or, for that matter, locating the persons authorized to make those decisions.[51] What was needed, therefore, was a vertically integrated system that not only tightly connected intelligence to command but also arranged all its components such that a warning signal almost automatically activated the rest of the system according to a preset formula. Systems science became prominent in the postwar era, as it was used to design that system.

Despite its military application, systems science does not take us too far afield from democratic theory. As the historian Hunter Heyck notes, we can see systems science as part of the postwar democratic discourse characterized by a deep pessimism about ordinary citizens' capacity to reason and the strong urge to defend democracy—a double-sided pressure that, as we saw in the previous chapter, catalyzed the instrumentalization of democracy. How can the rule by the people be justified if people are not rational? The social scientists who embraced systems science found an ingenious answer to this dilemma, Heyck suggests, by shifting the focus from "the decider to the decision, from the person to the process."[52] The underlying thinking was that even if people are not rational, rational decisions can still be made by a system populated by those people, if the system is designed smartly enough. Herbert Simon's famous concept of bounded rationality, which he had already adumbrated in his early work but refined partly through his engagement with W. Ross Ashby's cybernetic theory, captures this modified commitment to rationality.[53] Simon criticizes neoclassical economics and game theory for constructing an unrealistically demanding concept of rationality: the rational actor is assumed to possess "at least impressively clear and voluminous" knowledge of his environment, "a well-organized and stable system of preferences," and "a skill in computation" that enables him to determine which course of action will "permit him to reach the highest attainable point on his preference scale."[54] None of these assumptions correspond to reality, Simon complains. Individuals make decisions with much more limited information, choose among a small number of available alternatives rather than all possible ones, and settle on a sufficiently satisfactory payoff ("satisficing," in Simon's well-known terminology) instead of trying to maximize the benefit to the fullest extent. (In one of Simon's examples, the seller of a house, limited in her knowledge about the local real estate market and presented with just one offer at a time rather than having all potential offers on hand, would sell her house if the offer exceeds a certain amount, instead of seeking the highest possible profit.[55])

What is remarkable about Simon's theory of bounded rationality is that, unlike rational choice theory, it does not rule out emotion, passion, and subjectivity in general but manages those "irrational" traits so that people, and more importantly their organizations, could make (bounded) rational decisions. The key is to construct an adequate environment of choice. Simon's crucial point is not simply that people do make rational choices despite their limited capabilities and less-than-optimal conditions, but that because of those deficiencies, they cannot make rational choices unless they are placed in a carefully curated environment. As he puts it, "A higher degree of integration and rationality can . . . be achieved, because the environment of choice itself can be chosen and deliberately modified."[56] To an extremely limited extent, individuals can create such an environment for themselves, but since most important social issues are too complex for an individual's capabilities, designing a choice environment is primarily an "organizational matter."[57] And Simon's understanding of organization, which, in his cybernetic rendition, is essentially an information-processing mechanism of higher order, is distinctly hierarchical. He postulates that the organization has three principal functional levels: at the top, the organization's "values" or goals to which its members are to direct their activities are determined; in the middle, broad procedures are devised to guide members' attention, channel information, and organize their activities "to cause the specific day-to-day decisions to conform with the substantive plan"; and at the bottom, individual members make day-to-day decisions and activities, following the procedures and pursuing the organization's goals.[58]

Simon's theory shows that command-and-control's centralized decision-making is not attributable simply to the exigencies of nuclear war but stems from a more general desire to manage human irrationality to produce a rational decision. Mechanisms such as dispersed input collection and constant internal communication are devised for that purpose; they are meant not to decentralize power but to *eliminate* the independent judgment of members at the lower levels of the system and to *concentrate* decision-making power at the top. For a system to produce timely and efficient decisions in a highly complex and uncertain strategic environment, the reasoning goes, all the relevant factors—equipment, logistics, strategies, tactics, and costs—must be aggregated in a central location to allow analyses of different decisional paths' effectiveness, relative to cost, for a given task. (Unless all the elements of a system are compiled, for example, it would be impossible to determine how best to enhance the system's overall performance by eliminating redundancies and bottlenecks.) From that perspective, the chief function of multiple input sources and the continuous flow of information is to help the authorities at the top of an organization monitor and reinforce its subordinate units' compliance with the handed-down requirements more efficiently and constantly.

Systemic features of Simonian organization, in short, help create a more omnipresent centralized power.

Systems Science Goes to Washington:
Restructuring the Department of Defense

Systems science's centralizing tendency is illustrated by its most far-reaching application in the postwar era: the restructuring of the Department of Defense under secretary Robert McNamara through the Planning-Programming-Budgeting System (PPBS, discussed in more detail hereafter),[59] which was then used, for a brief period, as a template for other federal bureaucratic agencies.[60] Facing the notoriously daunting challenge his predecessors had tried to address without much success—the integration of fiercely competitive military services—McNamara brought systems analysis to the DoD.[61] He recruited a number of figures from the RAND Corporation, the birthplace and epicenter of systems analysis, and established an Office of Systems Analysis (OSA) within the Office of the Secretary of Defense. McNamara and the OSA group then developed PPBS, a management technique they implemented in military planning and procurement. PPBS was primarily a budget model. One of the most significant aspects of PPBS was to change "output" budget categories to reflect specific programs ("Strategic Retaliation," "Continental Defense," or "General Purposes Force") rather than, as in traditional budgets, particular objects needed ("personnel" or "equipment"), to allow for quantitative analysis of each program's relative-to-cost efficiency.[62] Once strategic objectives or programs *have already been determined,* each subunit would be required to justify its procurement requests in light of its contributions to those programs, and to supply data needed for the OSA to conduct quantitative analysis. In this respect, PPBS marked a significant departure from the traditional budget model.[63] Traditionally, a budget was put together from below. Each unit of a department prepared its own estimates and sent them up the chain of decision-making, going through various levels of authority. Because each unit was charged with identifying its own needs, the unit was not simply an informational but a decisional element in determining a department-wide budget. In PPBS, this decisional flow was reversed. Top policy was determined before the preparation of estimates and sent down to subordinate units as a guideline according to which they had to justify or adjust their requests.

PPBS was promoted as a neutral tool above partisan politics and also as a way of securing civilian control over the armed forces.[64] But if civilian control is justified on the principle that military decisions are to serve the ends determined by democratic authority, PPBS had the opposite effect; it technically shifted authority from the military to civilian policy makers but deepened the insulation of military decision-making from democratic politics. As Sonja Amadae points out, "The new policy elite were altering the rules such that authority over military procurement, strategy, and operations would be in the hands of 'objective' policy analysts, removed from democratic politics."[65] Despite its proponents' claims, PPBS was not simply a neutral tool that optimizes the use of resources relative to different objectives. Systems analysis is used in the strategic environment where objectives are unknown and uncertain; objectives *emerge through* systems analysis, rather than first being determined by democratic deliberation and then given to systems analysts. This is partly what distinguishes systems analysis from its progenitor, operations research. In operations research, the goals are relatively clearly defined—destroy as many German U-boats as possible, for instance—and analysts are tasked with finding the most efficient way to achieve that goal, by determining, for example, how best to allocate the existing fleet of fighter jets. In systems analysis, however, the very goals to be pursued are unclear. A variety of objectives can contribute to avoiding a nuclear war, and the question of how many nuclear warheads need to be produced as opposed to building up conventional armed forces or making more vigorous diplomatic efforts is inextricably linked to the numerical value assigned to each of those objectives by systems analysts. As Albert Wohlstetter, describing his study of US bomber bases (which is widely considered a classic example of systems analysis), stated, "The [systems] analysis ... not only was affected by the objectives considered, it affected them."[66] While in principle, representatives, experienced military experts, and the public could be consulted in identifying and weighing competing goals, since systems analysis requires taking into account the entire nexus of cost and benefit, the ultimate decision inevitably reflects the viewpoints and predilections of those who possess a "full view." In the DoD, McNamara, who had virtually no military background, handled the most crucial part of decision-making—determining strategic purposes and plans—with little discussion or consultation, meeting military services more abstractly as data points figuring in his quantitative analysis.[67] Capitalizing on the public anxiety about national security, stoked partly by claims about the so-called missile gap (which proved to be fictitious),[68] he presided over "the largest peacetime build up of the armed forces in

American history, with the annual budget rising from $41 billion in 1961 to $49 billion in 1962 and $54.3 billion in 1963."[69]

The presuppositions behind systems thinking—that complex problems can be captured by collecting homogeneous quantitative data and analyzed by the central authorities to produce an optimal decision—can mask a profound poverty in the understanding of the problems. Partly because the quantitative data that systems science relies on are massive in size and presented in apparently objective fashion, those data eventually constitute a kind of reality of their own, sidelining the question of whether the most relevant or important aspects of the problem are in fact measured. In a devastating account of America's attempt to measure progress during the Vietnam War, which was shaped importantly by McNamara's zeal for data, the military historian Gregory Daddis shows how McNamara's emphasis on "hard" numbers concealed the lack of clear strategic objectives, as well as the poor understanding of the highly unconventional nature of the war and of Vietnam's particular geopolitical conditions. The top policy makers failed to set priorities in the face of the complex mix of goals—helping to secure political stability and effective governance, pacifying the local population, fostering economic development, and using military force—and the military officers were poorly trained in counterinsurgency techniques. And this intellectual and conceptual vacuum was filled by numbers, creating the illusion of control and progress. "Left with insufficient foundational knowledge of counterinsurgencies and vague strategic objectives, MACV [Military Assistance Command, Vietnam] embraced Secretary of Defense McNamara's advice that everything that was measurable should in fact be measured.... MACV—and much of DoD—went about measuring everything and, in a real sense, measured nothing. In the process of data collection, the data had become an end unto itself."[70]

It was not conventional centralization that reinforced such intellectual poverty; systems science rejected such centralization. In *The Economics of Defense in the Nuclear Age* (1960), which served as an intellectual blueprint for the DoD restructuring, Charles J. Hitch and Ronald N. McKean criticized "large hierarchical organizations" for being "sluggish and hidebound by rules and regulations" and presented decentralization as an "extremely attractive administrative objective."[71] What they had in mind with decentralization, however, was not autonomy of the agents at the organization's lower levels. They warned that especially in the context of the Cold War, characterized by "great uncertainty" as to "when or whether there will be war, against whom, where, and what kind," it was not advisable to give military services autonomy over "budgeting, planning, and decision-making." Thus, much as Herbert Simon recommended, they called for a different kind of centralization that delimits and structures the choice environment so that members of a system, while not taking direct orders, have little choice but to conform to the systemic requirements: "Decentralized decisions work well only if the decision-makers at various levels can be given appropriate incentives and criteria."[72] In other words, the organization devised by systems science is still centralized, but less overtly hierarchical. Decisions made at the top are distributed downward not as direct orders but as guidelines its recipients technically choose to adopt, even though their only other "choice" would be suffering a budget cut, a bureaucratic equivalent of death. As Gene Rochlin observes in the context of business management (another area in which systems science exerted an enormous influence), command-and-control achieves top-down control "through compliance rather than hierarchical authority, allowing for formal decentralization while ensuring that the range of significant deviance from central plan and intent is narrow."[73] For this reason, those in a subordinate position in a command-and-control system often do not realize how much their autonomy is constrained and do not question the extent to which decision-making is centralized.

To be sure, the origins of certain conceptual apparatuses do not permanently dictate their application. Given the internal diversity of systems science and cybernetics, any blanket judgment about their political implications is difficult to sustain.[74] Indeed, there have been attempts to put systems science and cybernetics to democratic and progressive use.[75] Still, the foregoing discussion suggests that the technical requirements of systems science at once create and conceal from view tendencies toward centralized control. This does not mean that systems science is necessarily attached to command-and-control. But it does indicate that it is particularly vulnerable to it, and conditions for its application, especially to democratic politics, must be specified to address that vulnerability. In particular, it would be important to distinguish—more clearly than Easton did—between less overt hierarchy and high adaptability, on the one hand, and a system's consistency with the terms of democratic pluralism, on the other. In command-and-control, multiple information sources or constant communication does not make decision-making more diffused or competitive, "democratizing" the system, as postwar democratic theorists saw it. In fact, it can hide the degree to which decision-making is authoritarian. A system responds only to the inputs to which it is designed to respond, and that design is rarely determined or reviewed democratically.[76] In this respect, Easton may paint too benign a picture of the authorities as merely actualizing the outputs requested by the members of a system, and may overstate his case in claiming that the members "are able to regulate, control, direct, modify, and innovate with respect to all aspects and parts" of the system.[77] One must also acknowledge that the promise of efficiency tempts one to increase central control, and the system's apparently horizontal structure blinds one to how its purposes are determined, and by whom. When Easton portrays a system as a fully integrated entity into which all the inputs flow (see figure 1), he effectively intensifies that temptation.

And a related problem arises. Inputs, which Easton presumes to be spontaneous, can be manipulated and distorted by the requirements of system. This problem was fully and tragically dramatized in the Vietnam War, a test case of the supposedly universal science of systems. Washington's heavy demand for statistical data was profoundly at odds with the actual situation on the ground. Some of the factors that military planners weighed most heavily, such as factories, bridges, roads, and motor vehicles, did not hold an equivalent value in Vietnam. As Paul Edwards vividly describes, "The North Vietnamese Army (NVA) moved supplies by bicycle or oxcart or on foot, over ever-changing trails obscured by dense jungle canopies. When American planes blew up their bridges, NVA convoys simply forded the rivers. Communications relied on human couriers, not telephone lines. The guerilla forces used women, children, and old people ... as spies and part-time soldiers. Most wore no uniforms and so were indistinguishable from the civilian population."[78] Under the imperative of constructing a system via a single language (numerical metrics, in this case) to permit a comprehensive view for the authorities, gathering data became a priority, while the careful design and evaluation of metrics were sidelined. But a mismatch between reality and its representation in a system was not the only problem. An equally crucial issue was that aspects of reality that could not easily be translated into the dominant language of the system did not enter it at all. So, for example, the number of villages occupied by the South Vietnamese government was methodically counted, but popular support for the NVA, which turned those villages into hostile territory at night, was not measured and thus was not taken into account in systems analysis. Consequently, even as the war appeared doomed to many, those who were looking at the numbers—who happened to be the top decision makers—saw signs of "progress." The problem of input distortion, then, points beyond the problems of centralized decision-making and an over-blown faith in systems management. It compels us to confront another imperative to which systems science is susceptible: that everything, including human behavior, must be turned into measurable and predict-able units of a grand information-processing system. To operate, systems science had to reinvent the human.

Cybernetics: Reinventing the Human

Although it was not always explicitly acknowledged, operations research and systems analysis were premised on a crucial assumption. Systems science hinged on the ability to collect, transfer, and process data on a massive scale. As factors to be considered multiplied, it quickly became impossible to conduct systems analysis without relying on computers. (The calculation of the relative merits of two bombers with ten variables during World War II yielded already over a thousand combinations; raising the number of systems by just four resulted in over a million combinations for evaluation.[79]) Naturally, computers could not begin to perform their task until variegated pieces of information are translated into homogeneous and standardized units of analysis. Likewise, for computerized calculation to be possible, all the agents of a system, humans and machines, had to be assumed to behave in terms of the same informational codes. Cybernetics articulated this implicit assumption of systems science and generalized it as a theory of behavior by reconceiving living organisms and machines alike as an information-processing system.[80]

This implicit premise was articulated in a landmark article, "Behavior, Purpose, and Teleology," in which Norbert Wiener, with his colleagues Arturo Rosenblueth and Julian Bigelow, drew the basic outline of servo-mechanical or cybernetic theory. (The term "cybernetics" was not used until Wiener introduced it in his 1948 book; before then, he and others described their theory with the concept of servomechanism.) Through a series of conceptual divisions (active and nonactive behavior, purpose-ful and nonpurposeful behavior, feedback and nonfeedback behavior, and so on), they singled out a category of behavior—which they termed

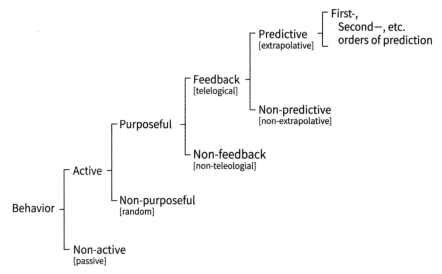

Figure 2. Cybernetic classification of behavior, based on Rosenblueth et al., "Behavior, Purpose and Teleology," 21.

"purposeful behavior"—that "reveals that a uniform behavioristic analysis is applicable to both machines and living organisms, regardless of the complexity of their behavior" (figure 2).[81]

For Rosenblueth et al., purposeful behavior denotes activities directed toward attaining a goal. They use the concept of purpose to characterize a cybernetic entity's voluntary activity: "When we perform a voluntary action what we select voluntarily is a specific purpose, not a specific movement."[82] (We simply choose to drink water rather than deciding each and every muscle movement involved in taking a glass of water from the table and bringing it to our mouth.) Despite the invocation of goal *selection,* however, what looms large in their discussion is goal-*directedness.* This subtle slide, as I will elaborate, betrays the problems of extending the cybernetic framework to politics. When goal-directedness is the criterion, a "torpedo with a target-seeking mechanism" is seen to perform a purposeful, and thus voluntary, activity.[83] Once purposeful behavior is thus understood, moreover, the concept of feedback takes on a particular meaning. Rosenblueth et al. focus solely on corrective (or "negative," as they call it) feedback, which refers to the process through which signals coming from the goal are used to restrict the entity's behavior when it strays from the goal, shaping outputs. (When we reach for the glass of water in the earlier example, we use visual signals coming from the glass to continuously, if almost unconsciously, correct our movements.) In this respect, "all purposeful behavior may be considered to require negative feedback."[84]

Rosenblueth and his colleagues conceived their universal theory of behavior at the level of a single entity functioning in a given environment. They did not explain how multiple cybernetic systems might interact with one another. That was the issue W. Ross Ashby tackled in *Design for a Brain* (1952). Like Rosenblueth et al., Ashby contends that living organisms and machines can be analyzed by the same criteria of goal-directed behavior and the feedback function they use to achieve their goals more successfully and reliably. But Ashby specifically explores the interaction—"joining" or "coupling," in his terms—of different cybernetic systems. Joining "occurs whenever we think of one system having an effect on another, or communicating with it, or forcing it, or signaling it."[85] When systems A and B are joined in a large system so that A affects B, what A does is not directly making B do certain things but changing the "parameters" of B's action, which refer to conditions not included in B's internal system. (The parameters of a pendulum, for example, would include the length of the pendulum and the lateral velocity of the air.[86]) When A affects B while not being affected by B in this way, it can be said that A "dominates" B.[87] To be sure, the relationship between the two systems does not have to be characterized by domination. In a machine Ashby designed to demonstrate his ideas—the homeostat—the subsystems (A, B, and C) are connected so that they exchange feedback with one another. Moreover, those subsystems are wired to a regulator that monitors the integrity of the whole system (F), so when signals from the subsystems indicate that they are too strained to maintain the stable functioning of the whole system, the regulator (F) alerts G to change the parameters for the subsystems' movement by, for example, slowing down the pace of the homeostat as a whole. In this way, not only do the subsystems adjust their movement in response to one another's reactions, but the whole system alters—though less frequently—its mechanism in response to its subsystems' feedback (figure 3).

For some observers, Ashby's idea of coupling embodied in the homeostat does not simply sketch a complex and interactive electromechanical device but adumbrates a dynamic social order that is abundant in

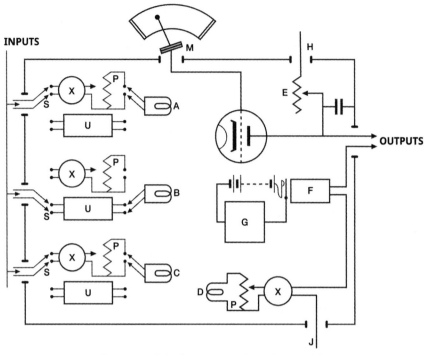

Figure 3. Circuit diagram of the homeostat, based on Ashby, Design for a Brain, *102.*

transformative energy produced by the unexpected encounters of diverse and open-ended agencies. The historian Andrew Pickering, for example, suggests that Ashby's "multihomeostat setup stages for us a vision of the world in which fluid and dynamic entities evolve together in a decentered fashion, exploring each other's properties in a performative back-and-forth dance of agency."[88] Thus interpreted, Ashby's cybernetic system can be regarded as an ideal to which postwar democratic theorists aspired. Ashby notes that when a system experiences a state that displaces its equilibrium, it is invariably only parts of the system, rather than the system as a whole, that are affected by that disturbance. So only the parts that lose their equilibrium will first change their states. But because all the parts of the whole are closely interlocked, this local movement will change the parameters of the other parts unaffected by the initial disturbance, so they will move as well. In consequence, what begins as peripheral instability ends up altering the whole system. In this sense, Ashby writes, "We can say (metaphorically) that every part has a *power of veto* over the states of equilibrium of the whole."[89] With quick terminological adjustments, this can easily describe the political system celebrated by postwar pluralists. In an ideal political system that accommodates change and stability simultaneously, a group of citizens (a subsystem) can react to a disturbance disproportionately affecting them in a way that compels other groups of citizens (other subsystems) to break out of their status quo, and through these voluntary actions, the political system (the whole system) alters its configuration and moves to a new point of equilibrium.

But a closer look at Ashby's "veto theorem" reveals distinct difficulties involved in achieving such a salutary condition in politics—difficulties understandably neglected by Ashby, who was thinking about a mechanical brain, not politics, but also underestimated by postwar democratic theorists. It is somewhat misleading to associate Ashby's "veto power" with political connotations of autonomy and agency. In Ashby's cybernetics, all systems, living and mechanical, are geared to "survival"—meaning that a system preserves certain "essential variables" within given limits.[90] (A cat approaching a fire will not get too close to it; a computer will turn on its cooling fan when the motherboard becomes too warm.) Now, suppose that two subsystems—a woman and a man, with the woman holding a fire—are joined to constitute a large system. Let's assume that both are content in their position, and the whole system is in equilibrium. Suddenly the woman with the fire moves closer to the man, and he moves as well to avoid getting burned. Because both of their positions have changed, the system has reached a new equilibrium. And since both of them are fully functioning, the integrity of the system has not been compromised. In this instance, the man is seen to have exercised veto power by moving, in the sense that he refused an equilibrium where he would be intolerably close to the fire, and instead effected an alternative equilibrium that allows him to stay without burn injuries.

Something is clearly missing here. Although Ashby took a step beyond Rosenblueth and his colleagues' foundational work by taking into account the interaction between cybernetic systems, he overlooked the fundamental condition of human relations, at least in politics: asymmetry of power. To be clear, Ashby's discussion of the joining of cybernetic systems can help expand our understanding of politics. The idea that domination can be understood in terms of one system's ability to set parameters for the other system's behavior offers subtle insights into how power operates in variegated ways, not simply in terms of command and obedience. Again, it was Herbert Simon who immediately noticed the potential. In an article published in the *Journal of Politics* (a journal founded in 1939 to promote behavioral approaches), Simon proposed to redefine the concept of power as the influence one exercises over the behavior of others. (He used the terms "power" and "influence" synonymously.) Although Simon did not cite Ashby specifically, he conceptualized the political relation in terms of the "joining" or "coupling" of cybernetic systems, and influence in terms of domination as Ashby used it—"A influences B, but B does not influence A."[91] But Simon was more explicit about the underlying premise of this conceptual approach: "This definition involves an asymmetrical relation between influencer and influencee."[92] For him, "A social structure [is] a network of (generally) asymmetrical relationships."[93] Simon allowed that power relations can be reciprocal, but he did not develop the point, focusing instead on how to distinguish dictatorship and democracy when both regimes have some feedback mechanism in place. (His suggested criterion: the time it takes for the authority to modify its policies in response to such feedback.[94])

What Ashby brings into focus is that a truly complex cybernetic system—a political system as Easton envisioned it, for example—is not monolithic but a densely layered entity consisting of multiple levels of cybernetic systems. It might not be impossible to create a system characterized by a perfect symmetry between its subsystems, but as Simon recognizes, it is not a general condition of politics; asymmetry is. A particularly crucial element of that asymmetry concerns the determination of purposes to be pursued by the whole system, which sets the parameters for—dominates—the subsystems' actions. And this is what remains in the background in the discussion of both Rosenblueth et al.'s and Ashby's accounts of a cybernetic system's goal-*directed* behavior. A self-guided torpedo adjusts its movement to follow the target, but someone has already decided the torpedo's mission, which justifies corrective feedback to which the torpedo is subject. Put differently, in a multilevel cybernetic system, a higher subsystem not only determines the whole system's purpose but constantly controls lower subsystems' behavior—by collecting and decoding signals "communicated" by those systems in its preferred way—so as to reinforce the purpose it has put in place. The lower subsystems may have veto power, but in the stark sense that they can resist feedback if it threatens their survival. In other words, veto power is granted not to promote the subsystems' welfare but to prevent their breakdown, which jeopardizes the smooth functioning of the whole system. Barring that extreme situation, the whole system forges ahead, continually exacting conformity from the subsystems through corrective feedback, rather than adjusting its goal or operation. The layered nature of a system, then, suggests the need to disaggregate Easton's broad discussion. He applies the cybernetic framework to conceptualize the political system as a whole, treating individuals merely as its parts, rather than cybernetic entities capable of adjustments and transformations themselves. But once we see a system as consisting of multiple cybernetic entities, it raises the question of which entity decides the whole system's goals and which is required to shoulder the burden of self-transformation pursuant to those goals. Seen from this perspective, Easton's theory neglects a crucial process that precedes the allocation of values: the *role designation* and the *positioning* of disparate cybernetic entities within a whole system.

To further illustrate this point, let us examine how Norbert Wiener initially developed the idea of cybernetics.[95] During World War II, Wiener was involved in a project that aimed to improve the performance of antiaircraft guns. His idea was to use electronic networks to predict the position of an attacking plane and use that knowledge to direct artillery fire. But the task of mechanically tracing an aircraft got mired in a difficulty stemming from a simple fact: the target was not entirely mechanical. The enemy pilot maneuvered the bomber to evade artillery fire and, in doing so, generated irregularities that could not be easily calculated. So in the summer of 1941, as Wiener was trying to make the actual device that would implement his ideas, he desperately needed to find a way to formalize the enemy pilot's behavior. As he later remarked, it was impossible to "eliminate the human element as far as it shows itself in enemy behavior." Thus, "To obtain as complete a mathematical treatment as possible of the over-all control problem, it [was] necessary to assimilate the different parts of the system to a single basis, either human or mechanical. Since our understanding of the mechanical elements of gun pointing appeared to us to be far ahead of our psychological understanding, we chose to try to find a mechanical analogue of the gun pointer and the airplane pilot."[96] This was the setting that made that assimilation look feasible:

> We realized that the "randomness" or irregularity of an airplane's path is introduced by the pilot; that in attempting to force his dynamic craft to execute a useful manoeuver, such as straight-line flight or 180

degree turn, the pilot behaves like a servo-mechanism, attempting to overcome the intrinsic lag due to the dynamics of his plane as a physical system, in response to a stimulus which increases in intensity with the degree to which he has failed to accomplish his task. A further factor of importance was that the pilot's kinaesthetic reaction to the motion of the plane is quite different from that which his other senses would normally lead him to expect, so that for precision flying, he must disassociate his kinaesthetic from his visual sense.[97]

Wiener's account here lays bare the possible cost of turning a human into a cybernetic entity. The enemy pilot could be assumed to behave like a servomechanism because he was in a high-stress environment. Once he is assigned to his airplane, the pilot has no choice but to dissociate his maneuvering acts from his normal senses to conform to its mechanical demands, or else he receives "feedback"—physical pain that "increases in intensity with the degree to which he has failed to accomplish his task." Here the pilot is the entity that is to prove its adaptiveness by pushing the limits of human physicality, not the military commanders who planned the air raid, not the political authorities that decided to go to war. Seen in this light, the image of a single cybernetic system freely exchanging influences with the environment is an untenably simplistic representation of reality. More often, a cybernetic system is nested in a hierarchy of cybernetic systems, as the pilot is embedded in a full chain of command. While the pilot may voluntarily adjust his behavior in response to feedback, that dynamism is not a manifestation of his freedom. Communication occurs between the pilot and the command center, but the latter wields the authority to interpret the former's movements through the language of success or failure. The pilot, on the other hand, is given a starkly different binary code: destroy or be destroyed.

The Quest for a "Viable Level of Support"

But can we apply this discussion to Easton's political system, the goal of which is to secure a viable level of support? Easton asserts that "divergences and variations" in his conceptualization of feedback stem from his emphasis on the concept of support as a central element of a political system, claiming that the problem of support has been neglected in other branches of systems science.[98] To investigate this point, let us examine

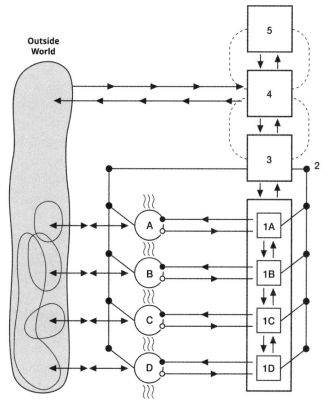

Figure 4. Structure of a cybernetic firm, based on Beer, Brain of the Firm, *130.*

one of the most earnest attempts to apply cybernetics to democratic government: Project Cybersyn in Salvador Allende's Chile. As the Allende government started nationalizing the country's major industries, the government enlisted Stafford Beer, one of the major theorists of cybernetic management, to undertake, in the words of Fernando Flores, who was in charge of the project, the "complete reorganization of the public sector of the economy."[99] Beer used the theory he developed for the purposes of corporate management to build a system of industrial control in Chile. Inspired by the living organism's neurophysiological control system, Beer imagined a firm as an "integral organism, with a vertical command axis consisting of five hierarchically arranged computer systems" (figure 4).[100]

Unlike Easton's portrayal, Beer's depiction shows that a cybernetic system consists of multiple levels of decision-making, which are hierarchically organized. It does not mean, however, that Beer intended cybernetic management to be centralized or authoritarian. He tried to transcend the "bogus dichotomy of centralization versus decentralization" by envisioning each system (S1 to S5) as "autonomic"—meaning that it can manage its affairs without intervention from an external authority, as long as it maintains internal homeostasis.[101] Workers at the lower levels of organization, for example, may receive a production quota from management, but they can decide specifics regarding their hours, rotation, and safety guidelines, as long as their output remains within a reasonable range of the given quota. Moreover, it is plausible to think that Beer had something even more democratic in mind. In explaining his theory, he resorted to Ashby's ideas of coupling and veto power. When systems A and B are coupled, Beer stated, A's departure from homeostasis causes B to change its state, which in turn causes A to change its state again—a process of mutual adjustments that is repeated until A returns to homeostasis. In this respect, "each system could *learn* about the other, not in terms of understanding all about it, but in terms of recognizing it *as being in normal operation.*"[102] So, in theory, if the workers feel that the production quota is set too high to ensure their safety or health, or to match their compensation, they can send their complaints up the command axis, demanding that management make necessary adjustments to the whole system. It is perhaps in this respect that Beer declared that his cybernetic organization was "designed for workers as well as ministers to use."[103]

Despite (or perhaps because of) his intentions, Beer may have interpreted autonomy and veto power too broadly and, as a result, overestimated the democratic potential of his cybernetic organization. First of all, even though workers in Beer's firm are allowed to make certain decisions, the actual freedom they enjoy is quite limited. Those in S1 can experiment with different ways of managing day-to-day production, as long as they carry out the goals determined by top management (S5, relying on the information supplied by S4, development management) within the operational environment created by S3. Most of the time, S1's "autonomy" makes no impact on the organization's goals or mode of operation. If it is autonomy, it is a radically diminished type, if not an entirely different conceptual category. What about veto power? From our discussion of Ashby, we know that in his cybernetic theory, lower systems' veto power is installed not to promote their welfare but to prevent interruptions to the efficient functioning of the whole system. Strikingly, this peculiar meaning is retained as Beer applies it to human organization. As Beer states, "As long as it still appears possible to carry out the board's [S5] instructions *within physiological limits,*" S3, operations management that coordinates different units of the firm and allocates resources among them, "will continue the task."[104]

The problem is not just the hierarchical structure of decision-making; the equally critical issue is the nature of communication that occurs between different levels. Perhaps one can make various factors, not just the ones straining workers' physiological limits, a legitimate ground for the use of veto power. Even so, in Beer's theory, veto power is not so much exercised as automatically activated. When, for example, the production level in S1 falls below a preset level, it triggers an alert mechanism that sends signals up the command axis so that upper-level systems can review and intervene. The responsibility of interpreting those data and deciding how to respond belongs to management. (Do the low production numbers indicate a bottleneck in operation, workers' lack of skills or motivation, unsustainably long hours, hazardous or discouraging working conditions, or low compensation? Should the firm bring in consultants to smooth out operation, hire more workers, replace them with potentially more motivated workers, or automate the production?) As Werner Ulrich points out, interlevel "communication" in Beer's cybernetic organization "merely serve[s] a *real-time location of internal symptoms, but not real-time explanation of problems nor real-time decision making.*"[105] Pickering glosses over this crucial point when he contends that Beer's theory "implied that the parties at different levels had to cast around for mutually agreeable initiatives and plans, precisely not the command-and-control mode."[106] The eventual decision reached through a process prompted by the alert signal might be mutually agreeable, but that does not mean it is agreeable to different actors to the same degree or in the same sense. For management, agreeable means that production is optimized again relative to cost; to workers (those who have not been laid off owing to the decision, that is), agreeable means that the new working hours, conditions, and compensation are within their "physiological limits."

This problem becomes more acute in democratic politics, in which the goal of optimizing production is enmeshed far more intricately with considerations of autonomy, fairness, equality, and a wide array of other values. Beer's ingenious attempt to reimagine democracy and incorporate it into Cybersyn throws this difficulty into sharp relief. Anticipating a concern that his cybernetic management is too technocratic to be justified in a democracy, Beer declared that "System Five [the goal-setting body] within a people's government cannot be an élite ruling class" but is "somehow the embodiment of the mass of the people themselves."[107] This, he suggested, would require a restructuring of conventional representative democracy. Traditional methods such as political parties, periodic elections, and representatives had been balancing democracy's two central needs—accommodating the variety of people's political demands and maintaining the regime's stability—primarily by reducing variety and slowing down response time. With the development of mass media, however, democratic government could now be more accountable in terms of the variety as well as the speed of its response, Beer claimed. His idea was to construct a direct, unmediated link between the government and the people via television, giving individuals a simple input device that he called an "algedonic meter." As the government broadcasts policies under consideration, people would turn the knob on the algedonic meter to indicate their level of satisfaction on a continuous scale between "unhappy" and "happy," and the TV screen would show the sum of people's responses. In this way, Beer reasoned, the government would instantly know how people feel about a particular policy, and in turn, people would know how responsive the government is by examining the changes it makes.[108]

Needless to say, this scheme is exposed to a number of serious problems, and it is uncertain how much, if at all, it can help democratize a cybernetic system's goal selection process. TV is a one-way communication technology and thus can facilitate the manipulation, rather than the unfiltered collection, of public opinion. Moreover, the technical integration of communication channels is amenable to the surveillance and control of inputs—a risk that does not abate even with the rise of two-way communication technologies such as the internet. Beer acknowledged some of these problems but insisted that they stem from the universal danger of political exploitation rather than from the cybernetic design of the system. But even when cybernetic democracy works ideally, people are still in a position that responds to policies merely by registering their instant feeling of happiness and unhappiness. As Beer stated, a citizen "does not have to explain anything—only to respond algedonically."[109] Despite its intentions to the contrary, then, the technical design of algedonic participation is likely to reinforce unreflective, impulsive judgment as a prevalent mode of democratic practice, amplifying the image that critics of the masses, from Gustave Le Bon to José Ortega y Gasset to Joseph Schumpeter, had long invoked to curb the extension of democracy. In fact, people do not speak at all in cybernetic democracy. Vox populi is not expressed by the people but deduced by someone who develops codes that reorganize people's utterances into information signals and attributes meaning to those signals. No utterance is unmediated, of course. But that is why democratic openness is a question of who gets to be involved in that mediation process. It is a question that is crucially omitted in the cybernetic vision of democracy.

Conclusion

As they reconstructed democracy as a variant of pluralism that accommodates diverse demands while at the same time maintaining stability, postwar democratic theorists rarely took the trouble to explain how that delicate task might be accomplished. They implicitly assumed that democracy is a self-regulating system moving from one state of equilibrium to another as it responds to its members' demands. In that sense, instrumental democracy was for them predicated not on mere stability but on dynamic stability. Unpacking this assumption adds an important layer to our understanding of postwar democratic theory. Typically, critics have stressed the anxiety produced by the experience of totalitarianism and the Cold War, depicting postwar democratic theory as an essentially conservative doctrine centered on stability rather than reform, narrowly conceived individual liberty rather than public engagement. In a representative statement, Edward Purcell Jr. observes that, under the pressure of the Cold War, many postwar democratic theorists implicitly equated the normative ideal of democracy with the empirical reality of postwar America and developed a "fundamentally complacent attitude" toward the status quo. As he writes, "[Postwar] social scientists were more concerned with the problem of conservation than of creation. As they devoted more and more research to the problem of stability, that stability took on the value of an end in itself."[110] Similarly detecting postwar democratic theory's bias toward stability, Graeme Duncan and Steven Lukes trace it specifically to the fact that it "rests upon a vague notion of equilibrium and *a priori* assumptions about the self-adjusting powers of the 'system.'"[111]

Duncan and Lukes's complaint identifies postwar democratic theorists' tendency to assume, rather than actually show, that postwar America was a self-regulating democratic system that reconciled pluralism and stability without sacrificing either. David Easton was an exception; his theory of political systems can be viewed as one of the rare attempts to explicate pluralist democracy's dynamics beyond vague notions and a priori assumptions. Ultimately, Easton's theory fails to offer a fully satisfactory account of how pluralist democracy treads a delicate line between the proliferation of political demands and the integrity of the whole system, achieving dynamic stability. In that failure, however, it reveals a crucial insight that most postwar democratic theorists ignored: that even a purportedly democratic system may be unable to achieve dynamic stability *unless it is supplemented by forces that undermine its democratic credentials.* Seen in this light, pluralist democracy's chief presuppositions—that the multiplication of interest groups (dispersion of input sources) would decentralize power, and electoral institutions and interest group activities (feedback mechanisms) would make government more responsive to popular demands—should be met with more skepticism. In Easton's general theory, those supposedly democratic traits uneasily coexist with more oppressive elements. Although Easton implicitly assumes that in a democracy those oppressive mechanisms will be less active, if operative at all, an analysis of systems science and cybernetics—which he explicitly acknowledges as his main intellectual inspiration—leads us to a different conclusion: that a system's adaptability and ostensibly diffused structure, on the one hand, and its oppressive and centralizing tendencies, on the other, may be not counterposed but mutually reinforcing.

The premise that a system functions as an integrated whole assumes that all the input elements are translated into homogeneous terms, which raises the politically charged question of who determine those terms, for what purposes, and at whose expense. Easton's portrayal of a system as a "flat" or single-level process in which individual inputs lead seamlessly to corresponding outputs obscures an adaptive system's upward and centripetal tendencies in its decision-making. As the case of PPBS illustrates, command-and-control's reliance on diffused information outlets rather than rigid hierarchy makes decision-making more, not less, centralized. And if Easton offers an overly sanitized image of systems by glossing over differential positions in which various inputs are placed, he also fails to fully interrogate the forces that circumscribe and regiment inputs, implicitly assuming that people's free and frequent communication with the authorities is positively linked to the latter's responsiveness. When Wiener's enemy pilot enters his aircraft, when Beer's workers walk into their factory, and even when Beer's citizens turn on their televisions with their hands on the algedonic meter, the range of relevant inputs is pre-programmed into their environment. Worse, their environment is often equipped with devices of negative feedback or manipulation that either punish them when they fail to react as they are supposed to or induce them to produce certain kinds of inputs. Stability is achieved, not by a system's responsiveness but by its normalizing, disciplinary mechanisms.

Postwar democratic theory's assumptions about dynamic stability, then, suggest that it may not simply have been a product of the rearguard action to protect the extant manifestation of democracy from the perceived threats of totalitarianism. What also underlay it may have been the ambitious idea that when we design it smartly enough—when, for example, we identify and connect its variegated parts, establish communication channels between them, and integrate them tightly into a functional whole—democracy can become a benevolent adaptive organism that responds deftly to changing conditions in a way that benefits all its parts. Behind postwar democratic theorists' implicit adoption of systems thinking, in other words, may have been a hope that democracy can be organized to produce good results without getting bogged down or imperiled by democratic politics that, from the standpoint of the cybernetic couplings regulated by the automated signaling mechanism, is hopelessly cumbersome and plagued by irrationalities. Despite the charge of conservatism, what animated postwar democratic theorists' defense of gradual and incremental reform may not have been just the fear-ridden belief that people's political freedom must be contained and displaced. It may also have been a faith in the power to create a controlled system in which people's unruly claims and interactions are managed—a system in which the disturbances that people create stay within preset parameters, and the signals they emit are instantaneously registered to ensure the system's ceaseless, ever-evolving operation. The system produces the optimal outcome that best accommodates people's aggregate demands without overly straining overall stability. The system, then, dispenses with the need for citizens to determine their collective goals through public deliberation. All citizens need to do is to register their individual preferences; the system takes care of the rest. In a democracy envisioned by systems thinking, in short, the demos becomes redundant.

CHAPTER FIVE

Cold War Neoliberalism and the Capitalist Restructuring of Democracy

Cold War neoliberalism has rarely been treated as an important part of postwar democratic theory. To be sure, most postwar democratic theorists did not accept what is often associated with neoliberalism today—an opposition to state intervention in the economy and a defense of laissez-faire economic programs. But portraying Cold War neoliberalism merely as an offshoot of market fundamentalism is inaccurate. As recent scholarship has begun to show, most Cold War neoliberals were neither unreserved opponents of the state nor unquestioning champions of the free market.[1] Perhaps more important, seeing Cold War neoliberalism as a purely economic doctrine is limited, if not misleading. This chapter analyzes Cold War neoliberalism as a distinctly political principle of social organization, situating it in the broader postwar debate over democracy and capitalism.

The relationship between liberal democracy and neoliberalism is the subject of an ongoing debate. Wendy Brown, for example, highlights the divergence between liberal democracy and neoliberalism. While wary of liberal democracy's limitations, Brown argues that its principles "hold, and hold out, ideals of freedom and equality universally shared and of political rule by and for the people," offering a basic platform from which more substantive democratic projects might be launched. According to her, neoliberalism stands opposed to, and is "evacuating," these liberal democratic ideals and desires.[2] In contrast, Antonio Y. Vázquez-Arroyo stresses the two doctrines' commonalities, pointing to shared features such as the separation of the economic and the political, the hostility to popular participation, and the generation of apolitical culture.[3] My own view is somewhat different from these perspectives. On the one hand, I suggest that liberal democracy was not simply hollowed out by neoliberalism but had already undergone an internal transformation in the postwar era so as to clear the hurdles for neoliberalism's subsequent rise. On the other hand, I suggest that significant differences do indeed exist between liberal democracy and neoliberalism. As I will elaborate, neoliberalism is far more radical than liberal democracy in its ambition to spread the market institutions and norms to noneconomic realms and is quite willing to violate the public-private distinction. The two systems' stark difference can be observed, for instance, in their approach to subjectivity. If postwar liberal democracy suspends the quest to form democratic subjectivity, Cold War neoliberalism actively seeks to replace democratic subjectivity with capitalist subjectivity attuned to price signals. Moreover, neoliberalism is far more aggressive in resorting to the authoritarian means to achieve its goal, partly because its own working incites democratic demands that cannot be contained within liberal institutions.

I reconstruct a political theory of neoliberalism and analyze its implications by drawing on the work of Friedrich A. Hayek. Hayek is a crucial figure in tracing the conceptual and organizational origins of neoliberalism: not only did he produce extensive work that helped codify neoliberalism, but he also mobilized various scholars with similar commitments and built an institutional basis, the Mont Pèlerin Society, for the elaboration and dissemination of neoliberalism.[4] I focus on Hayek's scholarly work, which I take to be the most comprehensive theoretical account of neoliberalism. Although he did discuss and advocate specific policies, Hayek, more than any other theorist of neoliberalism, articulated a general framework in which neoliberalism emerges not simply as an efficient economic system but as a superior form of social order. A close examination of his theory reveals that neoliberalism cannot be a purely economic doctrine, because its successful operation requires a restructuring of social relations. It also shows that democratic subjectivity is a chief barrier to, and thus a major target of, the neoliberal project. In this respect, postwar democratic theory's neglect of democratic subjectivity unwittingly cleared the ground for neoliberalism's germination.

Hayek was certainly not the only, nor the representative, theorist who wrote about capitalism and democracy in the postwar period. Capitalism, and the economic abundance it brought about, was one of the main concerns of postwar political and social thought. Even as they were impressed by economic growth, most postwar intellectuals ranged from cautious to critical in their assessment of capitalism. David Potter's *People of Plenty* (1954) might have been the most celebratory of the influential commentaries produced in this period, but even Potter registered serious worries about capitalism's corrosive effects on the "American character." Others—such as Daniel Bell's "Work and Its Discontents" (1956); John Kenneth Galbraith's *The Affluent Society* (1958); David Riesman's *Abundance for What?* (1964); Vance Packard's best-selling trilogy, *The Hidden Persuaders* (1957), *The Status Seekers* (1959), and *The Waste Makers* (1960); and Betty Friedan's *The Feminine Mystique* (1963)—evinced pointed criticisms of how industrial capitalism fell short of its promises and spawned new maladies, while largely accepting its basic structure. Still others—including Paul Goodman's *Growing Up Absurd* (1960), Rachel Carson's *Silent Spring* (1962), Michael Harrington's *The Other America* (1962), and Herbert Marcuse's *One-Dimensional Man* (1964)—were more radical, harboring deep doubts about whether capitalism could achieve universal opulence without generating psychological, environmental, and social pathologies that overshadowed its perceived benefits. These were all brilliant critiques, but they did not examine with sufficient focus how changing discourses of capitalism and democracy shaped each other, creating unique tendencies and tensions.

Hayek offers unique insights into the construction of postwar democratic theory. His work was an important catalyst in the political process through which capitalism became a correlate of democracy, and despite his belief that the West was making a regressive movement away from the neoliberal order, his theory helps capture powerful socioeconomic and cultural trends in postwar America that established market prices as a dominant social signal. Moreover, partly because he feared that capitalism was besieged by democracy (a particular variant of democracy, which, he lamented, was *eclipsing* instrumental democracy), Hayek was more sensitive than other postwar intellectuals to the tension between capitalism and democracy. While numerous postwar thinkers presumed that democracy and free-market capitalism were mutually supportive or at least reconcilable, Hayek believed that neoliberalism can thrive only when social relations are restructured in market terms, and such a restructuring can be achieved only when democracy is greatly circumscribed or, more precisely, when democratic subjectivity is thoroughly marginalized. In attempting to deal with this tension, his theory, finally, reveals instabilities of neoliberalism that were not clearly visible at the time.

Hayek was a remarkably prolific writer, and the three major statements of his neoliberalism on which I focus—*The Road to Serfdom* (1944), *The Constitution of Liberty* (1960), and *Law, Legislation, and Liberty* (1973, 1976, 1979)—were produced sufficiently far apart and in different contexts that treating them together may require some explanation. Hayek wrote *The Road to Serfdom* between 1940 and 1943, when he was at the London School of Economics, and its immediate impetus was not the debate over the New Deal that was raging in America but the socialist sympathies widely held among British intellectuals and especially the claim that National Socialism was a capitalist reaction to socialism.[5] *The Constitution of Liberty* was a product of Hayek's American years (1950–1962), during which he was on the Committee on Social Thought at the University of Chicago.[6] Finally, Hayek wrote *Law, Legislation, and Liberty* in Freiberg and Salzburg, and it was published in three volumes throughout the 1970s.[7]

Despite these different settings, his core themes remained remarkably consistent throughout those books: the significance of organizing knowledge to a free and prosperous civilization; his defense of the rule of law as an indispensable means to that end; his critique of "collectivism," including the welfare state, as a grave threat to the cardinal principles of free civilization; and his wariness that democracy deepens the perilous trend toward collectivism. All three books reiterate these themes in one way or another; in fact, Hayek is quite explicit about the intimate connections between them. As he remarked in 1953, Hayek conceived *The Constitution of Liberty* as a "positive complement" to *The Road to Serfdom*,[8] partly in response to the criticism that in denouncing collectivism while at the same time refusing to espouse laissez-faire, he failed to offer a clear alternative.[9] Likewise, *Law, Legislation, and Liberty* was intended as a companion to *The Constitution of Liberty*. In *The Constitution of Liberty*, Hayek already advanced his central claim that progress is the product not of a central plan but of an evolutionary process compiling individuals' innumerable local activities, as well as the idea that the rule of law provides a key condition for that evolution by setting up abstract rules that individuals can take into account as a sort of informational constraint in spontaneously adjusting their actions. In *Law, Legislation, and Liberty*, Hayek elaborated these ideas by relying more explicitly on evolutionary theory, trying to "fill the gaps" left in *The Constitution of Liberty*.[10] Moreover, the production of these two works was more proximate than suggested by the dates of publication. Although *Law, Legislation, and Liberty* came out in three volumes in 1973, 1976, and 1979, respectively, Hayek completed primary drafts of the book by 1970.[11]

In the politically charged reception of his work, Hayek's argument has often been associated with a "conservative" or "libertarian" stance. To be sure, a critique of collectivism and a defense of individual liberty are two of the principal themes he consistently foregrounds. But as in the case of cybernetics we examined in the previous chapter, Hayek's real faith lies not in the rationality of the individual but in the rationality of the free-market *system*. A close study reveals that he does not celebrate diverse forms of individuality but argues precisely the opposite: he proposes to discipline individuals so that they become a specific type of individual—one that responds to price signals. Despite their critique of consumerism, many postwar intellectuals failed to fully detect the forces that were establishing this capitalist subjectivity as a dominant social disposition, and they underestimated its implications for democratic politics—perhaps because they believed that commitment to democratic norms was secure enough. Hayek certainly thought so; if anything, he believed that it was too secure. He complained that a majority of people equated democracy with values such as equality and solidarity—which, for him, was a result of conceptual confusion, as well as an emotional remnant of the primitive past—and that they would resist the changes required by the capitalist civilization even though those changes would enhance their liberty and prosperity in the long run. The perceived gap between the capitalist civilization and its uncivilized inhabitants explains, finally, why Hayek finds political freedom, and democratic politics as its manifestation, so destructive. For him, when democracy becomes more than an instrument serving individuals' private interests, it encourages people to act on their "irrational" impulses and interfere with the working of the market at their own peril. In the end, Hayek's Cold War neoliberalism reaches a conclusion that is profoundly at odds with its libertarian rhetoric: democracy must be restrained so that people can be made to follow market rules against their wishes.

The Road to Serfdom and the Merger of Democracy and Capitalism

The Road to Serfdom: Context and Arguments

Hayek's *The Road to Serfdom* (1944) was, as he said, a "political book."[12] In it, he set out to unveil the forces that gave rise to Nazi totalitarianism, in the hope of dispelling the same forces he perceived to be at work, often under the name of socialism, in Western democracies. Reversing the Marxist diagnosis that Nazism was a twisted attempt to perpetuate capitalism, Hayek claimed that the rise of fascism and Nazism was "not a reaction against the socialist trends of the preceding period but a necessary outcome of those tendencies."[13] Maintaining that a society's political institutions are shaped by its economic system, he pitted capitalism organized by market competition against "collectivism," which encompassed all the other types of economic systems that apparently relied on central planning. "The various kinds of collectivism, communism, fascism, etc., differ among themselves in the nature of the goal toward which they want to direct the efforts of society," Hayek insisted, but "they all differ from liberalism and individualism in wanting to organize the whole of society and its resources for its unitary end and in refusing to recognize autonomous spheres in which the ends of the individuals are supreme." In this sense, he asserted, variants of collectivism are all "totalitarian."[14]

Hayek's Manichaean juxtaposition of individualism and collectivism, as well as his characterization of the latter as totalitarian, readily dovetailed with the dualistic politics of the Cold War, which were already beginning to harden by the time *Serfdom* came out. Those conditions probably accounted for the surprisingly popular and highly politicized reception in the United States of a book he had intended largely for an academic audience in Great Britain.[15] But as Hayek repeatedly complained, his arguments in *Serfdom* did not neatly fit the partisan debate between proponents of laissez-faire and advocates of state intervention, which was heating up against the fraught backdrop of totalitarianism.[16] He explicitly cautioned that his critique of collectivism should not be confused with a "dogmatic laissez-faire attitude."[17] Throughout the book, Hayek made remarkably large concessions to the role that the state may play in the economy. While competition "precludes certain types of coercive interference with economic life," he stated, "it admits of others which sometimes may very considerably assist its work and even requires certain kinds of government action."[18] He suggested that the state may impose certain regulations, concerning, for example, the use of poisonous substances, maximum working hours, and sanitary arrangements, and even provide an "extensive system of social services" without jeopardizing market competition.[19] When there is a "divergence between the items which enter into private calculation and those which affect social welfare," including the provision of public goods and the regulation of neighborhood effects, Hayek went so far as to contend that "we must find some substitute for the regulation by the price mechanism."[20] He explicitly endorsed measures of social protection and insurance, which, especially given his reputation, may seem quite strong. "In a society which has reached the general level of wealth which ours has attained," he maintained, "there can be no doubt that some minimum of food, shelter, and clothing, sufficient to preserve health and the capacity to work, can be assured to everybody"; nor is there any reason why "the state should not assist the individuals in providing for those common hazards of life" such as sickness and accident.[21]

In fact, even though Hayek proclaimed his desire to correct "the discussions of problems of future economic policy at the present time," which was "to an alarming extent guided by amateurs and cranks,"[22] *The Road to Serfdom* is striking for its relative lack of discussion of particular economic policies. Hayek did not try, for example, to expose the follies of the Beveridge Report, *Social Insurance and Allied Services,* which came out in 1942 and would serve as a blueprint for the postwar British welfare state.[23] Perhaps more surprisingly, he did not mount a challenge, as he had earlier, to Keynes, who, in *The General Theory of Employment, Interest, and Money* (1936), lent pivotal intellectual support to the state's active intervention in the economy. (Hayek mentioned Keynes only once, with reference to his obscure review, from 1915, of a book on the German economy.[24]) Rather, Hayek tackled a broader shift in thinking and sentiment that, in his view, made those policies look acceptable and indeed desirable to the majority of the population. The problem, he complained, was that "in the democracies the majority of people still believe that socialism and freedom can be combined."[25] According to Hayek, this belief took hold as socialists adulterated the original, purely political meaning of freedom ("freedom from coercion") by defining it so as to include "freedom from necessity"—liberation from physical wants and the structural constraints of the economic system. Through this obfuscation, socialists presented their movement as the "consummation of the age-long struggle for freedom," and many well-meaning liberals, ever the champions of freedom, embraced socialism as the "apparent heir of the liberal tradition."[26] Hayek sought to debunk this belief and show that, far from a natural extension of or precondition for political freedom, as insisted by socialists and their liberal allies, the pursuit of freedom from necessity actually undermines political freedom, threatening to turn democracy into dictatorship. *The*

Road to Serfdom was "political," not simply because it was intended as a contribution to a partisan debate but, perhaps more important, because it defended capitalism on political, rather than narrowly economic, grounds.

In this respect, *The Road to Serfdom* may be viewed as the first comprehensive statement of a shift in Hayek's approach to capitalism. Hayek had been consistently critical of state intervention in the economy, but until the early 1930s, his work remained narrowly economic and technical. His early sparring with Keynes and his followers focused on rather abstruse capital theory. (For example: "Even if it be true, as it probably is, that the rate of remuneration of the original factors of production is relatively more rigid than profits, it is certainly not true in regard to the remuneration of invested capital. Mr. Keynes obviously arrives at this view by an artificial separation of the function of the entrepreneurs as owners of capital and their function as entrepreneurs in the narrow sense."[27]) Hayek's perspective transformed in the middle of the decade as he engaged in the so-called socialist calculation debate. He launched an attack with the publication of *Collectivist Economic Planning: Critical Studies on the Possibilities of Socialism* (1935), in which he reproduced critiques of socialism made by Austrian economists such as Ludwig von Mises in the 1920s, along with a lengthy introduction and a survey of the current debate that he composed.[28] Following Ludwig von Mises, Hayek insisted that without market competition it would be impossible to determine the monetary value of goods in socialism, and thus economic managers would have no data with which to calculate the economic feasibility of their plans. Advocates of a socialist economy countered that when planners have relatively comprehensive knowledge of the economy, prices can still be determined outside the market. It is through his attempt to refute this claim that Hayek came to conclude that organization of dispersed knowledge, not just the production and distribution of goods, is a central feature of the economy. He first outlined this idea in his 1936 lecture "Economics and Knowledge." There, he identified the *"division of knowledge"* as "the really central problem of economics as a social science," declaring that the central question of economics is "how the spontaneous interaction of a number of people, each possessing only bits of knowledge, brings about a state of affairs ... which could be brought about by deliberate action only by somebody who possessed the combined knowledge of all those individuals."[29] "The problem of a rational economic order," as he later put it, is one of "the utilization of knowledge which is not given to anyone in its totality."[30]

The discovery of this insight was, in Hayek's own words, "the decisive point of the change in my outlook."[31] It marked the beginning of his move from the narrow modes of economic analysis to an integrative social philosophy that connects economics, politics, and law.[32] Some of the principal motifs stemming from this shift in perspective are clearly on display in *The Road to Serfdom*. Refuting the notion that the complexity of modern industrial society makes central planning inevitable, for example, Hayek reiterates his cardinal idea about dispersed knowledge. "Because nobody can consciously balance all the considerations bearing on the decisions of so many individuals, the co-ordination can clearly be effected not by 'conscious control' but only by arrangements which convey to each agent the information he must possess in order to effectively adjust his decisions to those of others."[33] Hayek advocates the free market not simply because he regards planning as a violation of the sanctity of private property but because he believes that the price system—in which "the individual producer has to adapt himself to price changes and cannot control them"—is the only arrangement that can make complex social coordination possible.[34] One also sees earlier indications of Hayek's attempt to link the market economy to the rule of law. He emphasizes that an "intelligently designed and continuously adjusted legal framework" is indispensable to the working of market competition,[35] going so far as to contend that the distinction between a competitive market system and central planning is "a particular case of the more general distinction between the Rule of Law and arbitrary government."[36]

The Road to Serfdom also contains early signs of a theoretical tension between Hayek's neoliberalism and democracy. One of his controversial claims is that planning is particularly dangerous when tried in a democracy. Here Hayek's argument almost exactly mirrors that of Joseph Schumpeter, another Austrian economist, whose concern about the threat to capitalism posed by the democratic inclusion of the working masses led him to espouse a radically diminished democracy (discussed in chapter 3). Hayek contends that economic planning, often justified by concepts such as the "common good," the "general welfare," or the "general interest," presupposes the existence of a "complete ethical code in which all the different human values are allotted their due place."[37] Because of this alleged requirement, planning puts an enormous strain on society by asking us to "agree on a much larger number of topics than we have been used to."[38] Given people's diverse interests, the more we extend the sphere regulated by common action, it becomes more difficult to reach agreement and thus more likely to suppress individual freedom in the name of collective agreement. Moreover, even if we somehow settle on the goal of planning, democratic governments will never be able to realize that goal in their doomed attempt to find common ground on all the particular aspects of devising and executing the plan. This incompetence will "inevitably cause dissatisfaction with democratic institutions" and eventually give rise to the belief that "if things are to get done, the responsible authorities must be freed from the fetters of democratic procedure."[39] This is why, as Hayek memorably declares, "the cry for an economic dictator is a characteristic stage in the movement toward planning."[40] Planning is, for him, like a train with a broken brake: once it is set in motion, one cannot stop it from overloading, paralyzing, and ultimately destroying democracy with an ever-increasing demand for social consensus.

While the emphasis on the diversity of viewpoints and the difficulty of forging social agreement is well taken as a general point, it is hard not to conclude that Hayek's argument here is too categorical. As numerous contemporaneous critics noted, Hayek's blanket treatment of "democracy" as a single system neglects specific empirical conditions—political history, the makeup of constituents, institutional configurations, political culture, and so on—that shape seemingly similar regime types in widely different ways.[41] Perhaps more fundamentally, he confounds the normative significance of fomenting democratic contestation *around* the common good with the empirical difficulty of attaining, once and for all, unanimous consensus *on* the common good. But the difficulty, even impossibility, of reaching a perfect consensus at a particular moment cannot be the reason to abandon the pursuit of the common good as such. Democracy is an indispensable political ideal, not because it is the most efficient way of realizing individual preferences but because it is built on the normative expectation that it values universal demands—demands for the sake of the common good and political equality—over particular ones. Unlike Hayek's suggestion, what political decisions effect is not so much an outright suppression of individual liberty as a shifting of the burden of proof such that those who disagree with a particular decision are now obligated to persuade their fellow citizens that the decision undermines the common good or political equality. And any generally applied political decision is not a permanently fixed decree but a temporary outcome of democratic processes. That is why it is crucial for democracy to ensure that contestation takes place, and again, on equal terms. Put another way, the most important task of democracy is to preserve and promote substantive political freedom, and other forms of freedom must be understood in terms of that central task.

Hayek argues the opposite: economic freedom must precede political freedom. He claims that "personal and political freedom has never existed in the past" without "freedom in economic affairs."[42] Again: "If 'capitalism' means here a competitive system based on free disposal over private property, it is far more important to realize that only within this system is democracy possible. When it becomes dominated by a collectivist creed, democracy will inevitably destroy itself."[43]

Certainly, attaining substantive political freedom requires a certain form of economic freedom. But Hayek does not construe the relationship between economic and political freedom as such a symbiotic one. On the contrary, he understands economic freedom and political freedom, capitalism and democratic politics, in antagonistic terms. And he contends that economic freedom must be preserved at the expense of political freedom or, more precisely, that political freedom must be restricted so as to guarantee the capitalist form of economic freedom to the fullest extent.

The uneasy relationship between neoliberalism and democracy in Hayek's theory surfaces more fully in his later works, but here I will note two related points. One is that he adopts a purely instrumental view of democracy. Warning against "making a fetish of democracy," he insists that democracy is "essentially a means, a utilitarian device for safeguarding internal peace and individual freedom."[44] Hayek considers democracy a least objectionable instrument, because it controls individuals' arbitrary will better than other types of political regime, but—and this is the second point—only when popular participation is curtailed. He displays the same low opinion of ordinary people that pervaded postwar political thought. Pointing out that what we often take to be the will of the people is nothing but an opinion of the largest group of society, he suggests that such a group is "not likely to be formed by the best but rather by the worst elements of any society." Hayek's reasoning on this point is swift. He begins by positing that the more educated and intelligent people are, the more diverse their views and tastes will be. This means that those who wish to rally a large number of people behind a unified position "have to descend to the regions of lower moral and intellectual standards where the more primitive and 'common' instincts and tastes prevail." In other words, a large group is likely to consist of "those who form the 'mass' in the derogatory sense of the term, the least original and independent."[45] From here the situation only gets worse. Once a large organization has gained momentum, it tries to mobilize even more people under a simple doctrine. Such ideological mobilization has the highest chance of success with "the docile and the gullible," who are incapable of independent thinking and swayed by passions and emotions.[46] In this way, popular democracy turns willy-nilly into totalitarianism. And totalitarianism perpetuates itself by suppressing "good people"—liberals who are committed to an individualist ethic. It rewards unthinking pawns whose only pleasure lies in the arbitrary and cruel exercise of power, and does little to "induce men who are good by our standards to aspire to leading positions in the totalitarian machine" and much to attract "the ruthless and unscrupulous."[47]

Turning Around the Anticapitalist Discourse

Some of Hayek's more polemical statements might be explained by his perception that democratic socialism was becoming dominant, irreversibly turning the tide against traditional liberalism. In the context of the 1930s, which is the primary historical reference of *The Road to Serfdom,* this was not an entirely groundless reaction. There was a lot of groping in the dark and a wide variety of views, but in the aftermath of the Great Depression many intellectuals grew impatient with liberalism and sympathetic toward some version of socialism, and this intellectual trend found its (limited and jumbled) way into mainstream politics. In 1930, John Dewey—whom Hayek singles out as the "leading philosopher of American left-wingism" and the "most explicit defender" of the muddied concept of freedom[48]—announced the "bankruptcy of the older individualism" and called for a fundamental reconceptualization of liberalism or, more precisely, a radical break from it, because "the new individualism cannot be achieved by extending the benefits of the older economic individualism."[49] According to Dewey, the "chief obstacle" to this goal was the "persistence of that feature of the earlier individualism which defines industry and commerce by ideas of private pecuniary profit."[50] Dewey insisted that American capitalism was fundamentally precarious, characterized as it was by the systematic gap between overproduction driven by overcapitalization and the majority's low purchasing power, and he predicted that the "problem of social control of industry and the use of governmental agencies for constructive social ends will become the avowed centre of political struggle."[51]

Dewey was hardly speaking from the margin. His diagnosis of capitalism was an iteration of what had then become a fairly standard view in mainstream liberal magazines such as the *New Republic* (where he delivered the foregoing indictment).[52] As Dewey predicted, the "social control of industry" indeed became a central theme in the early 1930s, reinforced by a chorus of influential books, including Adolph Berle and Gardiner Means's *The Modern Corporation and Private Property* (1932), Stuart Chase's *A New Deal* (1932), and George Soule's *A Planned Society* (1932). The argument of Stuart Chase, whom Hayek describes as "one of the most prominent economic planners,"[53] gives us a glimpse of the tenor of the time.[54] Although the title of Chase's book would be associated with Franklin Roosevelt's economic programs, Chase's proposals were actually far more radical than what was tried, let alone enacted, by the Roosevelt administration. Chase was more radical because he started from a different premise—that the prevailing system of capitalism was fundamentally out of step with the historical conditions. Sounding a theme that would continue to be central to postwar thought, Chase announced that "we have left the economy of scarcity behind and entered the economy of abundance."[55] But unlike postwar intellectuals, Chase contended that the age of abundance required a fundamental reconsideration of the very purpose of the economic system. He suggested that the economy be reconceived as a means for a specific function, "to provide food, shelter, clothing and comforts in as dependable and adequate quantities as natural resources and the state of technical arts permit," rather than remaining the arena for the pursuit of profit, which incidentally fulfills some social needs but inevitably generates staggering waste, imbalances, and instabilities.[56] The task, therefore, was not simply to mend the inadequacies of the current system, as Keynes and other reformers proposed, but to alter the way capitalism works as "a way of life" promoting excess, artificially created needs and wants, and frenetic speculation.[57] Chase proposed a broad array of ideas, but the gist of his reform agenda was the creation of a national planning board that would oversee the entire economy; identify and eliminate waste, duplication, and obsolescence; and regulate long-term investment to better meet genuine social needs. (Lest his vision look too sterile, Chase proposed to close up Wall Street as a "gambling joint" and open a new one in Washington so that people could sate their supposedly ingrained thirst for gambling.[58]) Few images could better capture what Hayek was arguing against than the national planning board as described by Chase: "a group which sees the whole picture, and how each segment dovetails with the next; a group which has access to a steady flow of facts and statistics covering all significant aspects of the country's economic life; a group which knows the past, can give capable advice as to the present, and sees into the future, especially the technological future."[59]

Whatever intellectual vitality inspired by visions of democratic socialism or a planned society existed in America in the 1930s, it had largely dissipated by the time *The Road to Serfdom* came out in 1944. Numerous factors accounted for this: the rise of fascism (from which America did not seem immune in light of the political ascendance of figures such as Huey P. Long and Father Charles E. Coughlin) led many leftist intellectuals to support the New Deal, at least temporarily, rather than criticize its lack of coherent vision and its haphazard, politically motivated, and chaotic nature; the collapse of the Popular Front dealt a serious blow to the hope for a united leftist alliance; and the threat of war posed by authoritarian regimes in Germany and Japan increased the appreciation of existing liberal and democratic values and institutions.[60] Perhaps most crucially, the succession of events from the Moscow trials to the fateful Nazi-Soviet nonaggression pact in August 1939 caused an irrevocable disillusionment with Soviet communism and intellectual paralysis.[61] Shocked and disappointed by the Soviet Union's political opportunism, intellectuals who had been arguing that fascism was a reaction to capitalism's instabilities and that communism was the only true bulwark against it found themselves in a highly defensive position vis-à-vis the charge, already percolating since the mid-1930s, that Nazism and Soviet communism were merely variants of the same totalitarian regime.[62] When the Committee for Cultural Freedom published a manifesto, a few months before the Nazi-Soviet pact, announcing that totalitarianism was "already enthroned in Germany, Italy, Russia, Japan, and Spain," and "unless ... combated wherever and in whatever form it manifests itself, it will spread in America,"[63] editors of the *New Republic* could still reproach the manifesto's signatories for complacently looking away from America's own suppression of freedom and for showing "a regrettable lack of historical perspective" by "lumping together the Fascist powers with the USSR." Insisting that suppression of political dissent in the Soviet Union had mostly to do with the "Russian tradition" rather than "socialist theory," the editors went so far as to suggest that a "socialist community, given proper conditions, should do more to liberate the human spirit than has ever been accomplished on this earth."[64]

But when Max Eastman, a disillusioned former champion of the Russian Revolution, wrote to the *New Republic* that October, demanding that the magazine acknowledge that "we were wrong. YOU CANNOT SERVE DEMOCRACY AND TOTALITARIANSM," the editors only protested that they "have never said nor believed that totalitarianism and democracy are compatible" and they "have repeatedly criticized the lack of civil and political liberties" in the Soviet Union.[65] As proponents of democratic socialism retreated, the enlarged discourse of antitotalitarianism, encompassing not just fascism and Nazism but now communism, served as a great simplifier that regimented diverse critical views in terms of the binary of democracy and totalitarianism.

Hayek built on, and contributed to, this discourse. Hayek cited Max Eastman, who followed up his angry letter with a book-length critique of the Soviet Union and, as an editor of *Reader's Digest,* would publish a condensed version of *The Road to Serfdom.*[66] Hayek also relied on James Burnham, another former radical, who argued that Nazi Germany, Stalinist Russia, and New Deal America were all manifestations of the same underlying shift from a capitalist economy to a collectivized and tightly managed mode of social production—the shift that Burnham famously called "the managerial revolution."[67] At least in one major case, Hayek was a direct influence. In one of the most high-profile ideological conversions of the late 1930s, Walter Lippmann, once an ardent supporter of economic planning, published *An Inquiry into the Principles of the Good Society* (1937), in which he defined the New Deal as "collectivism," which includes totalitarianism, socialism, and communism, presenting it as a grave threat to democracy. "A democratic people cannot have a planned economy," declared Lippmann. "In so far as they desire a planned economy they must suspend responsible government."[68] Lippmann acknowledged *Collectivist Economic Planning,* Hayek's intervention in the socialist calculation debate, as an intellectual inspiration.[69]

Neoliberalism would have to wait a few more decades for real dominance, to be sure, but the intellectual ground for its ascendance was long in the making. Hayek helped lay that groundwork, but not simply by drawing a firm line between the public and private spheres and using that distinction to delegitimize government's role in the economy. If so, he would have been more in line with classical liberals, with whom he aligned himself.[70] But Hayek's neoliberalism departs from classical liberalism in striking ways. Instead of enlisting market capitalism as a tool of material production that individuals may use to pursue their goals as they see fit, he tries to establish it as an organizing principle of social relations in all aspects—a principle that people prioritize over all else and blindly obey. And to achieve that goal, Hayek is quite willing to violate the public-private distinction. Even in *Serfdom,* he flummoxed his readers by insisting that the target of his criticism was only "planning against competition" and endorsing "the very necessary planning which is required to make competition as effective and beneficial as possible."[71] Inconsistencies like this become less confusing once we understand Hayek's radical ambition, which becomes clearer as he elaborates a positive theory of neoliberalism.

Hayek's Theory of Neoliberalism and the Capitalist Restructuring of Democracy

What Makes Hayek's Theory *Neo*liberalism?

Many of Hayek's works following *The Road to Serfdom* can be seen as an extensive elaboration of some of the chief motifs he laid out in it. In response to the criticism that his critique of collectivism lacked a positive alternative, Hayek articulated pieces of his neoliberalism in the 1940s and 1950s, eventually bringing them together in two of his most systematic works, *The Constitution of Liberty* and *Law, Legislation, and Liberty.* Building on the foundational insight about dispersed knowledge that he discovered in the mid-1930s, he set out to outline essential norms and principles that could help form a best knowledge regime. In Hayek's view, knowledge in a given society could never be known in its totality by an individual mind, not just because such knowledge is vast but also because it changes constantly according to individuals' actions and reactions. Therefore the most beneficial, if not the only, way to organize knowledge is to let each individual decide the purpose and the mode of using the bits of knowledge in her possession. This is why individuals must be given as much liberty as possible. Individuals' maneuverings cannot be limitless or isolated, however, for then their actions will generate chaos and prevent people from achieving their goals. Without deliberate or overarching plans, individuals must still somehow coordinate their activities and adjust their behavior to that of others. For that purpose, they must share some information on which they can rely in determining what to do with the pieces of unique knowledge they privately own. That common information helps individuals predict the consequences of their actions, including others' potential reactions, with a level of reliability. Market prices are a crucial component of that common information, but more generally it consists of a set of rules regulating social relations. These two needs—safeguarding individual liberty and securing a level of predictability in social relations—delimit the state's power, so political measures that restrict individual liberty or reduce predictability in interpersonal relations are inherently suspect and require a particularly stringent justification.

While it may not be readily clear in this summary account, Hayek's neoliberalism is in many ways a significant departure from classical liberalism. One of the most striking—and ironic, given his polemic against totalitarianism's smothering of individual spontaneity—aspects of his theory is the pains he takes to delegitimize the conventional conception of individualism. Classical liberals, even those who do not adopt the doctrine of natural rights, assign some intrinsic value to the individual. The realization of individuality is the ultimate goal, and their various ideas about political arrangements—basic individual rights, the public-private distinction, laissez-faire, and so on—are all to serve it and to make it attainable for more people.

In Hayek's neoliberalism, liberty appears not as a state or capability of the individual but as a feature of a particular social order, namely, the market order. The relation between a social order and its members, then, is reversed. A society does not exist to support its members' exercise of liberty; the members help maintain the capitalist civilization by engaging in social interaction as dictated by it, and may receive liberty in return for their conformity.[72] On these grounds, Hayek rejects the belief that individualism is premised on "the existence of isolated or self-contained individuals instead of starting from men whose whole nature and character is determined by their existence in society" as the "silliest of the common misunderstandings."[73] But he is not just acknowledging the socially embedded nature of individuality. He goes on to assert that the notion of "original personalities" is not just unrelated to, but potentially in conflict with, individualism, and he insists that the "cult of the distinct and different individuality" belongs only to the German intellectual tradition and is "little known elsewhere," though its influence has found its way, partially yet still unfortunately, into the British tradition in the form of J. S. Mill's *On Liberty*. "This sort of 'individualism,'" Hayek remarks with disdainful quotation marks, "not only has nothing to do with true individualism but may indeed prove a grave obstacle to the smooth working of an individualist system."[74] Speculating that "so-called German individualism is frequently represented as one of the causes why the Germans have never succeeded in developing free political institutions," Hayek raises doubts about "whether a free or individualistic society can be worked successfully if people are too 'individualistic' in the false sense, if they are too unwilling voluntarily to conform to traditions and conventions, and if they refuse to recognize anything which is not consciously designed or which cannot be demonstrated as rational to every individual."[75] In Hayek's theory, the individual is subordinated to the individualist *system* or the individualistic *society.*

Hayek formulates another pillar of his neoliberalism—coercion and the rule of law as its only acceptable form—with the same logic. Noting that "coercion is nearly as troublesome a concept as liberty itself," he maintains that coercion occurs "when one man's actions are made to serve another man's will, not for his own but for the others' purpose."[76] As in the case of Hayek's individualism, the problem is not that coercion intrudes on certain fundamentals of intrinsically valuable individuality. Rather, coercion is "bad because it prevents a person from using his mental powers to the full and consequently making the greatest contribution that he is capable of to the community."[77] As noted earlier, Hayek justifies law on the grounds that it facilitates organization of fragmented knowledge by increasing predictability in social relations and thereby allowing individuals to make decisions already adjusted to their social environment—that it makes possible, in other words, unplanned social coordination. To use his example, we do not build a bonfire in our living room because we can foresee its consequence; likewise, we do not set our neighbor's house on fire because we can predict its consequence, too. In both cases, the individual's knowledge of law, either natural or man-made, "enables him to foresee what will be the consequences of his actions," and "helps him to make plans with confidence."[78] It is in this sense that Hayek states that "the ideal type of law ... provides merely additional information to be taken into account in the decision of the actor."[79] And that is why he argues that laws are "instrumental" at the disposal of each individual and should be judged by their "usefulness" in producing overall social benefits.[80]

Relying on this argument, Hayek goes so far as to suggest that individual liberty and the rule of law are not just consistent but inextricably intertwined with each other. He asserts that as long as laws do not dictate individuals' particular actions and apply equally to everyone, "the laws of the state have the same significance for me as the laws of nature," and in obeying those laws, "we are not subject to another man's will and are therefore free."[81] In the real world, Hayek concludes, "freedom can never mean more than that they are restricted only by general rules."[82] This particular argument has drawn criticisms from libertarians, otherwise his sympathetic readers.[83] Taken alone, Hayek's claim here is difficult to sustain in terms of logical consistency. One can easily imagine situations in which certain laws, even if they are general and universally applied, may be viewed to severely restrict individual liberty (e.g., mandatory military service, imposition of religious or moral customs, prohibition of trade in certain areas). Hayek later defended his rather idiosyncratic position as a realistic concession, noting that complete elimination of coercion is impossible and that the only viable alternative is to reduce coercion as much as possible by anchoring it in general, abstract rules.[84] But Hayek's embrace of the rule of law is not a reluctant compromise. Rather, it is a necessary conclusion stemming directly from the way in which he constructs his theory. As I have discussed, Hayek's neoliberalism conceives individual liberty as a precondition for, and an outcome of, a particular social order in which individuals follow certain rules. For Hayek, individual liberty is not potentially threatened by laws; it *rests on* them. "Life of man in society, or even of the social animals in groups, is made possible by the individuals acting according to certain rules."[85]

But if following rules is essential to the capitalist civilization, exactly what rules must individuals follow? How should those rules be determined? Put differently, what is the *substance* and *procedural basis* of the rules that Hayek stresses so much? The distinction between these two questions is often blurred in his discussion, but a careful examination reveals that his answers are not consistent, at least not consistent with his professed commitment to individual liberty and democracy.

Neoliberalism versus Democracy

At first glance, Hayek seems to focus solely on the formation of rules, leaving the substance of those rules open. As he frames his ideas explicitly as a general theory of social and political order, he distinguishes two types of order according to the manner in which order is formed: one deliberately designed from outside (made order, or *taxis*), and the other emerging spontaneously from within (spontaneous order, or *kosmos*).

He highlights the absence of a predetermined, particular purpose as the most important aspect of that distinction. The spontaneous order, Hayek claims, is created not by "human design" but by the "action of many men."[86] This conception of spontaneous order, however, is immediately crosscut by another strand of thought. After stating that rules are but a regularity exhibited by individuals' actions, Hayek adds that "not every regularity in the behavior of the elements does secure an overall order."[87] He now contends that society can exist "only if . . . rules have evolved which lead individuals to behave in a manner which makes social life possible."[88] Here Hayek clearly indicates that he endorses certain rules not because they result from individuals' spontaneous interactions but because he considers them to be favorable to producing "an overall order." This latter formulation, then, points to a strikingly authoritarian impulse in Hayek's neoliberalism that competes with its libertarian motifs. As he ominously notes, while some rules facilitating spontaneous order will be followed voluntarily, "there will be still others [rules] which they [people] may have to be made to obey, since, although it would be in the interest of each to disregard them, the overall order on which the success of their actions depends will arise only if these rules are generally followed."[89]

Although Hayek casts the problem in general terms, one can easily discern that his idea of spontaneous order centers on his image of free-market capitalism. He even coins a new term, "catallaxy," to signal that he approaches capitalism not merely as an economic system but more broadly as a particular type of spontaneous order. One of the principal merits of the capitalist society, Hayek writes, is that it makes individuals behave in "a manner which makes social life possible," in the sense that it enables people to "live together in peace and mutually benefiting each other without agreeing on the particular aims which they severally pursue."[90] "Peaceful reconciliation of the divergent purposes," he insists, "not only is the effect of the market order but could not have been brought about by any other means."[91] The salutary outcome of the market order does not end there, either, for it is also the best way to enhance collective prosperity. Hayek describes catallaxy as a "wealth-creating game" (as opposed to a zero-sum game) that improves all the participants' prospects while still rewarding them differentially depending on their skill and luck.

This feat of catallaxy, however, relies on a set of assumptions. It is possible when individuals are motivated chiefly by "the striving for the better satisfaction of their material needs," social relations are organized exclusively by money ("cash-nexus"),[92] and people act "within the rules of the law of property, tort and contract."[93] The integrity of prices was already central to Hayek's thinking in the 1930s, as exhibited in his polemic in the socialist calculation debate, and the price mechanism became the focal point of his political theory as well. The gist of his neoliberalism lies in social coordination, and prices are what make that coordination possible. As he puts it in *The Road to Serfdom*, "Any attempt to control prices or quantities of particular commodities deprives competition of its power of bringing about an effective co-ordination of individual efforts, because price changes then cease to register all the relevant changes in circumstances and no longer provide a reliable guide for the individual's actions."[94] In the wealth-creating game of catallaxy, too, players inadvertently provide for a wide array of needs only because prices alert them to opportunities for profit and give them rough ideas about what they might need to do to take advantage of those opportunities.[95]

Because the substance of the rules of spontaneous order is not as open-ended as it first seems, Hayek's account of the procedural basis of those rules oscillates between different poles of thought. On the one hand, he endorses democracy as the legitimate basis of law. He can hardly not, for it follows from his commitment to legal equality as the core of "true" individualism. As he puts it, "Equality before the law leads to the demand that all men should also have the same share in making the law."[96] On the other hand, however, this endorsement is beset by the apprehension that the majority might make decisions damaging to their own liberty and long-term interest. In fact, this worry is so acute that it continually destabilizes his support for democracy. For example, announcing that "while individualism affirms that all government should be democratic, it has no superstitious belief in the omnipotence of majority decisions," Hayek suggests that "one of the most important questions" for future political theory is to find "a line of demarcation between the fields in which the majority views must be binding for all and the fields in which, on the contrary, the minority view ought to be allowed to prevail if it can produce results which better satisfy a demand of the public."[97] In *The Constitution of Liberty*, he reiterates his equivocal support for democracy. But here even a line of demarcation is apparently not enough: "Liberalism regards it as desirable that only what the majority accepts should in fact be law, but it does not believe that this is therefore necessarily good law. Its aim, indeed, is to persuade the majority to observe certain principles.

It accepts majority rule as a method of deciding, but not as an authority for what the decision ought to be."[98]

The notion that liberalism aims to "persuade" the democratic majority raises a series of troubling questions: Who, exactly, should do the persuading? What would be the sanctioned means of persuasion? What happens when the "right" rules do not emerge spontaneously from democratic processes? When pressed, these questions reveal that Hayek's neoliberalism and democracy are in conflict with each other *except when citizens in a democracy have already internalized the norms of the capitalist market.* And this—the dominance of capitalist subjectivity—is a key element that sustains Hayek's reluctant embrace of democracy. But in his theory, it is indeed an exception; the rule is democracy's encroachment on neoliberalism.

Sometimes Hayek downplays the severity of the tension at the heart of his neoliberalism by suggesting that an agreement on basic rules is easier to attain in the market order. When people are trying to determine the rules of the market, he asserts, they need only to agree on how economic resources are to be valued and exchanged. They do not have to settle on a set of desirable social ends, nor do they have to justify the goals they pursue with their economic gains. Because what happens in the market is merely "an allocation of means for the competing ultimate resources which are always non-economic,"[99] it allows those who might otherwise be mortal enemies to set aside their differences and work together.

But Hayek may have passed over the real difficulty of his neoliberalism too quickly. Consider the following thought experiment, which he introduces to illustrate the "abstract" nature of rules. Imagine mothers whose children are sick. While it is hard for them to decide whose child should get the doctor's care first, Hayek reasons, it is far easier for them to reach an agreement, before their child gets sick, on certain rules that will be used to determine the order of medical care. When actually implemented, those rules might benefit some more than others. But when they are trying to establish the rules, mothers do not know for sure who will be in a favorable position; that is precisely why they could agree. They can adopt the rules that they believe, on the basis of their current knowledge, would be better for all of them.[100] Generalizing this point, Hayek concludes that the most desirable order of society is "one which we would choose if we knew that our initial position in it would be decided purely by chance."[101] Here is a problem, though: would the mothers adopt rules that auction the right to see the doctor, awarding the privilege to the highest bidder? If this sounds unlikely, it raises serious questions about why people would choose capitalism as the principle of their social interaction. As Hayek emphasizes, the market rules do not recognize needs or merits that are not merely an aggregation of private preferences expressed via market prices, because that would require an unacceptable presumption that certain needs are more urgent and certain merits more admirable than others.[102] If people establish a society imagining their position would be determined purely by chance, would they choose the rules that completely disregard nonmarket needs and merits?

They would not. And Hayek knew it. He lamented that most people are still not used to the idea of regulating society solely by abstract rules, which is a relatively recent discovery. Instead they are profoundly affected by "emotions deeply ingrained in human nature through millennia of tribal existence." Emotions are by nature attached to "concrete objects" and to the "visible needs of the group to which each person belongs," so people's keenly felt needs often prevent them from realizing the superior significance of abstract rules.[103] For Hayek, it is unfortunate that so many people retain the "emotional traits of primitive man," because it is only by disciplining and restraining supposedly natural instincts that we were able to proceed to civilization.[104] (He singles out "sharing" and other forms of "solidarity" as some of the "habits [that] had to be shed to make the transition to the market economy and the open society possible."[105])

The apprehension toward "the masses" Hayek expressed in *The Road to Serfdom* only deepened over time.[106] In *The Constitution of Liberty,* characterizing the demand to extend the principle of equality to the "rules of moral and social conduct" as the expression of the "democratic spirit," he asserted that it is rooted in "envy," and declared that "the modern tendency to gratify this passion [envy] and to disguise it in the respectable garment of social justice is developing into a serious threat to freedom."[107] Similarly, he complained that the New Deal and the embedded liberalism of the postwar era discredited the market order as a tool of "some sinister power," stimulating the rise of "the long-submerged innate instincts" and "primordial emotions" that manifested themselves in people's "demand for a just distribution in which organized power is to be used to allocate to each what he deserves."[108] As evidenced by these two remarks, Hayek rarely made a meaningful distinction between democracy and socialism. "The Rousseauesque nostalgia" for a community bound by "natural" emotions, he asserted, leads "directly to the demand for a socialist society."

For him, both democracy and socialism ensue from the attempt to erect a social order on archaic instincts rather than on rationality. And insofar as they subject the entire population to decisions that abuse the name of "common purposes" merely to satisfy those instincts, both "must produce a totalitarian society."[109]

Despite all his dire indictment, Hayek does not propose to abandon democracy altogether.[110] According to him, democracy's destructive tendencies currently on display stem not from some fundamental defect of its principle but from its perverse development. As we saw earlier, Hayek's conception of democracy is unreservedly instrumental. Originally, he insists, democracy referred to nothing but a method for changing government and making political decisions peacefully. And as far as that function is concerned, democracy is still an "ideal worth fighting for to the utmost." The problem arises when people take democracy out of its proper domain and try to dictate substantive political goals such as equality under its name.[111] Thus, to bring democracy back to its worthy form, Hayek proposes, we need to limit it again. His argument here centers on creating a particular breed of constitutional democracy equipped with a set of constraints on the power of the majority and the representative organs supposedly beholden to them. Because the "prevailing form of democracy is ultimately self-destructive," Hayek declares, "it is clearly legitimate to provide against our inadvertently sliding into a socialist system by constitutional provisions which deprive government of the discriminating powers of coercion."[112]

We need to examine more closely what it is that Hayek tries to achieve with his constitutional democracy. On the surface, it seems like a classic liberal argument that purports to protect individual liberty and civil society from the coercive power of government. That is certainly how Hayek presents his case when speaking in general terms. He states that the "basic clause" of his constitution is that government coercion is justified only by publicly known "universal rules" that apply consistently to all future cases regardless of their particularities.[113] As Hayek elaborates his arguments, however, it becomes clear that he is at least equally keen to protect government from civil society. One of the central themes of the last volume of *Law, Legislation, and Liberty*, where he develops his theory of neoliberalism most fully, is that democratic government is particularly vulnerable to the pressure of interest groups. Hayek argues that government has become an entity that dispenses "subsidies, privileges and other benefits" to particular groups.[114] Once civil society groups realize that there are benefits to be extracted from government, they have a strong incentive to organize themselves as political pressure groups—which, in his view, was exactly what was happening in his time. Eventually, political parties, once guided by coherent principles, are captured by these organized interests. The ultimate outcome is not just a corrupt but a highly perverted form of government that is "oppressively powerful" in relation to "a minority" but entirely dominated by organized groups such as "trade associations, trade unions and professional organizations."[115] Hayek's proposed constitutional measures, which "would make all socialist measures for redistribution impossible,"[116] are intended to forestall that situation by eradicating the root cause of civil society's politicization—government's ability to provide or distribute benefits outside the capitalist market.

Ultimately, however, eliminating government's autonomy vis-à-vis the market is not enough to safeguard the neoliberal order, because overblown expectations about the welfare state are not the only, not even the most important, reason for civil society's politicization; the very working of neoliberalism is. Thus Hayek's neoliberalism requires not just a noninterventionist government that keeps out of the market but also a strong government that actively depoliticizes civil society.

To understand why this is the case, let us recall Hayek's worry that most people would not voluntarily follow market rules. He never goes so far as to suggest that those rules must be forcibly drilled into people, but he does argue that the capitalist market has a built-in mechanism to discipline and induce people to become economically rational. Market rules, asserts Hayek, gradually emerged through a "process of selection guided not by reason but by success."[117] As in natural selection, those rules were chosen because a few rational individuals who followed them happened to be successful, compelling others to emulate their behavior. "Competition will make it necessary for people to act rationally in order to maintain themselves." In this respect, market competition is not simply a way of maximizing the use of dispersed knowledge; it is "a method for breeding certain types of mind."[118]

But if market rules could emerge spontaneously in this way, why is Hayek so anxious to keep civil society depoliticized? According to his reasoning, as long as we secure the autonomy of the market, people will, over time, realize the merits of the capitalist order and voluntarily develop a "rational" mind-set and pattern of behavior. There is an odd rift between Hayek's portrayal of market rules as evolution's winner and his urgent warning about their endangerment. Even if we accept Hayek's account of the persistence of "primitive feelings," it sits uneasily with his analysis of civil society's behavior as calculated responses to economic incentives. So if he is genuinely concerned about the crisis of capitalism, it is probably because he realizes that people have reason to resist market discipline. As just noted, the adoption of market rationality occurs when a few individuals enjoy affluence while others are put under pressure to adapt their behavior or languish. Hayek stresses this point time and again, if in more benign language. He states that the "intellectual growth of a community rests on the views of a few gradually spreading, even to the disadvantage of those who are reluctant to accept them."[119] Similarly, he describes competition as "a process in which a small number makes it necessary for larger numbers to do what they do not like, be it to work harder, to change habits, or to devote a degree of attention, continuous application, or regularity to their work which without competition would not be needed."[120] In this sense, Hayek concludes with striking candor, *"Man has been civilized very much against his wishes."*[121]

A group of mothers voluntarily agreeing to the rules that they believe will be in their best interest, then, turns out to be a highly misleading illustration of Hayek's neoliberalism. Its unstated premise is that most people would resist the rules they ought to adopt—so they must be made to do so. This point, at last, reveals why Hayek is so ambivalent about democracy. The neoliberal order inflicts too great a pain on the majority while conferring privileges on the few, and democracy is what allows the many to contest that order. Unless it is restrained from interfering with market rules, therefore, democracy is incompatible with neoliberalism. Hayek frankly acknowledges this point: "I doubt whether a functioning market has ever newly arisen under an unlimited democracy, and it seems at least likely that unlimited democracy will destroy it where it has grown up."[122] Crucially, the more he highlights the antagonism between democracy and capitalism, the less spontaneous the neoliberal order becomes. Some of the scenarios he considers as a rather remote possibility suddenly proceed to the center of his theory. Hayek points out, for example, that "it is at least conceivable that the formation of a spontaneous order relies entirely on rules that were deliberately made."[123] But if new democracies thwart the emergence of neoliberalism, such a deliberate design may become not just conceivable but necessary. Even in established democracies, if market rules are so wantonly violated, government may need to play an ever-increasing role to ensure "that those rules are obeyed."[124] With no small irony, Hayek's purportedly libertarian creed morphs into a paternalistic and authoritarian doctrine.

The Allure of Abundance: Postwar Critiques of Capitalist Democracy

Keeping Faith with the New Deal

Once we recognize that neoliberalism is not simply a set of market-friendly economic policies but an organizing principle of social order, it becomes possible to assess critiques of capitalism that were prevalent in the postwar era in a different light. One of the main presuppositions of postwar political thought was that the question of political economy that Marx raised—which centered on the related concepts of the volatile and exploitative economic structure and class struggle as a means of changing it—had been solved. The issues of volatility and exploitation had been addressed by the so-called mixed economy that complemented free-market capitalism with some degree of state action, especially in regard to the infrastructure, business cycle management, limited wealth redistribution, and welfare provision. As Arthur Schlesinger Jr. declared, "The liberal democratic state ... has brought about a redistribution of wealth which has defeated Marx's prediction of progressive immiseration; and it has brought about an economic stabilization which has defeated Marx's prediction of ever-worsening economic crisis."[125] And as business and labor found common ground in the mixed economy rather than engage in a zero-sum struggle, class struggle had been superseded by electoral competition between various interest groups. The working class organized themselves into trade unions that are "clearly [as] indigenous to the capitalist system as the corporation itself."[126] "The capitalist state," Schlesinger concluded, "has become an object of genuine competition among classes."[127] Given this reality, Daniel Bell complained, "to see political history as a shift in the power position of 'institutions' rather than, say, of concrete interest groups, or classes, is to read politics in an extraordinarily abstract fashion."[128] For Bell, what the New Deal did was not to change the economic structure in any direct way but to *legitimate the idea of group rights, and the claim of groups, as groups, rather than individuals, for government support."*

An "extraordinary social change" did come about, but only as a salutary by-product of intergroup competition.[129] Similarly, Seymour Martin Lipset analyzed class struggle exclusively as a matter of group competition organized by the Democratic Party, which represented "lower-status groups," and the Republican Party, which spoke for "the more privileged."[130]

None of these thinkers was oblivious to or complacent about postwar America's problems, but they insisted that those problems could be solved within the dominant political and economic framework, given its essentially beneficent nature, and they ought to be solved within the existing framework, given the threat of totalitarianism. Thus, while predicting that "there will certainly be changes in the economic structure," Schlesinger adamantly maintained that the process of bringing about those changes "must be parliamentary."[131] Likewise, Bell contended that the debate over social reform should be "an empirical one," involving questions of "*where* one wants to go, *how* to get there, the costs of the enterprise, and . . . *who* is to pay."[132] This reform effort should presumably take place through "democratic politics" ("bargaining between legitimate groups and the search for consensus") and, more specifically, within the two-party system, which he praised as "one of the sources of flux and stability" that could accommodate "countless social movements" without being overwhelmed by them.[133]

What really prompted postwar intellectuals' embrace of postwar America's political and economic framework—whether it was its putative material accomplishments, perceived external and internal threats, or a theoretical validation of its merits—was never clear, but its intellectual consequence was momentous. It marked a shift in the understanding of what democracy is. The general tenor of this shift was signaled by President Harry Truman in a speech he gave shortly before the announcement of the Truman Doctrine. The stakes of Truman's speech become clear when it is compared to Franklin D. Roosevelt's famous "Four Freedoms" speech (1941).[134] In that speech, Roosevelt linked America's war aims to the nation's identity, which he described as comprising not simply civil liberties (freedom of speech and worship) but also social and economic rights (freedom from want and fear). By weaving the effort to promote socioeconomic rights into the nation's history, Roosevelt skillfully turned the charge that the New Deal was a violation of individual freedom and thus "un-American" on its head, implying that, in fact, clinging to laissez-faire liberalism was what effectively betrayed America's founding sprit and undermined the nation's standing in the world. Building on this broadened notion of freedom, Roosevelt later called for a "Second Bill of Rights" in his 1944 address, listing the universal right to adequate employment, to basic social goods such as housing, medical care, and education, and to social insurance programs as its major components. Although Roosevelt's emphasis on individual rights, rather than the political and economic structure, already signaled a certain diminution of the New Deal, the idea of the Second Bill of Rights showed the awareness that unbridled capitalism weakens citizens' "moral fiber," erodes their allegiance to democratic institutions, and ultimately threatens democracy's integrity.

Three years after Roosevelt's Second Bill of Rights speech, Truman, too, talked about America's identity, reiterating his predecessor's claim about the supremacy of freedom.[135] But what Truman offered in the name of freedom was something starkly different. Instead of Roosevelt's Four Freedoms, Truman now spoke of three essential freedoms: freedom of speech and worship remained on the list, but freedom from want and fear was replaced by freedom of enterprise. More significantly, Truman claimed that freedom of enterprise is what underpins the first two freedoms, asserting that "throughout history, freedom of worship and freedom of speech have been most frequently enjoyed in those societies that have accorded a considerable measure of freedom to individual enterprise." Thus, Truman declared, "Our devotion to freedom of enterprise ... has deeper roots than a desire to protect the profits of ownership. It is part and parcel of what we call American." The symbolic significance of this new frame of thinking cannot be overstated. By presenting freedom of enterprise as a safeguard of individual freedom, Truman overturned the prevailing notion of Depression America, expressed partially in Roosevelt's speeches, that regarded freedom of enterprise as a source of privilege for the few, a cause of insecurity for many, and a germ of alienation for all.[136] For Truman, a social order that would be most conducive to freedom was no longer one in which all citizens are provided with basic resources to take part in democratic life. Rather, it was "one in which the major decisions are made, not by governments, but by private buyers and sellers, under conditions of active competition ... relying for guidance on whatever prices the market may afford."

The resemblance between the democratic society Truman depicted and the neoliberal civilization Hayek envisions is striking. In fact, they are almost indistinguishable, insofar as both are a social order in which citizens act primarily as "buyers and sellers" and make decisions by relying on market prices as a central guide. Truman's redescription of democracy, then, helps reveal the blind spots of postwar critiques of capitalism. Postwar intellectuals believed that the political and economic framework established by the New Deal—the mutually reinforcing amalgam of the mixed economy and interest group politics—would progress so as to make capitalism beneficial and deepen democracy. But this faith led them to understate the attenuation of the New Deal—the dilution of the Full Employment Act, which abandoned full employment as the government's responsibility, for example, or the passage of the Taft-Hartley Act of 1947, which seriously curbed the power of organized labor—as a temporary setback, rather than as a permanent transformation driven by the same force that sensitized them to the virtues of balance, compromise, and capitalism: antitotalitarianism qua anticommunism.[137] Perhaps more important, they passed over the structural limitations of the New Deal framework. Its modus operandi was such that the state adjudicates between competing claims of organized groups, which circumscribed the nature and scope of possible economic reforms. It created disproportionate difficulties for more populous, diffused, and thus hard-to-organize groups, such as labor. And it made the entry of new groups into the decision-making forum exceedingly difficult relative to already entrenched groups. As the historian Nelson Lichtenstein notes, in the postwar period the American working class was divided into relatively favorably placed union members and "a still larger stratum, predominantly young, minority, and female, that was left out in the cold."[138] This segmentation not only weakened organized labor but made further economic reforms politically infeasible. Once they had accepted private corporate welfare such as pensions and health insurance, for instance, unionized workers had an economic incentive to resist extending state-funded welfare to unrepresented workers and the general populace (agricultural or domestic workers, who were predominantly African American or "nonworking" women)—an incentive that would intensify as the tax code became increasingly regressive in the subsequent decades.

Seen from this perspective, the political consensus that postwar intellectuals touted may not attest to the New Deal regime's inherent strengths. Rather, it may have been a sign of depoliticization—which was effected by the pressures of anticommunism and, perhaps even more powerfully, induced by the promise of a consumers' utopia. As many historians have shown, unexpected and astonishing economic growth, which materialized

in the form of a cornucopia of mass-produced goods, thoroughly permeated people's lives and imaginations in postwar America.[139] And that astonishing growth indelibly shaped politics. Business and labor, liberals and
conservatives, debated how to encourage consumption, not whether it was
desirable. No ideological divide seemed insurmountable when the presumably virtuous cycle of mass consumption and economic growth promised
universal abundance. The prospect of continuous economic growth made
employers concede wage increases and enhanced benefits to a certain
degree, and made workers give up their power in managerial decisions in
exchange for those material benefits. It persuaded conservatives to accept
government spending on defense and even some of the public assistance
programs and led liberals to believe that the formation of mass markets,
where more individuals could purchase the same product for the same
price, was a harbinger of the deepening of democracy. Difficult political
questions concerning inclusion and equity were perpetually delayed, with
the hope that as long as economic growth continued, its benefits would
eventually reach the currently marginalized and the unorganized. Despite
its stable appearance, therefore, the regime that solidified in the midst of
postwar prosperity contained the seeds of volatility, insofar as it lacked
independent political grounds for legitimacy and depended entirely on
constant economic growth for popular allegiance.[140]

Democratic Thought in the Age
of Economic Prosperity

Not surprisingly, the issues of economic abundance and mass consumption stimulated and shaped political thought as well. The appeal of
economic abundance was so strong that, in some cases, intellectuals let
it subsume democracy. In reframing America's national identity around
the theme of economic abundance, the historian David Potter insisted
that "there is a strong case for believing that democracy is clearly most
appropriate for countries which enjoy an economic surplus."[141] While
this was not a particularly novel idea, his reasoning was peculiar. In
Potter's view, a democracy, "setting equality as its goal, must promise
opportunity. But in promising opportunity, the democracy is constantly
arousing expectations which it lacks the current means to fulfil and is
betting on its ability to procure the necessary means by the very act of
stimulating people to demand them and go after them."[142] In his formulation, then, democracy shades into capitalism: it is democracy, not sellers

or advertisers, that incites people's appetite for material acquisition; it is the prospect of rising absolute standards of living, not the right to make collective decisions independently of the wherewithal in one's possession, that defines democratic equality. For Potter, the New Deal was not even an institutionalization of interest group politics, as Daniel Bell described, but merely a different method of carrying out what had been the consistent goal of government throughout American history: to "make the economic abundance of the nation accessible to the public."[143] When American democracy had encountered challenges, Potter observed, it tended "to overleap problems—to bypass them—rather than to solve them." That America had rarely tested or honed its problem-solving abilities did not alarm him. If anything, it was a laudable tendency that allowed Americans to achieve social reforms without, as Europeans did, "necessarily treating one class as the victim or even … the antagonist of another." In the end, in Potter's analysis, economic abundance emerged as a looming impera-tive that reduces democracy to its instrument. Pointing out that America had achieved democracy "less by sheer ideological devotion to democratic principle than by the creation of economic conditions in which democracy will grow," Potter counseled that one should "make his political system as one of the instruments" for economic abundance. Only when "democratic devices" are successfully applied to enhance economic abundance, he asserted, can one *then* "use abundance as a base for the broadening and consolidation of his democracy."[144]

While many postwar intellectuals were less sanguine about economic abundance than Potter, their critique was inflected by their acceptance of the New Deal regime, which increasingly pivoted on the expectations of continual economic growth. Because they decided that the political and economic framework was essentially sound, postwar intellectuals approached capitalism's troubling ramifications, even when they de-tected them, primarily as a cultural matter. Writing in 1960, for example, Schlesinger was less cheerful about the free market, which, a decade earlier, he had insisted must be primarily responsible for making eco-nomic decisions.[145] He now described the 1950s as an era of "quiescence and respite" during which America took "holiday from responsibility" and resorted to the "policy of drift."[146] Likely goaded by John Kenneth Galbraith's *The Affluent Society* (1958), a powerful indictment of the gap between lavish private consumption and impoverished public services, Schlesinger regretted, in particular, that the nation allocated resources to "undertakings which bring short-run profits to individuals rather than to those which bring long-run profits to the nation."[147] Thus, looking forward to the new decade, he called for a "reorganization of American values"—a shift from the belief in the "sanctity of private interest" to a renewed dedication to the "supremacy of the public interest."[148] Despite the stern tone of his critique, however, Schlesinger did not call for a radical revision of the New Deal regime. He proposed no structural change to the economy, nor did he question the prevailing practice of democracy or the distribution of power. How, then, could the reorientation of values come about? The answer, for Schlesinger, lay in people's shifting tastes generated by the "economy of abundance." Now that matters of subsistence had largely been solved (besides "pools of poverty which have to be mopped up"), he conjectured, people might want different things, like "individual dignity, identity, and fulfillment," and care more about issues such as "education, health, equal opportunity, [and] community planning" than about acquiring private goods.[149]

Daniel Bell also advanced an extended critique of postwar capitalism, contending that the "cult of efficiency" relegated workers to the "grinding mill" of work deprived of satisfaction and meaning.[150] To make work itself meaningful, Bell argued, one must challenge the concept of efficiency itself, realizing that an individual's work "must not only feed his body" but "sustain his spirit." Making work meaningful would involve reorganizing the work process itself, altering job rotation patterns, making the division of labor less rigid and monotonous, and increasing the work cycle. These changes, of course, cannot be achieved unless workers are able to affect management decisions. As Bell recognized, "Short of pressure from the workers themselves, there is no action which would force modern enterprise to reorder the flow of work." But that was precisely what labor unions forwent as they partook in the dealmaking he celebrated, and became, in his words, "part of 'the control system of management' itself."[151] Moreover, there was the reality of mass consumption. Bell lamented that workers were still forced to work, no longer by physical hunger but no less strongly by a "new hunger": "the desire for goods" and the concern with the "standard of living." For him, the American worker "has been 'tamed'" by the "possibility of a better living," and instead of trying to transform the nature of work itself, he either puts up with it to maintain his "style of life" or engages in "escapist fantasies." But even as Bell excoriated "advertising and the installment plan" as the "two most fearsome inventions of man since the discovery of gunpowder," which amplified individuals' new hunger and encouraged their escapism, he offered no political arguments, let alone alternatives. He looked instead to technological change, hoping that, by eliminating drudgery and encouraging the cultivation of more integrative skills, automation may bring a "new concept of self" to the workers.[152] In a way, both Schlesinger and Bell were betting on the predictive power of Potter's hypothesis: that America could, again, overleap its problems.

So even in their more critical moments, postwar intellectuals tended to view economic abundance as a given condition that could be harnessed for different purposes without fundamentally altering the prevailing political and economic framework. They refused or failed to confront the extent to which mass consumption was integral to the model of economic growth that postwar America adopted,[153] and the extent to which the government actively encouraged it.[154] They interpreted exponential increases in consumer spending too quickly as a sign of real wealth. As a recent study suggests, much of postwar consumption relied less on savings or rising incomes than on consumer credit (which was buoyed by tax deductions). The apparent relative equality of lifestyle in the present obscured the fact that people were obtaining it by taking on future burdens, which were distributed differentially. (Clerical or factory workers were more likely to borrow than managers, owners, or professionals. And blacks borrowed far more relative to their incomes than whites and paid higher interest.[155]) Similarly, that everyone could purchase, say, the same refrigerator for the same price shrouded the fact that the mass consumption economy was structured so as to increase inequality between lenders and debtors.

Perhaps more fundamentally, postwar intellectuals may have underestimated the extent to which the instrumental conception of democracy they endorsed—which casts democracy as an instrument that various organized groups use to advance their private interests—aided neoliberalism in what Hayek identified as its most daunting task: persuading people to act primarily as buyers and sellers and follow market prices over all else. Hayek perceived the postwar welfare state as a grave threat to neoliberalism, not simply because he regarded its economic policies as arbitrary interference with the free market but because he believed it was an expression of "substantive" democracy—of the continuous and vigorous public debate about collective goals and values. In light of the foregoing analysis, Hayek's assessment may have been unfounded. But postwar intellectuals shared his assessment, confounding intergroup competition over the benefits dispensed by the welfare state with democratic contention over the goals of collective life. They saw the need for a reorientation of public values but did not realize that the political and economic framework they embraced depleted the very source needed for that reorientation.

David Riesman, one of the early enthusiasts of interest group liberalism and the economy of abundance, came to see the limitations of that position. Writing in 1960, Riesman regretted some of his main arguments in *The Lonely Crowd* (1950): his uncritical depiction of American democracy as a rivalry of "veto groups" taking place against the backdrop of the public's political apathy (Riesman actually took a step further from postwar pluralism by interpreting apathy as an individual's attempt to maintain a measure of privacy from the pressure to join); his "complacent" assumption that the economy of abundance would continue and that the New Deal's accomplishments "would not be reversed and would in fact be extended"; and his suggestion that play and leisure could become the sphere in which a modern individual could liberate herself from the social pressure to conform and develop genuine autonomy.[156] Riesman now felt that in making these claims, he had "understated the depth of our political despair."[157] Interest group competition could not be seen to attest to or protect democracy's autonomy vis-à-vis capitalism, since "these groups, quite apart from the specific economic interests they may draw upon, are inevitably shaped in their ways of perceiving and acting by the climate of a business culture." By the "climate of a business culture," Riesman refers not simply to the clout of corporations or the emphasis on individual profit but to the broader and surreptitious ways in which social relations are organized. Business culture tends to reward expansion for expansion's sake, and to readily recognize measurable and calculable values while barely registering, let alone supporting, others. As different organized groups clamor to gain advantage in the name of democracy within that structure, individual groups' wins and losses alike serve to further entrench the "business culture," and it ultimately becomes like a bad climate for most people—something they dislike but cannot change. "Men no longer conspire enthusiastically in their own alienation: they are often somewhat disaffected, but they lack the conviction that things could be done any other way—and therefore cannot see, save in a peripheral way, what is wrong with how things are."[158]

Ultimately, however, Riesman could not see how things could be done differently, either. Reflecting yet again on *The Lonely Crowd* in 1969, he reiterated that his assumptions about the economy of abundance were "mistaken."[159] But now his focus was not the overwhelming and debilitating effect of business culture but, circling back to Potter's concern, the need to ensure continual economic growth. He agreed with other critics such as Galbraith, Schlesinger, and Bell that "the pursuit of production as an end in itself is pathological." But Riesman insisted that its significance to democracy should not be downplayed: "Given the political structure of veto groups," he reasoned, integrating the really poor would be politically possible only by "greatly raising the levels of living of lower, but not poor, socioeconomic groups" as well. Unless "they themselves do not live on an ever-rising incline of consumer satisfaction," the "still only insecurely affluent lower-middle and upper-working classes cannot be persuaded to be generous to the truly deprived, especially if these are black and obstreperous."[160] Indeed, "obstreperous" radical movements—the coalition of "the poor ... and their conscience-stricken affluent allies"—often backfire, in that such movements awaken widespread yet dormant conservatism into a conscious political movement. Thus, Riesman concluded, a fundamental condition for further reform is "the expansion of resources to moderate the envies and resentments of the morally indignant not-quite-poor."[161]

In falling back on the idea that economic abundance driven by the market economy is a precondition for democracy, Riesman, like other postwar intellectuals, underestimates the tension between them. Some of the sources of that tension are already discussed. The political legitimacy of the postwar welfare regime was more precarious than postwar intellectuals assumed, resting as it was on continual economic growth and little else. But there is reason to believe that simply underwriting the "ever-rising incline of consumer satisfaction" cannot even sustain the coalition supporting the postwar regime. It is not just because material welfare is a relative concept and so the middle class will likely be under constant pressure to "level up." Rather, it is because economic growth tends to undo its promise.

In an insightful critique, Fred Hirsch challenges the notion that continual economic growth would simultaneously promote individual and social benefits without collective coordination—the foundational promise of economic liberalism that also lies at the heart of Hayek's neoliberalism. In advanced industrial societies where basic material needs are met, Hirsch theorizes, scarcity becomes increasingly social in its nature. In other words, the satisfaction and value that individuals draw from the consumption of a certain good depends less on the innate quality of the good and more on what others do. As he puts it, in deceptively simple terms, the value of my education depends "not only on how much I have but on how much the man ahead of me in the job line has."[162] Under these circumstances, the link between private self-interest and social welfare is broken. In the world of natural scarcity, any increase in material wealth at the individual level directly translates into social welfare. In the world of social scarcity, however, most individuals cannot attain what they desire, no matter what they do as isolated individuals and regardless of the absolute levels of their wealth. (In a society that, say, disproportionately prizes an Ivy League diploma, most people cannot access that "educational good," regardless of their absolute level of education, unless they collectively decide to value it less.) In this situation, free-market competition among isolated individuals results only in social waste, deepening social inequality, and widespread frustration. Thus, Hirsch concludes, the age of affluence makes economic liberalism outmoded and accentuates the need for collective coordination. "The only way of avoiding the competition in frustration is for the people concerned to depart from the principle of isolated individual competition and to coordinate their objectives in some explicit way. Only a collective approach to the problem can offer individuals the guidance necessary to achieve a solution they themselves would prefer."[163]

As clearly indicated in the foregoing passage, Hirsch does not view the matter simply as one of creating government agencies and policies regulating the market. He criticizes the attempt to erect institutions of explicit social coordination without a "supporting social morality," stressing that "correctives to laissez-faire increase rather than decrease reliance on some degree of social orientation and social responsibility in individual behavior."[164] Seen from this perspective, one of the most perilous aspects of capitalism is that it tends to undermine the very social orientation it needs to address its deficiencies. An increase in the output of material goods relative to the time remaining constant means that time becomes scarcer in industrial capitalism. Insofar as individuals are disposed to maximize their private material consumption, therefore, they are more likely to spend their time on activities that yield immediate and tangible benefits rather than on activities that may be economically inefficient but are nonetheless essential to building lasting social relations (such as having an aimless conversation with friends or aiding a stranger in need). It is important to stress again that people's disposition to disengage from public activities is a consequence of the expansion of economic liberalism that bases social coordination exclusively on the isolated individual's pursuit of private material welfare. As Hirsch writes, "Perception of the time spent in social relationships as a cost is itself a product of privatized affluence."[165] Free-market capitalism is not simply an inadequate solution to the problem of social scarcity; it undermines the foundation on which an adequate solution can begin to be devised.

This is not to dismiss or downplay the postwar welfare state's role in providing basic social goods and promoting relative equality. But a close examination of postwar critiques of capitalism alongside Hayek's neoliberalism raises a different set of questions. To what extent was the postwar welfare state an expression of vigorous public efforts to organize collective values?[166] How successful was it in keeping the inexorable spread of capitalist subjectivity at bay? Did it lay the groundwork for further democratization or inadvertently pave the way for neoliberalism's domination of democracy in the following decades? The New Deal consensus that postwar intellectuals cherished was never as robust as they believed, reliant as it was more on the suspension of, or distraction from, democratic debate. Disillusioned with socialism, intellectually intimidated or militarized by anticommunism, and impressed by unexpected economic growth, postwar intellectuals embraced free-market capitalism as a correlate of democracy, treating them both as instruments that can be combined to improve the welfare of the people. Ironically, it was Hayek who was more keenly aware of the difficulties of fusing free-market capitalism and democracy. When scrutinized, his neoliberalism reveals the volatilities of capitalist democracy, over which postwar intellectuals passed too quickly. With its tendency to penalize all but the most successful and its inability to address the ineradicably social nature of goods, the very working of free-market capitalism necessitates and incites "substantive" democracy, even as it needs continually to deprive democracy of that substantive character. Capitalist democracy at once gives rise to and suppresses attempts at the collective organization of values, hurtling toward each next crisis it is increasingly less capable of managing.

Conclusion

Despite the marginality of neoliberal economic policies, the postwar era brought American democracy remarkably close to the neoliberal social

order envisioned by Hayek. The attempt to put capitalism under democratic control—which was admittedly scattered but serious—was greatly
reduced in its range as well as intensity, as anticommunism regimented
the intellectual universe and economic abundance stunned its inhabitants.
Catallaxy, Hayek's wealth-creating game, became the singular center of
attention that sharply refocused the political imagination. The desirability
of political and social relations was now gauged in terms of material pos-
sessions. Thus, when then vice president Richard Nixon visited Moscow
in 1959, he was able to boast without irony that America had achieved a
"classless society," presenting as evidence "a total of 56 million cars, 50
million television sets and 143 million radio sets" that Americans owned
and "an average of 9 dresses and suits and 14 pairs of shoes per family
per year" they were buying.[167] True, postwar intellectuals lamented the
crudity and emptiness of that reality, but even so, they failed or refused
to reconsider the relationship between democracy and capitalism in any
fundamental way. Instead they oscillated, touting labor's abdication of
the demand to participate in management at one point and reprimanding
workers for being unable to manage their working conditions at another;
defending the free market against the menace of "totalitarian" government
control, praising it for generating the conditions for political compromise
and "free play," and then castigating it for its aimlessness and excess; and
encouraging people to see democracy as the arena for dealmaking while
deploring the lack of public spirit and common purpose. In an intellectual
climate that was more forgiving to contradictions and ironies than to dissent, incongruities in their thought were never severely tested, and postwar
intellectuals put forth opposing strands of thought without explaining how
they might coexist, let alone hang together. They saw problems but were
not certain where to trace those problems other than to people's mind-set.
Haunted by the vague fear that trying to alter the existing political and
economic framework might only make things worse, they kept returning
to the promise of economic abundance.

It is for this reason that Hayek's neoliberalism, even though it stayed
in the margin of postwar political thought, is illuminating. Because he
believed, though mistakenly, in my view, that capitalism was threatened
by democracy, he took pains to specify the conditions that must be satisfied for the marriage of democracy and capitalism to be a sustainable one.
Because he did not regard the merger of democracy and capitalism as a
settled fact, he was also far more attuned to the difficulties of achieving

and maintaining that union. As a result, Hayek's neoliberalism brings out the tension inherent in capitalist democracy with a clarity that no other postwar political intellectual provided. Although he presented himself as a guardian of individual liberty, what he actually defended was the individualist social order, which he insisted could be secured only by restricting individual liberty by the norms of free-market capitalism. Because individual liberty, a person's ability to develop and act on one's beliefs, entails the right to challenge the rules of the market, it poses a potential threat to the individualist order. In fact, it is a likely threat, because, as Hayek acknowledges, capitalism works by conferring disproportionate privileges and benefits on a minority while pressuring the majority to play incessant and unwinnable catch-up. Despite Hayek's claims to the contrary, in other words, the rules of the capitalist market cannot emerge spontaneously from below but have to be imposed from above. He is acutely aware of this problem, and when that awareness comes to the fore, his purportedly libertarian neoliberalism resorts to strikingly authoritarian measures to reinforce the market rules against spontaneous democratic demands. By instrumentalizing democracy, postwar intellectuals deprived it of the ability to organize democratic spontaneity into a force that could contest the inadequacies and volatilities of capitalism. In doing so, they did not simply debilitate democracy; they unwittingly prepared the ground for its negation.

CHAPTER SIX

The Erosion of Democratic Attunement and the Crisis of Democracy

What was totalitarianism's lesson for democracy? Was it really a sober warning against the faith in "the people," as many postwar intellectuals believed? Or was totalitarianism an outlier that, horrendous as it was, could not be generalized to justify a fundamental revision of the democratic ideal, as their critics contended? This chapter articulates a perspective that derives general insights about modern democracy directly from reflections on totalitarianism but diverges from the prevailing views of the postwar era. I develop my argument through a critical engagement with Hannah Arendt's political theory. While Arendt's influential account of totalitarianism was received by many postwar intellectuals as an affirmation of their diagnosis—which focused on the political danger of the masses and ideology—I suggest that the core themes she broaches actually contain a critique of the dominant postwar reaction to totalitarianism. Specifically, I argue that for Arendt, the masses are not a root pathology but a manifestation of modernity's deeper problems, which she theorizes, admittedly in a preliminary fashion, in terms of the mutually reinforcing relationship between the instrumentalization of politics and the attendant rise of antipolitical subjectivity. This concern, I suggest, remains central to her political theory even as she moves beyond the context of Nazism, and reappears in her more general account of modernity that is characterized by world alienation and the triumph of the *animal laborans*.[1]

In emphasizing the significance of subjectivity to Arendt's theory, I follow a number of recent scholars who have proposed to shift the interpretive focus from her unique concept of action to that of the context for action, especially a particular mode of reception as its essential component.[2] A crucial question for Arendt is less whether we are able to engage in action—in some respects, we always already do—than whether action's unique qualities can be recognized and activated. That recognition and activation require a particular kind of receptiveness from those who inhabit the public realm and experience what is potentially initiated by action. Rereading Arendt's discussion of Kant and Montesquieu, I conceptualize that receptiveness as attunement to public claims appealing to political equality inherent in the democratic ideal. Democratic attunement, as I interpret it, does not refer to a cognitive state or a practical act of response. Rather, it is an affective force that precedes cognition and activity, animating, orienting, and shaping them. I find conceptual insights in Arendt's political theory that allow us to see democratic attunement as a public entity whose vitality neither fluctuates randomly nor rests on individual feelings but is deeply entwined with material conditions and ideological constructs. In this way, her theory points not just to the ethics but to the political economy of democratic attunement. I develop this point by disentangling Arendt's theory of the social from her notorious critique of the "social question" in *On Revolution,* and considering it instead in light of thematic parallels between *The Human Condition* and her earlier and contemporaneous works. Although Arendt failed or refused to clarify this strand of thought and occasionally ventured reductive remarks about economic issues, I suggest that it reflects her particular assessment of modernity rather than inherent flaws in her general theory of the social.

Diverging Roads from Totalitarianism

One of the fatal consequences of totalitarianism, Arendt noted, was the destruction of liberals' belief in "some innate goodness of the people."[3] As discussed in chapter 3, the encounter with totalitarianism greatly accentuated the danger of "the masses," allegedly characterized by their conformity and blind submissiveness and, as its flip side, sharply focused attention on individual autonomy. As Arthur Schlesinger Jr. declared in

The Vital Center (1949), "The essential strength of democracy as against totalitarianism lies in its startling insight into the value of the individual."[4] In book after book, postwar intellectuals produced a portrait of postwar America where conformity reigned, smothering individuality. Even a brief glance at some of the era's major works—Erik Erikson's *Childhood and Society* (1950), David Riesman's *The Lonely Crowd* (1950), Eric Hoffer's *The True Believer* (1951), C. Wright Mills's *White Collar* (1951), Sloan Wilson's *The Man in the Gray Flannel Suit* (1955), William Whyte's *The Organization Man* (1956), Vance Packard's *The Hidden Persuaders* (1957) and *The Status Seekers* (1959), and commentaries, in journals such as *Partisan Review, Dissent,* and *Commentary,* by cultural critics including Clement Greenberg, Dwight McDonald, Harold Rosenberg, and Ernest van den Haag—reveals the dominant intellectual trend of the time. While not everyone drew an explicitly political message, they shared an uneasy sense that what they were observing could not be auspicious. When the literary critic Bernard Rosenberg announced that mass culture threatened "not merely to cretinize our taste, but to brutalize our sense while paving the way to totalitarianism,"[5] his tone may have been grandiose, but his underlying argument was not far from the prevailing sentiment.

Arendt's *The Origins of Totalitarianism* (1951) was, and often is, viewed as part of that trend. Many postwar intellectuals received her account as an affirmation of their reaction to totalitarianism. Schlesinger drew on Arendt to identify the totalitarian dynamic of communism "toward the unlimited domination and degradation and eventual obliteration of the individual," which "achieve[s] its evil perfection . . . only in the concentration camps."[6] Daniel Bell treated Arendt as a representative of the theory that sees the mass as "mob," and chided her, along with other theorists of mass society, for defending "an aristocratic cultural tradition" and propagating "a doubt that the large mass of mankind can ever become truly educated or acquire an appreciation of culture."[7] While Schlesinger and Bell drew these conclusions exclusively from *The Origins of Totalitarianism,* Sheldon Wolin, whose critique of modernity in *Politics and Vision* (1960) actually overlaps significantly with Arendt's, detected antidemocratic tendencies in the larger body of her work, contending that "it is not difficult to show that many of the major categories that compose and distinguish her political outlook were either critical of or incompatible with democratic ideas." Wolin did note that "a change is evident" in Arendt's later writings, but it was, in his view, inconsistent and logically strained because of her theory's basic architecture.[8] Wolin's critique was repeated by later historians as well. Wilfred McClay perceived a paradox in Arendt's approval of participatory democracy and her alleged distaste for real-world politics and attributed it to "her attraction to elements in the conservative critique of mass society, which in turn informed her (and [Emil] Lederer's) understanding of totalitarianism," also noting "the influence of Martin Heidegger upon her thinking" as "a channel for this influence."[9] For McClay, these influences cast doubt on the validity, if not the sincerity, of Arendt's political theory as a whole. There was "a strong element of sheer romanticism in her esteem for the participatory polity," he declared, "as if it were a compensatory fantasy of some early lost love-object, some form of social connectedness that could never be replaced."[10]

But numerous difficulties trouble the view that places the aversion to the masses at the center of Arendt's analysis of totalitarianism, let alone her overall political theory. Although she did make seemingly disparaging remarks about the masses that echo the elitist critiques of mass society, Arendt expressed her sympathy toward "the common people," the political mobilization of "the down-trodden," and workers' cooperatives in her early works, well before the publication of *Origins.*[11] Her admiration for popular movements is visible in *Origins,* too, though it tends to appear in brief asides in her discussion, otherwise devoted to the unfolding of a calamity. When she criticized imperialism and the political ascendance of the bourgeoisie as an event prefiguring totalitarianism, for example, she contrasted its logic to that of the French Revolution, noting that the latter's "conception of man as lawmaker and *citoyen* ... had almost succeeded in preventing the bourgeoisie from fully developing its notion of history as a necessary process."[12] Even when she turned her critical eye to the mob and the masses, Arendt took pains to distinguish them from "the people" and the working class.[13] In fact, she explicitly assailed the "great historians of the nineteenth century" who warned of the rise of the mob for failing to grasp that "the mob could not be identified with the growing industrial working class, and certainly not the people as a whole," but was the "distortion and caricature" of the people.[14] She insisted that this category mistake not only permeated the blind faith in vox populi, vox dei in nineteenth-century Europe but also underlay the "common error of our time," which posited that people could be completely manipulated by propaganda.[15] So when Arendt stated, in *On Revolution* (1963), that Cold War liberalism's tendency to demonize the masses and dismiss political freedom rests on dubious assumptions, the "most pernicious" of which is the "equation of 'people' and masses,"[16] she was repeating the same warning about the widespread yet misguided generalizations she had observed a decade ago, rather than expressing her newly acquired radicalism.

The distinction between the masses and the people goes to the heart of Arendt's diagnosis of totalitarianism and sharply distinguishes it from the dominant view of the postwar era. Many postwar intellectuals presupposed that the venerable tradition of liberalism is predicated on individual autonomy, and regarded the masses, prone to conformity, as a threat to it. On the contrary, Arendt thought that the mass mentality was a perverse culmination, rather than an antithesis, of the liberal mind. According to her, liberalism is at its core a contradictory doctrine whose subordination of politics to the bourgeoisie's economic interests undercuts the basis of its own legitimacy. Concerned exclusively with the endless accumulation of wealth, the bourgeoisie enter politics only because they realize that their economic pursuits require political power. And they fashion political institutions "exclusively as an instrument for the protection of individual property" and as an engine for generating economic wealth.[17] Despite classical liberals' claims, the instrumentalization of politics does not limit politics vis-à-vis the economy. On the contrary, the imperative of perpetual economic growth requires the expansion of political institutions to support it. And this requirement for continual political expansion creates an unsustainable dynamic, since, unlike the production of wealth, "the political structure cannot expand indefinitely . . . because the genuine consent at its base cannot be stretched indefinitely."[18] Liberalism, in other words, ends up with a continually expanding political structure sitting on a constantly eroding foundation of citizens' loyalty, trust, and consent. It is a fundamentally volatile arrangement charged with destructive energy that is ready to burst through the weak seams of society.

Arendt draws on Hobbes to elaborate liberalism's perilous dynamics. Hobbes shows with unmatched clarity, she says, the consequences of a politics engineered to meet the needs of the bourgeois individual who "consider[s] his advantage in complete isolation . . . and then realize[s] that he can pursue and achieve his interest only with the help of some kind of majority."[19] Because he looks to politics with the sole aim of acquiring power to advance his private economic interest, the bourgeois's membership in the political community "does not change the solitary and private character of the individual . . . or create permanent bonds between him and his fellow-men."[20] In fact, the isolation of individuals is intensified when they build a political structure that endlessly accumulates power. From a purely private perspective, it is rational to seek power at the expense of others, so Hobbesian individuals are engaged in a constant power struggle, generating social disorder and dimming economic prospects. In those circumstances, the only way to serve the "law" of perpetual economic growth is to concentrate power in the hands of the state. The result is that even as the state dramatically increases power, its members lose access to politics and experience them as "absolute necessity," something beyond their control and concern.[21] Their isolation and their concern for private welfare deepen, as do their competition and the perceived need for a stronger and more distant power. In the end, liberalism, which begins with self-interested individuals, re-produces them as subjects whose undiminished concern with private economic interests is now conjoined with political submissiveness.

Things do not stop there. Since it completely lacks legitimacy, the liberal state can maintain itself only by acquiring ever more power, and thus the accumulation of power becomes an end in itself. This marks the arrival of a new kind of politics. Although power and violence have always been a central element of politics, they have been subordinate to purposes determined by the members of a political community. It has been possible, at least in principle, for citizens to determine whether power is used well or not. In liberalism, however, power is self-justifying as "the never-ending, self-feeding motor of all political action that corresponds to the legendary unending accumulation of money that begets money."[22] From here it is a short but crucial step for perpetual economic growth—and the endless accumulation of power as its counterpart—to transcend particular political communities and redefine the meaning of history itself. Whereas the eighteenth-century vision of progress was aimed at the "emancipation of man," the bourgeois concept of progress "not only did not want the liberty and autonomy of man, but was ready to sacrifice everything and everybody to supposedly superhuman laws of history."[23] The liberal state becomes a giant machine "whose only purpose is the generation and accumulation of power" and whose functioning requires individuals to be "degraded into a cog."[24] In this way, the radical individualist doctrine of liberalism ends in a radical negation of individuality, neither by accident nor by the distortion of its principles but through its own logic.

The mob and the masses, which fueled imperialism and totalitarianism, respectively, are for Arendt both by-products of this volatile arrangement of liberalism. The mob appeared when the bourgeoisie tried to salvage the liberal political and economic structure beset by numerous difficulties, including overproduction, the saturation of the domestic market, lack of raw materials, superfluous capital without investment opportunities, increasing social conflicts, and declining political legitimacy. They found a cure-all in imperialism, which "spirited away all troubles and produced that deceptive feeling of security."[25] Its immense profitability and its safe distance from domestic politics made imperialism irresistibly attractive; the bourgeoisie did not have to confront the contradiction of their demand for profits accompanied by their refusal to fulfill any real social function. But imperialism was a smoke screen, not a solution. If anything, it spread liberal subjectivity to wider sections of the population, aggravating the underlying problem. The bourgeoisie drew "prospecters, adventurers, and the scums of the big cities," who had been leading an idle, superfluous existence to their profit-making excursions, awakening in them "the new desire for profit-at-any-price."[26] The mob that was "begotten by the monstrous accumulation of capital," Arendt observes, "betray[s] a surprisingly strong affinity with the political attitudes of bourgeois society."[27]

If the mob was a product of liberalism's desperate attempt to extend its life span, the masses came into being when it finally began crumbling. Here Arendt points specifically to the fall of the hierarchical class system as the immediate catalyst for the production of the mass man and his psychology.[28] But this does not mean that she favors the hierarchical class system as a necessary check on the masses.[29] As we saw, the fundamental problem for Arendt is the very construction of liberalism, which combines the exclusive concern with private interest and political submissiveness. The class system, like moral hypocrisy and the Christian tradition that temporarily chastened the bourgeoisie,[30] was a remnant of the past that had somewhat delayed the march of liberalism's inexorable logic. It is completely extraneous to the central problem Arendt grapples with. In fact, she explicitly rejects the elitist critique of mass society that the masses "result from growing equality of condition, from the spread of general education, and its inevitable lowering of standards and popularization of content."[31] To Arendt, the masses do not signify the invasion of liberalism by democracy. Like the mob, the masses are an embodiment of liberal subjectivity; their political indifference exactly replicates that of the bourgeoisie.[32] So when Arendt declares that "the chief characteristic of the mass man is not brutality and backwardness, but his isolation and lack of normal social relationships,"[33] she is not lamenting the breakdown of the social hierarchy; she is referring to the unleashing of liberal subjectivity embodied by the bourgeoisie, the mob, and the masses.

The masses displayed the same underlying subjectivity differently, however, because they faced dire circumstances. Whereas the bourgeoisie and the mob were able to deflect liberalism's inherent tension, enjoying the profits and the political stability temporarily provided by imperialist adventures, the masses emerged when the destabilizing forces of constant economic and political expansion could no longer be contained. In the period leading up to the rise of totalitarianism, there was no profit to assuage and distract the masses, and no political community to give them even a semblance of social security. Even as they were ravaged by economic depression and social upheaval, moreover, the masses were abandoned by all the prevailing political parties for being "too apathetic or too stupid for their attention."[34] Hence the masses' fanatical devotion to ideology, their refusal to acknowledge reality as they experienced it, and their participation in atrocious violence, all in the service of the complete overthrow of the status quo. "The masses' escape from reality is a verdict against the world in which they are forced to live and in which they cannot live."[35] Met with radical social abjection, the masses' exclusive concern with private interest metamorphosed into its polar opposite: radical disregard for self-interest. Arendt repeatedly describes lack of self-interest as the most striking, unprecedented trait that distinguishes the masses as a political subject and totalitarianism as a political movement.[36] Arendt's critics found this aspect of her analysis overdrawn and almost mystifying,[37] but it is important to note that she makes her characteristic, if methodologically controversial, move here. While apparently describing historical events, she at once distills theoretical categories from them while at the same time projecting those categories back onto them. In other words, her *description* of the mass overlaps with her *theorization* of the mass as an ideal type—which represents one extreme of the spectrum including various distortions of the people that are caused by liberalism's inner contradictions. The other extreme, of course, is occupied by the mob, whose single-minded obsession with profit making may also be found wanting if judged exclusively by the standard of descriptive accuracy.

If the real target of Arendt's criticism is indeed not the masses but the instabilities latent in liberalism, then from her perspective, postwar

intellectuals were misguided to believe that liberalism was assailed from
without by the masses. The problem is liberalism itself, or more precisely
its instrumentalization of politics, which hollows the liberal polity out from
within. This fundamentally different diagnosis of totalitarianism explains
why, unlike postwar intellectuals who were fixated on conformity, Arendt
placed far more emphasis on social fragmentation and alienation (in a special sense, as we will see). As she put it, "Social atomization and extreme
individualization preceded the mass movements," and "the masses grew out
of the fragments of a highly atomized society whose competitive structure
and concomitant loneliness of the individual had been held in check only
through membership in a class."[38] The masses' blind faith in ideology, which
postwar intellectuals attributed to their deep-seated psychological tendencies, was for Arendt "the result of their atomization, of their loss of social
status ... and [of] their situation of spiritual and social homelessness."[39]

   That Arendt's diagnosis of totalitarianism is informed by her theoretical
critique of liberalism as the archetypal political form of modernity also
clarifies why she insisted from the beginning that the subject of *Origins* was
not Nazism as such but "the underlying real political problems" it manifested in an unprecedented way.[40] In an outline she sent to her publisher
in 1946, Arendt wrote that she "assumes that the destruction of nazism
[crossed out] is only the destruction of one particularly dangerous and ter-
rible amalgam which automatically leaves behind it all the older elements
which, though more or less harmless in their separation, may find a new
amalgamator any time as long as they have not found genuine political
solutions."[41] As she widened her research after the publication of *Origins*
to track "totalitarian elements in Marxism,"[42] her belief that, despite all
its atrocities, totalitarianism was still a symptom, rather than a pathology,
seemed to grow only stronger. In "Ideology and Terror," first published in
1953 and included in *Origins* as a new conclusion in 1958, Arendt insisted
that the "crisis of our century" manifested in totalitarianism is "no mere
threat from outside, no mere result of some aggressive foreign policy of
either Germany or Russia," and "will no more disappear with the death
of Stalin than it disappeared with the fall of Nazi Germany."[43] "Insofar as
totalitarian movements have sprung up in the non-totalitarian world,"
she wrote in an almost contemporaneous essay, "the process of understanding [totalitarianism] is clearly, and perhaps primarily, also a process
of self-understanding."[44] The works Arendt produced in the 1950s and
early 1960s—the ones usually considered to contain her political theory,

including "Ideology and Terror," *The Human Condition* (1958), *Between Past and Future* (1961; with two essays added in 1968), and *On Revolution* (1963)—were driven by this concern. In these works, she would suggest that the political pathologies she partially identified through her interpretation of Hobbes and imperialist political philosophy and illustrated in the context of Nazism were plaguing not just the midcentury totalitarian regimes but all modern societies, including liberal ones such as postwar America.

The Context for Action, or Democratic Attunement

Once we see Arendt's political theory as a response to the mutually reinforcing relationship between the instrumentalization of politics and liberal subjectivity she put forward in *Origins,* its otherwise disparate elements come into focus. Her chief aim, I suggest, is to identify the forces that were consolidating that relationship and to outline conditions that might foster an alternative subjectivity. In making this claim, I follow a number of recent readers of Arendt and propose to shift the focus of her political theory away from the concept of action to its context.[45] Arendt's unique concept of action, which she often illustrates with reference to ancient Athens, has been the center of attention for many of her proponents and critics alike. Proponents appreciate the redemptive power of her glorification of action,[46] while critics accuse her of romanticizing political action, celebrating elitism, and bypassing the concerns of morality and justice.[47] Given the overwhelming experience of totalitarianism, which seemed nothing short of a death sentence to action, it is not surprising that Arendt tried to recover the lost meaning of action and that her portrayal of action sometimes took on an urgent tone. She was not alone. French existentialists such as Sartre and Camus, who exerted significant influence on postwar intellectuals, similarly emphasized the responsibility of taking action even when its meaning seemed utterly absent.[48] But insofar as her diagnosis of totalitarianism does not simply bemoan the disappearance of action but traces, in admittedly preliminary fashion, the process through which action is eclipsed, we need to consider her theory of action not in isolation but in relation to other pieces of her thought.

Although Arendt's use of ancient Greece (whose residents she describes as avid seekers of immortal fame and distinction[49]) and the Heideggerian concept of disclosure[50] (which is geared to the exceptional individual's authentic accomplishments) can give the impression to the contrary, her concept of action is not an expression of heroic individualism. What is unique about Arendtian action—the act of beginning something new—lies in its embeddedness in the interrelated conditions of plurality, common sense, and world. Her distinct view is already glimpsed in *Origins,* where every time she laments the demise of individuality, she repeatedly calls attention to the conditions under which it can exist. When she discusses the masses' refusal to acknowledge "reality" as they experience it in favor of ideology, for example, she attributes this refusal to their "essential home-lessness" and the loss of "common sense" that preceded the totalitarian mobilization.[51] Likewise, when she describes how totalitarianism prepared the ground for complete conformity, Arendt notes, citing David Rousset, how Nazi operatives made protest and even martyrdom impossible by depriving individual action of the basis of its meaning: "human solidar-ity."[52] Perhaps the clearest anticipation of her later focus appears in her account of stateless people. She argues that, by losing their political status, stateless people lost the very ground of their standing as individuals.[53] For an individual to exist as such, she must belong to a "world" that human beings consciously erect so that its different and unequal members are recognized as political equals. Individuality, Arendt writes, depends on political life, and political life "rests on the assumption that we can produce equality through organization, because man can act in and change and build a common world, together with his equals and only with his equals."[54]

Action's context-dependent nature is a consistent refrain in Arendt's work. As she argues that one discloses or reveals one's distinctness through speech and action, she states that this "revelatory quality of speech and action comes to the fore where people are *with* others," not-ing that both the anonymous do-gooder and the criminal who must hide from public view are "lonely figures" and thus politically marginal.[55] Ac-tion can disclose a person's individuality—not her place in the existing system of social roles and functions ("what" she is) but her uniqueness that calls the very system into question ("who" she is)—only when she "appears" in a setting shared by others who are plural as well as equal.[56] Action takes effect, in other words, only when it is received in a particular way.[57] Because action can occur only in an "already existing web of human relationships," it always has a measure of unpredictability; as she puts it, action "never achieves its purpose" as intended by the actor.[58] But the fact that action takes the form of a story that is read in multiple, unexpected ways is also a vital condition that explains its power to preserve plurality from the established causal patterns threatening to reduce distinct human beings into mechanical and replaceable units. Because action depends on how it is received, it does not have to be a heroic, rare exertion aimed at singular achievements. Arendt makes numerous remarks concerning this point, which are incomprehensible when seen in light of her alleged glorification of heroic action. "The hero the story discloses needs no heroic qualities; the word 'hero' originally, that is, in Homer, was no more than a name given each free man who participated in the Trojan enterprise and about whom a story could be told."[59] And again: "The smallest act in the most limited circumstances bears the seed of the same boundlessness, because one deed, and sometimes one word, suffices to change every constellation."[60]

The concern with a particular mode of receptiveness extends to Arendt's conceptualization of the public realm. One of her central arguments is that the public realm is not natural but artificial; it requires material underpinnings and institutional shapes. Because action is by nature transitory, it needs a "stable worldly structure."[61] A story, after all, can be read only when it is recorded in "documents and monuments," "use objects or art works," and "all kinds of material."[62] Like action, however, those tangible conditions need to be activated, and that activation has less to do with any special qualities they might possess than with how people treat them. This peculiarity is intimated in her brief account, in *The Human Condition,* of artworks as the archetypical physical objects that sustain a common world and protect action from oblivion. At first, Arendt seems to try to designate a certain class of objects for that purpose. She contends that to perform this indispensable task, to provide "a reliable home for men," objects must be liberated from concerns of immediate utility, as in the case of artworks.[63] But as she does with regard to action, Arendt almost imperceptibly shifts her attention from the production to the reception of objects. She suggests that not just artworks but *anything* can contribute to the permanence of a common world, because "whatever has a shape at all and is seen cannot help being either beautiful, ugly, or something in-between" and can elicit a response.[64] Naturally, a lot hangs on what kind of response an object receives. Writing that everything "transcends the sphere of pure instrumentality once it is completed," Arendt says that "even use objects are judged not only according to the subjective needs of men but by the objective standards of the world," as those objects help construct a "home for mortal men."[65]

What might judging by the "objective standards of the world" mean? On the one hand, it undoubtedly has a cognitive component. It is about whether we are able to recognize action as a singular act that discloses human plurality and contributes to common sense, and an object as a building block of the world that invites our thoughtful reaction. Arendt complains that the tradition of Western political philosophy—its "well-worn notions and categories"—is poorly equipped to aid us in that comprehension.[66] And her search for the lost meaning of key philosophical concepts such as action, freedom, authority, and revolution can be seen as her attempt to alter the frame of our thinking. Roy Tsao has recently called attention to this aspect of Arendt's thought, suggesting that her aim in dividing human activities into labor, work, and action is "not so much to prove that free human actions are possible as it is to answer how it is possible for us to comprehend action, given the fact that we do."[67] Based on this insight, Tsao suggests, with more than an echo of John Rawls's concept of the veil of ignorance, that citizens' freedom for Arendt derives from "their capacity to *disregard* the fact" that they are constrained by their biological needs and by the demands of utility.[68]

This argument is compelling in its own terms, but too much stress on the cognitive dimension can be misleading unless considered in relation to other elements of Arendt's political theory, which are overtly skeptical about the cognitive approach to politics. Tsao interprets Arendt's task as a Kantian one (as pursued in the *Critique of Pure Reason*) that tries to establish principles for our experience and action by elucidating cognitive constraints on our understanding. Seen in that light, for Arendt, as for Kant, what we can do depends on, and is delimited by, what we can understand; thinking and action merge. Tsao even suggests that Arendt consciously frames her theory in the Kantian fashion.[69] This Kantian rendition of Arendt is problematic for several reasons, however. First of all, the seamlessly favorable relationship between thinking and politics that Tsao implicitly assumes overlooks the deep tension between philosophy and politics that remains unsettled in Arendt's thought. Even as she seeks to rescue thinking from the shibboleths of the Western philosophical tradition and stresses, most notably in her account of Adolf Eichmann, the political danger of thoughtlessness, she remains uneasy about thinking's antipolitical implications.[70] More important, although Kant is one of the major figures on whom Arendt draws to develop her ideas, her appropriation of Kant is highly idiosyncratic and based on a willful neglect of the first two *Critiques* and an almost oddly single-minded focus on the *Critique of Judgment*.[71]

Arendt's unconventional interpretation of Kant's theory of aesthetic judgment strongly suggests that the particular mode of reception required by Arendtian action is not just, and not even primarily, cognitive. Kant asserts that aesthetic judgment is public in the sense that when we declare something to be beautiful, we demand others' agreement. We are inclined to respond to that demand because we like to reflect on beautiful objects regardless of whether we derive any material benefits from that activity. And because we feel our aesthetic judgment is independent of our private interest and impartial in that sense, we believe that our liking "must contain a basis for being liked [that holds] for everyone."[72] In other words, aesthetic judgment always lays claim to universal validity or, as Arendt puts it, "appeals to common sense."[73] Aesthetic judgment's validity claim is unique, however, in that it is premised not on truth (deduced by logic) but on the subjective feeling of pleasure and displeasure. Truth claims can be proved or refuted by a set of procedures about reasoning on which everyone has agreed. But the price of that certainty is the restricted nature of truth; it is entirely contained within the parameters of those procedures. Truth, in short, is unable to transcend. When it comes to beauty, in contrast, "there can be no rule by which someone could be compelled to acknowledge that something is beautiful."[74] Instead of deriving its validity from its compliance with a set of predetermined universal standards, aesthetic judgment demands that the beauty it claims to identify in particular objects be acknowledged as universal, continually expanding, challenging, and reconfiguring people's perception of what is beautiful   or, more fundamentally, what should be looked at.

It is not hard to see why Arendt was attracted to Kant's aesthetic theory rather than his transcendental idealism or moral philosophy. His aesthetic theory comports well with her emphatic focus on plurality—which unfolds through the almost intermingling back-and-forth of action and reception that ensues—as the only, if constantly shifting, ground of the public realm. She states that the public realm is characterized by the "presence of others who see what we see and hear what we hear."[75] But even what we see and hear is not a given starting point, a solid foundation that stabilizes the contention between different perspectives. Aesthetic judgment "decides how this world, independent of utility and our vital interests in it, is to look and sound, what men will see and what they will hear in it."[76] Owing to aesthetic judgment's subjective basis and inherent contestability, the very nature of the public realm is constantly disputed. As a product of, not a precondition for, judgment, the common world does not have a fixed content but is always in the process of becoming.

Arendt sometimes seems to theorize judgment in cognitive terms, as when she discusses it by relying on Kant's concept of "enlarged mentality."[77] Put simply, enlarged mentality refers to the ability to think not just from one's own point of view but from diverse standpoints. As she explains, it is neither "empathy" that blindly adopts someone else's viewpoint nor an estimate that derives a majority view from the arithmetic mean of multiple opinions. Rather, it involves imagining, and evaluating from one's own perspective, different viewpoints.[78] Crucially, however, Arendt's account of how we engage in enlarged mentality is significantly different from Kant's. For Kant, enlarged mentality is possible because of an ability shared by all individuals—an ability he describes with the term *sensus communis*: "a power to judge that ... takes account (a priori), in our thought, of everyone else's way of presenting [something]." We use that ability, Kant continues, as follows:

> We compare our judgment not so much with the actual as rather with the merely possible judgments of others, and [thus] put ourselves in the position of everyone else, merely by abstracting from the limitations that [may] happen to attach to our own judging; and this in turn we accomplish by leaving out as much as possible whatever is matter, i.e., sensation, in the presentational state, and by paying attention solely to the formal features of our presentation or of our presentational state. Now perhaps this operation of reflection will seem rather too artful to be attributed to the ability we call *common* sense. But in fact it only looks this way when expressed in abstract formulas. Intrinsically nothing is more natural than abstracting from charm and emotion when we seek a judgment that is to serve as a universal rule.[79]

In her Kant lectures, Arendt cites this passage at length but then moves to extrapolate from it an idea strikingly at odds with Kant's. She argues that what Kant means by *sensus communis* is an "extra sense—like an extra mental capability—that *fits us into a community*." She even calls it "community sense."[80] But this is not Kant's view at all. What he describes in the quoted passage is a cognitive process by which we rule out subjective or contingent factors ("charm and emotion") and deduce conclusions from the "formal features" of the mental structure we supposedly have in common. If Kant presupposes a community, it is a prepolitical community par excellence, of rational human beings capable of such cognitive abstraction—a community one can access in the solitude of one's own mind. Arendt presumes no such community. Her community is eminently political in the sense that it is grounded not in the amorphous concept of human nature but in specific laws, institutions, and material objects, and it emerges when citizens act and react in that particular setting. Elsewhere Arendt explicitly rejects a cognitive rendering of common sense, though with reference to Descartes, lamenting that in the modern age, common sense "became an inner faculty without any world relationships," and "what men now have in common is not the world but the structure of their minds."[81]

In fact, taken on its own terms, Kant's formulation of *sensus communis* threatens to undermine the very reasons why Arendt finds aesthetic judgment so relevant to political theory. Kant's enlarged mentality operates by not questioning certain precepts presumed to exist, contradicting Arendt's notion of contending particularities that continually remake the world and its established predicates. Moreover, by trying to achieve impartiality by purifying aesthetic judgment of sensation, Kant risks depriving it of its unique motivating force—the uncalculated joy we take in the presence of beautiful objects—and the emotional check that reminds us of the ultimately subjective foundation of our view even as it connects us to others. Although Arendt did not elaborate the affective aspects of aesthetic judgment in her account of Kant, it is, in my view, one of her central concerns and is possibly projected onto her interpretation of *sensus communis* as community sense. The "fitting into a community" to which Arendt alludes cannot mean a state of cognitive consonance with the community's shared standards, because for her no such community exists before the exercise of judgment. Rather, it involves our entering a particular mode of affective attunement,[82] which gives primacy to certain issues over others, recognizes certain aspects of a given issue more readily than others, and leads us to engage with the political world independently of our immediate private interests without presuming the universality of our impartiality. What matters is not just whether we are able to perform certain cognitive functions; equally important are whether we are *disposed* to do so, and whether our cognitive exercises are *oriented* away from so-lipsism as well as from hubristic certainty.

The significance of affective attunement to Arendt's thought comes into view when we consider another major inspiration for her revision of traditional philosophy: Montesquieu. Montesquieu appears frequently in the transitional essays she wrote between *The Origins of Totalitarianism* and *The Human Condition,* and they leave little doubt about the profound influence his thought had on her. Arendt's generalized account of totalitarianism in "Ideology and Terror," for example, draws heavily on Montesquieu's distinction between the "essence" and the "principle" of government. (She frames terror as the essence of totalitarianism, and ideology as its principle.) While stressing that politics cannot simply count on norms and customs but requires the "stabilizing force" of laws, another insight of Montesquieu's,[83] Arendt states that the "laws hedge in each new beginning and . . . guarantee the pre-existence of a common world" but do not "inspire" actions.[84] "Therefore," she concludes, "what the definition of government always needed was what Montesquieu called a 'principle of action' which, different in each form of government, would inspire government and citizens alike in their public activity and serve as a criterion, beyond the merely negative yardstick of lawfulness, for judging all action in public affairs."[85] In a lecture unpublished at the time, Arendt went so far as to suggest that when "these principles are no longer valid . . . each [corresponding] form of government comes to its end."[86]

Although Arendt cautions that principles "should not be mistaken for psychological motives,"[87] we must understand the statement in the context of her general argument that action must be free from the actor's motives,[88] and more specifically her notorious critique of the politicization of private emotions such as compassion.[89] She deploys the contrast between motives and principles in her criticism of Robespierre, writing that action "makes manifest its principle" but "does not reveal the innermost motivation of the agent."[90] We should not take this as a wholesale rejection of the affective nature of principles, however. After all, Montesquieu defines principle as "the human passions that set [government] in motion."[91] Arendt herself distinguishes principles from the will and the intellect in unmistakably Kantian fashion (reason, will, taste),[92] clearly indicating that principles belong to the aesthetic realm. And she invokes explicitly affective terms to describe principles. She states that the principle of a republic is "the joy not to be alone in the world."[93] Similarly, she maintains that for the

American revolutionaries, "public happiness," which involves "a feeling of happiness they could acquire nowhere else,"[94] was the principle that *"prepared the minds* of those who then did what they never had expected to do, and more often than not were compelled to acts for which they had no previous inclination."[95]

What Arendt seems to be getting at in her account of principle, then, is the peculiar kind of universality that she seeks to theorize through her idiosyncratic reading of Kant, but with a collective and institutional dimension that is more pronounced in Montesquieu. For action to take effect, citizens must treat it as they would beautiful things, beholding and discussing even when (or perhaps because) it does not affect their immediate material interest, and evaluating it by the standard of political freedom rather than with considerations of survival or utility.[96] Arendt may have been inclined to call this attunement "republican,"[97] but we might call it democratic attunement, since her focus on political equality, plurality, and natality is antithetical to militarism, chauvinism, and the extremely narrow composition of the citizenry characterizing the republican tradition. Arendt's engagement with Montesquieu implies that democratic attunement is not a private feeling that comes from within the individual but a public force that animates and orients individuals.[98] (Thus understood, the concept of democratic attunement helps us come to terms with her furtive crossing of the boundary between the individual and community in her account of Kant's *sensus communis.*) By the same token, what threatens such dispositions is not, contra Kant, our inability to understand the formal features of our cognitive faculty but the construction of modern politics, which breeds political subjectivities indifferent, if not hostile, to action.

It warrants emphasis that Arendt never provided a full-fledged account of these issues despite the demands of her theory. She unequivocally implies that a particular subjectivity is essential to creating the context for action. And Montesquieu's insight that political regimes have different dominant principles clearly indicates that the political salience of democratic subjectivity is not given but shaped by historical conditions. Indeed, that is exactly how Arendt frames her critique of modernity. Despite all of this, however, Arendt resolutely refrained from considering what we might do to change unfavorable structural conditions or to foster more favorable ones, limiting her discussion to what we might do under those conditions. This is perhaps because she was hesitant to adulterate the spontaneity of action (she may have made a point by declining to give a corresponding subjectivity only to action, a privilege she grants to labor and work), but whatever the motivation, Arendt's ambivalence on this point sometimes led her to make rigid and overdrawn distinctions, as in her much-criticized account of the social, and created deep indeterminacies in her theory.

Modernity and the Challenge of Democratic Regeneration

Although some of Arendt's most memorable statements are devoted to recovering the lost meaning of action, there is reason to believe that its resuscitation is not the most urgent and difficult task for her. She believes that action is grounded in the ontological condition of natality, "the new beginning inherent in birth," so that its complete eradication is an anomaly, if not an impossibility; the concentration camps are all the more shocking precisely for that reason.[99] The proper reception of action qua action—which discovers and actualizes ubiquitous but latent action—does not have such an ontological grounding, however. Consider the requirement that individuals in the public realm regard each other as political equals. There is nothing natural about treating plural and unequal human beings as peers; human beings must decide and work to organize their relations in that way.[100] The same holds true for "common sense," the only thing, for Arendt, that keeps plurality from degenerating into radical doubt, which perversely generates a longing for ironclad certainty. In the absence of religious, moral, or philosophical absolutes, we can trust that our private experience is "real" only because others experience the same thing, but from a different perspective. "Only where things can be seen by many in a variety of aspects without changing their identity, so that those who are gathered around them know they see sameness in utter diversity, can worldly reality truly and reliably appear."[101] This, too, is a quite demanding condition, insofar as it asks people to accept the partiality of their own perspectives that feel so certain to them, and to work through differences to find a (still less than absolutely secure) footing for their judgment and action.

Still, lack of ontological grounding is not the most serious obstacle to cultivating democratic attunement, for Arendt finds that all the major trends of modernity suppress and displace it. What began as an investigation of Marx led her to generalize the problem of social alienation, which she had already emphasized in *Origins* as the seedbed of totalitarianism, as a main feature of modernity itself—a problem neglected and even deepened by traditional political philosophy's inadequacies. In *The Human Condition,* Arendt clarifies her unique understanding of alienation as "world alienation"—a situation in which people lead their lives with "an exclusive concern with the self" and "without any care for or enjoyment of the world"—and identifies it as the "hallmark of the modern age."[102] In fact, although *The Human Condition* is apparently a philosophical work, the bulk of which is devoted to elucidating the meaning of labor, work, and action, a close reading suggests that it is actually much closer to *Origins* in its historical motivation. Arendt's main concern is to understand how radical self-care came to prevail in modern politics. One of the central tasks of *The Human Condition,* she writes, is "to trace back modern world alienation ... to its origins."[103] Continuities do not end there, either, as her substantive argument also proves strikingly similar in both works.

Arendt analyzes world alienation in terms of the successive rise of two subjectivities, which she calls *homo faber* and the *animal laborans.* First elevated is *homo faber,* whose chief concern is to use tools and make durable things or, in Arendt's terminology, work. *Homo faber's* ascendance is expected because its disposition coincided with modernity's ideal of control, creativity, and productivity. But modernity also intensifies the volatility latent in *homo faber,* eventually putting it at the service of yet another subjectivity, the *animal laborans,* preoccupied exclusively with sating biological needs and desires through what Arendt terms labor. As a fabricator, *homo faber* works strictly within the means-ends category; he uses a particular means to produce a particular product, which also means that his work has a definite beginning and a definite end. The problem is that the principle of utility governing *homo faber's* activities cannot help him determine to what end his work should be performed and, unless it is overridden, demands that an end product prove its worth by becoming again a means for some other end, creating an "unending chain of means and ends."[104]

Homo faber gives way to the *animal laborans* when the principle of utility is supplanted by the utilitarian principle of "happiness"—which is premised on the assumption that "what all men have in common is not the world but the sameness of their own nature," sameness rooted in their concern with pain and pleasure.[105] For the *animal laborans,* the ultimate goal of activity is to sustain the "life process," subsisting, most basically, but also satisfying or releasing one's appetites, desires, and bodily urges.[106] When *homo faber* no longer serves to erect and maintain a world by giving it durability with the things he makes,[107] and comes under the reign of the life process, his latent tendency to get caught in an endless process of production is radicalized. Things made for the life process are the most ephemeral of all, as they are produced for immediate consumption, which, by reproducing labor power, feeds right back into production. When work is governed by the life process and the recurring cycle of production and consumption, therefore, the very distinction between means and ends ceases to make sense. In that way, Arendt writes, *homo faber*'s "free disposition and use of tools for a specific end product is replaced by rhythmic unification of the laboring body."[108] At that point, the victory of the *animal laborans* marks the end of individuality, and Arendt ends *The Human Condition* there, unmistakably echoing the closing of *Origins,* with a grim description of dehumanizing metamorphosis.

> The last stage of the laboring society ... demands of its members a sheer automatic functioning, as though individual life had actually been submerged in the over-all life process of the species and the only active decision still required of the individual were to let go, so to speak, to abandon his individuality.... [Seen from afar] all [human] activities ... would appear not as activities of any kind but as processes, so that ... modern motorization would appear like a process of biological mutation in which human bodies gradually begin to be covered by shells of steel.[109]

The similar endings of *Origins* and *The Human Condition* are not just a stylistic touch; they point to far more systematic parallels between Arendt's account of totalitarianism and her critique of modernity. In "Ideology and Terror," Arendt makes an early attempt to elucidate the problem of social alienation by introducing two concepts, isolation and loneliness. Isolation results from the destruction of the public sphere, where people "act together in the pursuit of a common concern," leaving them powerless. While isolation is totalitarianism's "most fertile ground" and "always its result," it is not unique to totalitarianism but characteristic of all tyrannies.[110] What makes totalitarianism a truly new form of politics is its reliance on "loneliness," on the "experience of not belonging to the world at all, which is among the most radical and desperate experiences of man."[111] With this distinction, Arendt again gestures toward the problem of subjectivity. Isolation denotes a tangible condition ("I cannot act, because there is nobody who will act with me"), whereas loneliness refers to a not readily observable situation ("I as a person feel myself deserted by all human companionship"). As such, these two conditions do not necessarily follow each other. On the one hand, even when I am isolated, as I must be to engage in productive activities through which I contribute to the material construction of the common world, I can be not lonely and remain "in contact with the world as the human artifice."[112] On the other hand, even when I am not isolated and technically act together with others, I may well be lonely and my action an expression of alienation rather than freedom.

Already in "Ideology and Terror," Arendt links this distinction to *homo faber* and the *animal laborans* and their activities—still inchoate concepts— and she does the same when she elaborates this theme in *The Human Condition*.[113] If the distinction between work and labor is an "unusual" one, which by her own admission has scant supporting evidence,[114] it plays a crucial role in Arendt's theory by helping to identify different underlying dynamics hidden behind the same surface phenomenon, as do isolation and loneliness. Is isolation, the surface phenomenon, manifesting loneliness or only a temporarily suspended but still robust connection to the world? This question, I suggest, is what Arendt consistently brings to her analysis of some of the defining events of modernity. Her discussion of the labor movement—which, it is worth noting, is included in the chapter titled "Action"—perfectly illustrates her approach. Arendt observes that the European working class "has written one of the most glorious and probably the most promising chapter of recent history."[115] But she bases her praise on "one of the important side effects" of the labor movement, rather than on its intended goal, which, she insists, was the elevation of the laboring activity itself.[116] What impresses Arendt is that, in the early stages of the labor movement, "a whole new segment of the population was more or less suddenly admitted to the public realm, that is, *appeared* in public."[117] The distinguishing achievement of the modern labor movement, she claims, lies not in securing personal liberties but in establishing workers as citizens with an equal, if only formal, political standing. (She mentions the abolition of property qualifications for voting rights as a "turning point."[118]) In that salutary period, workers attempted to found "a new political space with new political standards" without being "absorbed by the social realm and, as it were, spirited away from the public," and even fought "against society."[119] But the apparently same labor movement can no longer be counted on for that "political and revolutionary role," because it is now driven by a different dynamic. As Arendt ruefully notes, today the workers are not rebels against society but its members, and "the political significance of the labor movement is now the same as that of any other pressure group."[120]

Here we encounter Arendt's notorious concept of "the social" or "society." Her theory of the social, which is often counterintuitive and at times maddeningly abstruse, has provoked a great deal of criticism. In particular, Arendt's highly controversial and startlingly sweeping claim that "the social question"—the problem of poverty that the poor brought to the forefront of revolutionary politics—was culpable for the "failure" of the French Revolution and bedeviled "all revolutions that were to follow" cast a long shadow over the reception of her theory of the social.[121] But in my view, Arendt's concept of the social comprises two disparate strands, one designating a set of substantive issues such as poverty, and the other describing a Montesquieuian principle empowering a particular subjectivity, namely, the *animal laborans*. Although Arendt is not particularly careful about differentiating these meanings, critics are often too quick to establish a causal connection between the two registers. In other words, critics interpret Arendt's argument as a warning that the introduction of "economic" issues into the political realm *will produce* destructive political outcomes, and for that reason, politics should not open itself to certain types of issues and those who are supposedly concerned exclusively with those issues. As Hanna Pitkin concludes, "It seems that for Arendt, because political action cannot solve economic problems, and because misery can become active only in destructive ways, it is best for the poor and the laborers to be kept out of the public sphere. Like women, they belong in the household, with concerns of the body."[122]

Ample evidence in Arendt's writing, especially in *On Revolution*, supports this reading. But when we see her discussion of the social question not as a direct elaboration of her general theory but as its (mis)application, and focus instead on her account in *The Human Condition*, with particular attention to the problem of subjectivity, a different reading comes into view. As I suggested, Arendt's main concern in *The Human Condition* is to understand the ascendance of a particular public disposition, world alienation or loneliness, and a subjectivity that embodies that disposition, the *animal laborans*. This concern is not clearly visible when we focus on chapter 2, where she presents the social in contradistinction to the public and the private illustrated by the example of ancient Greece. The basic structure of her argument in that chapter, which erects rather rigid ideal types, amplifies the impression that a "spatial" reading of the social is warranted. The problem with the social, according to this reading, is that it brings into the public realm economic issues that ancient Greeks reserved for the private realm. The idea that certain issues must remain outside politics follows. In one passage, Arendt indeed defines "the rise of society" as "the rise of the 'household (*oikia*)' or of economic activities to the public realm, housekeeping and all matters pertaining formerly to the private sphere of the family," apparently confirming the spatial reading.

However, those are not her final words on the matter. A few pages later, she introduces another idea, claiming that the rise of the social "has not only blurred the old borderline between private and political" but "changed ... the meaning of the two terms and their significance for the life of the individual and the citizen."[123] To be sure, this remark does not necessarily invalidate the spatial interpretation, if we can read these two descriptions of the social as causally sequenced, that is, if Arendt means that the public and private realms lost their previous meanings *because* the line between them was blurred and *because* they were infiltrated by issues supposed to belong to another realm. But we cannot quite settle the matter in this way. Later she discusses a situation in which economic activities take place in the public realm but do not amount to the reign of the social. Her example is the exchange market in the ancient world, where *homo faber* "show[ed] the products of his hand and receive[d] the esteem which is due him."[124] The exchange market was not a political realm, she says, but it was not a radically antipolitical realm, either. It was a place suspended between *homo faber*'s commitment to absolute standards and the purposefulness of production and the demand by the *animal laborans* for incessant and mindless production geared solely to consumption. It is interesting in this respect that merchandise and producers' skills ("conspicuous production," as Arendt calls it) existed side by side in the exchange market. So even though the exchange market had the public realm filled with economic activities, and was favored by tyrants for that reason, it did not (yet) effect an irrevocable transformation of the public realm—until it was overtaken by "the rise of the social realm."[125]

Arendt's argument here almost exactly mirrors her discussion of the successive rise of *homo faber* and the *animal laborans*. The exchange market has volatilities, she argues, because the imperative of exchange exerts pressure on *homo faber* to make things with the sole aim of selling, in accordance with buyers' fleeting preferences rather than with the standards of craftsmanship. These volatilities are amplified and radicalized as the ancient exchange market gives way to "the labor society," in which productive activities become "a mere function in the regeneration process of life and labor power."[126] The problem, then, is not simply that economic activities appear in the public realm, which is a constant in the ancient market and the labor society; it is a surface phenomenon. The real issue is *how* and *for what purposes* apparently economic issues are dealt with in public. Again, the distinction between isolation and loneliness, corresponding to work and labor, respectively, is illuminating. Arendt notes that despite the public display of his activities, *homo faber* remained isolated in the exchange market, and the walls of that isolation crumbled in the labor society, where everyone came to participate in the work process. On the surface, the end of *homo faber*'s isolation, along with the political impotence it entailed, seems like a celebratory event that would usher in an age of political freedom. That was, says Arendt, what many well-meaning observers, Marx most notably, believed. For her, however, such a belief confounded isolation with loneliness. The "emancipation" of workers did not lead to political freedom, despite promising achievements that the early labor movement did make toward that goal. Rather, it ended up being absorbed by the social as a collective organizing principle. The end of isolation in the modern age did not set the stage for political freedom; it set in motion a process that, if uninterrupted, would lead to political freedom's complete eradication.

Thus viewed, the real tragedy of modernity is not necessarily that "inappropriate" economic issues have become the subject matter of politics. It is that we have come to approach our entire life predominantly *in terms of* labor—subsistence, gratification of appetites, and private "happiness" completely severed from the common world we inhabit with others—and to model politics on the same principle, so much so that we care about, recognize, and judge political claims only in those terms. The trouble is not that we use a political means to achieve wrong ends, but that a distinction between means and ends disappears altogether in politics—that politics becomes a perpetual motion beholden to never-ending economic growth. The problem is not just homogeneity, which Arendt insists is inherent in certain economic issues ("in so far as we all need bread, we are indeed all the same, and may as well unite into one body"[127]), but that assumptions about our supposed sameness are allowed to grow to such an extent that those assumptions redefine the meaning of both the public and the private. It is "not merely against society, but against a constantly growing social realm, that the private and the public have proved incapable of defending themselves," Arendt writes.[128] That constant growth surely cannot be animated by the mere nature of economic issues; it happens only when people conduct and support the kind of politics that spur it on.

What we see here is yet another iteration of Arendt's critique of instrumental politics and the bourgeois subjectivity, a combustible combination that fuels continual growth, which in turn increases its volatility even further.[129] In this setting, citizens' political passivity and indifference deepen not despite but *because of* economic prosperity. Unless this basic political arrangement is challenged, the hope that the liberation from drudgery and the availability of "free time" made possible by modern technologies will create a more vibrant political life, making Pericles's Athens a "reality for all," remains an illusion. "The spare time of the *animal laborans* is never spent in anything but consumption, and the more time left to him, the greedier and more craving his appetite."[130] And Arendt perceives a similar dynamic at work in "what we today call democracy." Representative government, which is taken to be democracy's chief expression, is predicated on the view of citizens as "the represented." By definition, it elevates their "interest," which is supposed to be uniform and can thus be aggregated and represented by an external agent without losing its substance, while marginalizing their "actions and opinions."[131] While "the voter acts out of concern with his private life and well-being," representative institutions operate as "the very efficient instruments through which the power of the people is curtailed and controlled."[132] The prevailing form of democracy, then, perfectly replicates the double-sided instrumentality of liberalism: an instrument for the pursuit of private happiness, from each individual's perspective, and an instrument of political oppression, from the societal perspective.

This critique of instrumental democracy latent in her general account of the social, however, is hopelessly entangled with her critique of "the social question." Although her own theory clearly points to the problem of subjectivity embedded in broader social processes, when it comes to the solution, if we can call it that, she focuses exclusively on purely political institutions, supporting people's councils and Jefferson's ward system.[133] Deliberate or not, Arendt's refusal to confront the implications of her theory on this point creates a serious theoretical tension. What is at stake is not simply the feasibility or effectiveness of the institutional measures she apparently favors. Rather, the problem is that in Arendt's theory, institutions need to be continually activated by people to serve their functions and yet cannot by themselves generate the energy required for that activation. Institutions offer stability but cannot inspire action: that is the fundamental insight Arendt has drawn from Montesquieu. Arendt champions councils as the locus of people's "power," which, in contradistinction to strength or violence, "springs up between men when they act together and vanishes the moment they disperse."[134] But if power is by nature transient, how can we secure its reappearance? How can we regenerate democracy in its original meaning (*demos-kratos*)? Or, more precisely, how can we prevent the disappearance, not of people's power as such, which is by definition bound to disappear, but of the democratic attunement that promises its renewal?

Arendt's theory suggests that thinking about how we might alter the historical and structural forces that marginalize and displace democratic attunement might represent a step toward answering these questions, but it was a step she was unwilling to take. At times she almost sounds fatalistic about the waning prospect of democratic regeneration. "The rather uncomfortable truth of the matter," she writes, "is that the triumph the modern world has achieved over necessity is due to the emancipation of labor, that is, the fact that the *animal laborans* was permitted to occupy the public realm."[135] If this is true, we are at an impasse. Freedom from necessity, an essential prerequisite for political freedom that was achieved by slavery in ancient Greece, is essential to democratizing political freedom. But if it can be achieved only by letting the *animal laborans* dictate the public realm, it would dissolve political freedom. In a moment like this, Arendt indeed seems to present political freedom and democratization as a nonnegotiable trade-off, making her advocacy of both either inconsistent or romantically tragic insofar as she continues to defend political freedom while fully knowing that its possibilities are constantly shrinking. Arendt's view that economic liberation can be achieved only by subordinating politics to the logic of labor seems to me what makes her account of the social every so often reductive. It is a surprisingly stark claim that is hard to understand except as a projection of her interpretation of Marx—to whom she turned, as noted earlier, to find the intellectual origins of Stalinism.[136]

Her theory of the social, which contains important insights about the perils of modern democracy, slides into an overly rigid argument about keeping the public realm "pure" from the social question's adulterating effect, because she assumes that economic issues have already and irrevocably been colonized by the *animal laborans.* It is an assumption that, I think, we should reject so as to push the alternative path from totalitarianism charted by Arendt to its logical end.

Conclusion

The imagery of totalitarianism irrevocably shaped postwar democratic theory. Most postwar intellectuals became highly hesitant about, if not averse to, the increase of state power and the political inclusion of the masses. They took those worries to redefine democracy with an almost singular focus on civil liberties and institutional mechanisms, in explicit juxtaposition to the construction of a politically empowered and engaged citizenry. Critics protested this trend but mainly complained that it was an overreaction that tilted the balance between institutional stability and political participation too heavily in favor of the former. Partly because they were keen to break the spell that antitotalitarianism cast over postwar political imagination, they did not explore totalitarianism's implications in depth. Without an alternative interpretation, however, critics wound up conceding to their opponents the power to shape the narrative of the indisputably momentous political event of the time.

I suggested that we can find an alternative reading of totalitarianism in Hannah Arendt's account, and that it leads us to a democratic theorizing that throws into sharp relief the problems of the postwar reconstruction of democracy. Postwar intellectuals attended to only one part of Arendt's diagnosis: individuality and plurality were destroyed by the totalitarian state, which rested on the political mobilization of the masses. But Arendt was unequivocal in stating that totalitarianism, atrocious though it was, was a symptom, a manifestation of a deeper pathology. Forces that are endangering individuality and plurality are found in modernity itself and cannot be equated simply with the overgrowth of the state or the political awakening of the masses. Rather, the problem is the spread of the bourgeois subjectivity and the resultant instrumentalization of politics. For Arendt, individuality and plurality can have meaning only in a particular environment—people who are disposed to engage with public claims independently of their private welfare. Seen in this light, postwar democratic theorists' authorization of private interest claims as the sole basis of democratic politics is a profound mistake that not only suppresses popular participation to an unwarranted degree but imperils the very concerns they aimed to protect by instrumentalizing democracy: individuality, plurality, and stability.

To be clear, this is not to suggest that instrumentalized democracy pushed American democracy to the brink of totalitarianism. Nor is it to suggest that the legitimation of the bourgeois subjectivity would automatically give rise to the growth of state power and the diminished respect for individuality as if following a script. The problem, rather, is that instrumental democracy was a stopgap that deflected attention away from the real challenge and delayed a direct response to it. In fact, it was more than that. Like imperialism, instrumental democracy bought temporary stability while deepening unsustainable and ultimately destructive underlying trends. Apparent stability gained through targeted political repression and aggressive economic growth was mistakenly attributed to the instrumental construction of democracy, solidifying postwar intellectuals' faith in their endeavors and masking the volatilities growing from within. In the midst of that strange mix of fear and self-assurance, the eroding foundations of political legitimacy went virtually unnoticed. When economic growth inevitably stalled, American democracy was left without a cogent intellectual defense against neoliberalism's drive to completely remold democracy after the image of the free market.

CHAPTER SEVEN

Conclusion

When the triumph of democracy was announced after the end of the Cold War, political theorists did not fully consider how the Cold War might have transformed democracy itself. It was not just those who assumed that democracy as witnessed in the late twentieth century represented a culmination of the modern democratic ideal. Critics acutely aware of democracy's deficiencies at the turn of the new century attributed them primarily to neoliberalism's rise since the 1980s. Neoliberalism's challenge to democracy is undoubtedly a crucial concern. But we cannot fully understand the current crisis of democracy—and the ascendance of neoliberalism—without taking into account what happened to democracy in the middle of the twentieth century, or so I have argued in this book.

The reconstruction of democratic theory in the post–World War II era warrants a fresh look. It has been predominantly described in terms of the denigration of popular political participation in favor of existing institutional mechanisms. Some of the best-known critiques of postwar democratic theory—encapsulated in labels such as "elitist," "minimalist," "competitive," or "procedural"—all operate within that framework, contrasting political participation to postwar democratic theory's narrow focus on elections and its neglect of broader political and socioeconomic arrangements that distort the distribution of actual political power beneath the surface of formal equality. These prevailing critiques are correct as far as they go. But the exclusive focus on participation can also obscure our purview. In chapter 1,

I discussed some of the blind spots created by the activist conception of the demos—the demos as those who make claims—that most critics of postwar democratic theory adopted. Another way of putting it would be that the critics remained beholden to the exercise concept of power. The exercise concept of power focuses on individual empowerment—namely, the extent to which each person can realize her sovereign will. So the critics parted company with their opponents only in their understanding of what constitutes the sufficient condition of individual empowerment; they did not contest it as a primary measure of democracy. If postwar democratic theorists took a legalistic approach, emphasizing suffrage and other formal rights, their critics took a more substantive approach, highlighting practical constraints that hinder individuals from imposing their will on the world despite the apparent absence of legal barriers. The critics' main objection, in other words, was that postwar democratic theory does not give individual citizens—each of them—enough power.

This line of critique elides an essential dimension of democracy. What is unique about democracy is not simply that collective decisions in it reflect the will of a multitude rather than a single person or a group. Rather, it is that private wills undergo transformation to become a public will that does not exist before citizens' mutual engagement. Thus it is misleading to understand democratic empowerment exclusively at the individual level. Democratic empowerment is not equal to the absolute amount of resources available to each individual but rests crucially on the institutional setup and the broader configuration of social relations that enable and dispose citizens to address their collective problems according to the principles of the common good and political equality. Only against the backdrop of a public thus enabled and disposed—the demos as a responsive public—can the empowerment of individual citizens democratize their community.

I have sought to show that the displacement of the demos, rather than the suppression of popular political participation, is postwar democratic theory's most distinct and perilous aspect. Postwar democratic theory does not simply narrow the scope of political participation but alters its terms and changes the environment in which it takes place. It does so by redefining democracy as an instrument that individuals use only to pursue their private interests, and by effectively reinforcing a distinctly undemocratic political subjectivity. By changing the narratives about what kinds of public claims warrant citizens' primary attention and response and are to be weighed more heavily in their political judgment, postwar democratic theory creates a framework in which the general public's indifference is not only a justified but natural state—a state that is only occasionally interrupted when people's private welfare is directly and immediately at stake. Postwar democratic theory, most fundamentally, is not elitist but instrumental; its real problem is not that it justifies asymmetrical distribution of power but that it deprives democracy of its most fundamental source of vitality—(temporary and incomplete) transcendence of private wills through public engagement—and reduces it to a contest of sovereign wills.

The formation of instrumental democracy cannot be attributed to a single driving force. While the pressures of totalitarianism and anticommunism were overwhelming, they did not directly cause so much as activate a number of motifs with their own histories and intellectual architecture. This multilayered construction, rather than the preponderance of particular political discourses, accounts for instrumental democracy's resilience. In the preceding chapters, I examined instrumental democracy's three constitutive motifs: fear of the masses, faith in rational systemic management, and ambivalence about the relationship between capitalism and democracy. These motifs, while stemming from disparate intellectual traditions, compounded and strengthened one another in forging instrumental democracy. Mass politics appeared particularly undesirable to postwar intellectuals, for instance, not simply because of the vivid memories of Nazism, but also because they believed there was a superior alternative—an elaborate system of feedback and communication that can accommodate individual citizens' demands without going through collective mobilization and public appeal. Similarly, postwar intellectuals' acceptance of free-market capitalism as a correlate of democracy, their qualms about its culturally corrosive effects notwithstanding, was driven not simply by anticommunism. It was also encouraged by the stark contrast they drew between economic competition with perhaps morally reprehensible ramifications and the power struggle that could end in the obliteration of individuality.

Still, instrumental democracy endures not because it is innately stable or even sustainable but because it continually shifts around rising risks of political crisis. It exists not as a public institution but as a mechanism for distributing economic benefits. In fact, it is not even a mechanism. Since instrumental democracy displaces a citizenry that can judge competing public claims' congruence with the principles of the common good and political equality, its distribution of benefits is invariably ad hoc, contingent on the outcome of a particular power struggle. This setup heavily favors well-organized and well-resourced minorities, not only in specific instances of political conflict but in the long term. "Reform" in instrumental democracy is rarely institutional and structural but almost always takes the form of extending additional benefits to the dissatisfied segment of the population. Without altering the basic structure of the economy within which profits flow unevenly to employers and employees and externalities are not recognized at all, for example, the after-the-fact distribution of wealth by political means only sets up further conflict, especially among ordinary citizens, on whom the burden of expanding the distributive regime is frequently and disproportionately imposed.

Seen in this light, the dichotomous structure of the current debate on the crisis of democracy—which echoes the structure of the debate over postwar democracy—needs to be reconsidered. Scholars are divided between those who highlight institutional failures to respond efficiently to citizens' demands and those who stress the rise of unconventional political activities. Both views are limited, however. The focus on institutional optimization fails to question the underlying conception of democracy shaping current representative institutions, which envisages citizens as consumers whose political claims are considered equivalent by default for the sole reason that each of them is willing to pay the same price: a vote. But especially in an advanced industrial society where more goods take on social and positional character, it is impossible to satisfy all the constituents' demands at once; collective decisions inevitably advantage some members while disadvantaging others. Unless the grounds for those decisions—broad principles governing the conditions of citizenship—are continually formed and reformed through public debates, therefore, people have no reason to accept those decisions' uneven effects, and democracy is bound to get caught in the unbridgeable gap between unyielding expectations and persistent frustration, no matter how refined its institutions are. For similar reasons, we should meet the claims about the emergence of a new participatory democracy with caution. Insofar as the instrumental construction of democracy goes unchallenged, increasing extrainstitutional political activities, even if they amount to a durable trend, are exposed to the perennial danger of co-optation, leading not to lasting institutional change but to social conflicts that will ultimately benefit already powerful minorities.

This point, then, brings us back to the debate about neoliberalism. While correctly calling attention to neoliberalism's penetration into politics, the economy, social relations, and subjectivity as a threat to democracy, critics often find an alternative in the postwar regime, which combined the welfare state and interest group pluralism.[1] But the concept of instrumental democracy helps bring some of the postwar regime's limitations into sharp relief. The apparent compromise between business and labor that is touted by contemporary theorists was highly contingent on the urgency of an ongoing, albeit "cold," war, as well as on unexpectedly strong economic growth. Anticommunism shifted the direction of the New Deal from a structural and regulatory approach to a compensatory one that focused mainly on boosting demand rather than regulating the capitalist market. The main impetus of the "second" New Deal—which was the framework of postwar economic policies—was not the supposedly democratic imperatives of a mass-production and mass-consumption economy but the hope for continuing economic growth, which could assuage its multiple constituents, including, most importantly, capital-intensive multinational corporations. The economic structure dominated by corporations remained intact, and the Kennedy and Johnson administrations financed social programs not by making the income tax more progressive or raising corporate tax rates but mostly by raising the social security tax, whose immediate burden is felt most acutely by lower-income citizens.[2]

The neoliberal revolt was led by corporations and the upper class, but they found their way to success by exploiting fissures among ordinary citizens (e.g., workers versus the poor, lower-class whites versus African Americans) created and deepened under the postwar regime. In important respects, then, the engine and the fuel of neoliberalism—the unchallenged dominance of corporations and the growing social divisions—were supplied by postwar democracy. These unintended effects were not the outcome of postwar democracy's failure to live up to its ideals; they resulted directly from its instrumental character. Postwar democracy refused to articulate broad principles of citizenship and left collective decisions to be made exclusively by the struggle between competing groups. As a result, powerful minorities that were largely insulated from public scrutiny dictated the structure of the postwar period's welfare regime, and the further inclusion of marginalized groups became a zero-sum game among ordinary citizens.

It did not *feel* like a zero-sum game, however, in times of extraordinary economic growth; many individual citizens' absolute standards of living were on the rise. As we saw, most postwar intellectuals failed to see through this deceptive impression and to investigate the extent to which the postwar welfare regime rested not on any agreement about the guiding principles of democracy but on its constituents' (unevenly) rising bottom line, especially that of corporations. In fact, they participated in the consolidation of that unsustainable arrangement, insofar as they naturalized—and thereby implicitly authorized—democracy that was divorced from citizens' commitment to the common good and political equality. And as the zero-sum nature of postwar democracy's distributive regime became evident in the 1960s and especially in the 1970s with the slowdown of the economy, postwar intellectuals' embrace of instrumental democracy led to intellectual paralysis. When the denunciation of "democratic excess" quickly occupied the center of democratic discourse in the mid-1970s to become a unifying platform for the multipronged attack on government, social democratic visions, and participatory democracy (with thinly buried racial undertones),[3] postwar liberals had little to offer in response.

Thus the call for "discipline" came to serve exclusively as a justification for reducing public spending, repressing radical political action, and relying further on the market's allegedly rationalizing forces while deflecting attention away from increasing "permissiveness" toward the wealthy, the powerful, and the market. For example, the state's quiet deregulation of the financial industry, in the late 1960s and the 1970s, as a solution to swelling public-sector liabilities and the ensuing inflation almost entirely escaped postwar intellectuals' critical interrogation.[4] Unwilling to confront the politically difficult task of setting priorities in the tightening credit market, the state let the market (i.e., commercial banks) do the work by, for instance, deregulating interest rates. In the resulting environment of rising interest rates, an illusory division formed between consumer-spenders and consumer-savers (artificially separated figures who were often embodied by a single individual), apparently rewarding the latter for their "discipline" with higher interest on their savings and deepening the former's dependence on credit (i.e., debt), all the while hiding that public benefits were being replaced by privatized access to credit—a privilege differentially extended according to the ostensible virtue of creditworthiness determined by the financial industry. Neoliberalism would intensify these trends, but it did not invent them.

Seen in this light, neoliberalism's aggressive spread over the past few decades should not be taken as evidence of its intrinsic strength; it should alert us to the weaknesses of postwar democracy that preceded neoliberalism's emergence. On its own, neoliberalism's attempt to absorb democracy is ultimately self-undermining. In a drive to regulate multidimensional human relations with a single yardstick of market prices, it lavishly rewards the winners of market competition while punishing those who fall behind, magnifying capitalism's tendency to increase inequality. For all the pressure it exerts on people to extract their conformity to market norms (e.g., the imperative of competition that dictates longer hours, ever-higher productivity, and more "flexible"—unstable—employment), neoliberalism cannot offer people a secure sense of social standing, as it rests heavily on social and positional goods whose value is determined not by market prices but only by their peers' recognition. And neoliberalism's singular focus on wealth as a measure of worth and its externalization of risks encourage reckless economic adventures bound to generate a crisis, for which the public, the unaware bearer of risks, is forced to assume responsibility. Even as neoliberalism tries to mobilize individuals as market subjects, therefore, its operation incites an aspiration to a different principle of social organization that acknowledges the fact of social interdependence, the value of fairness, and the plurality of human values.

The question is whether such an aspiration could find a venue for materialization in institutional and discursive space and be organized into a democratic subjectivity. Neoliberalism may not be as ironclad as it is sometimes made out to be today, but its demise alone would not automatically put an end to the crisis of democracy. In a tumultuous time when conventional fabrics of political relations seem to be fraying, it is tempting to counsel a restoration of the status quo ante. But a clearer understanding of democracy before neoliberalism should help us resist that temptation. Instead we must envision a different democracy—one that rests on a demos engaging in collective inquiry and judgment, rather than on a group of individuals concerned exclusively with their private welfare. Such a democracy would require intellectual persuasion; the blind veneration of traditional institutions, the dream of efficient technocratic management, and the obfuscation of the politically constructed nature of the economy are still weighing on our political imagination and need to be dispelled. Moreover, as Dewey and Arendt recognized, a new democracy would need to create institutionalized space in which citizens are actually tasked with the responsibility of discussing and addressing their collective problems. Finally, a new democracy would require efforts to reset the priorities and pace of social life. As long as life is dictated by the terms of the *animal laborans*—that is, when life is nothing but a scramble to gratify appetites that are constantly stimulated but forever unsated by endlessly proliferating objects of desire—those terms inexorably overflow and shape our political disposition. The affective energy now released through the cracks of the neoliberal reign seems furious because it is directionless. We need radical ambition, not a retreat to the "vital center," to prevent its destructive crystallization.

Chapter 1. Democratic Theory and the Crisis of Democracy

1. Freedom House, *Democracy's Century: A Survey of the Global Political Change in the 20th Century* (New York: Freedom House, 2000).
2. Francis Fukuyama, "The End of History?" *National Interest* 16 (Summer 1989): 4.
3. Francis Fukuyama, *The End of History and the Last Man* (1992; New York: Free Press, 2006), xi.
4. Fukuyama, *The End of History,* xx.
5. Freedom House, *Freedom in the World 2016,* 3, https://freedomhouse.org/report-types/freedom-world.
6. Joshua Kurlantzick, *Democracy in Retreat: The Revolt of the Middle Class and the Worldwide Decline of Representative Government* (New Haven, CT: Yale University Press, 2013); Anna Lührmann, Valeriya Mechkova, Sirianne Dahlum, Laura Maxwell, Moa Olin, Constanza Sanhueza Petrarca, Rachel Sigman, Matthew C. Wilson, and Staffan I. Lindberg, "State of the World 2017: Autocratization and Exclusion?" *Democratization* 25, no. 8 (2018): 1321–1340.
7. Wolfgang Merkel, "Embedded and Defective Democracies," *Democratization* 11, no. 5 (2004): 33–58.
8. David Waldner and Ellen Lust, "Unwelcome Change: Coming to Terms with Democratic Backsliding," *Annual Review of Political Science* 21, no. 1 (2018): 93–113.
9. Matthijs Bogaards, "De-Democratization in Hungary: Diffusely Defective Democracy," *Democratization* 25, no. 8 (2018): 1481–1499.
10. Joseph S. Nye Jr., Philip D. Zelikow, and David C. King, eds., *Why People Don't Trust the Government* (Cambridge, MA: Harvard University Press, 1997); Mariano Torcal and José R. Montero, *Political Disaffection in Contemporary Democracies: Social Capital, Institutions and Politics* (London: Routledge, 2006); Russell J. Dalton, "Political Support in Advanced Industrial Countries," in *Critical Citizens: Global Support for Democratic Government,* ed. Pippa Norris (Oxford: Oxford University Press, 1999), 57–77; Colin Hay, *Why We Hate Politics* (London: Polity, 2007); Thomas E. Patterson, *The Vanishing Voter: Public Involvement in an Age of Uncertainty* (New York: Vintage, 2003).
11. Susan J. Pharr and Robert D. Putnam, eds., *Disaffected Democracies: What's Troubling the Trilateral Countries?* (Princeton, NJ: Princeton University Press, 2000).
12. Peter Mair, *Ruling the Void: The Hollowing of Western Democracy* (London: Verso, 2013); Donatella Della Porta, *Can Democracy Be Saved?* (Cambridge, UK: Polity, 2013); Wolfgang Streeck, *Buying Time: The Delayed Crisis of Democratic Capitalism* (London: Verso, 2014); Nadia Urbinati, *Democracy Disfigured: Opinion, Truth, and the People* (Cambridge, MA: Harvard University Press, 2014); Larry Diamond, "Facing Up to the Democratic Recession," *Journal of*

Democracy 26, no. 1 (2015): 141–155. See also the special issues of the *Journal of Democracy* 26, no. 1 (2015) and *Democratic Theory* 1, no. 2 (2014).

13. Nadia Urbinati, "Reflections on the Meaning of the 'Crisis of Democracy,'" *Democratic Theory* 3, no. 1 (2016): 9.

14. Pharr and Putnam, *Disaffected Democracies,* esp. chaps. 1 and 3.

15. James S. Fishkin, *The Voice of the People: Public Opinion and Democracy* (New Haven, CT: Yale University Press, 1995); Fishkin, *When the People Speak: Deliberative Democracy and Public Consultation* (New York: Oxford University Press, 2011); Bruce A. Ackerman and James S. Fishkin, *Deliberation Day* (New Haven, CT: Yale University Press, 2004); Michael R. James, *Deliberative Democracy and the Plural Polity* (Lawrence: University Press of Kansas, 2004); Mark E. Warren and Hilary Pearse, eds., *Designing Deliberative Democracy: The British Columbia Citizens Assembly* (New York: Cambridge University Press, 2008); Archon Fung, *Empowered Participation: Reinventing Urban Democracy* (Princeton, NJ: Princeton University Press, 2006); Archon Fung, Erik Olin Wright, and Rebecca Abers, eds., *Deepening Democracy: Institutional Innovations in Empowered Participatory Governance* (London: Verso, 2003).

16. Colin Crouch, *Post-Democracy* (Malden, MA: Polity, 2004), 85–102; Wolfgang Merkel, "Is Capitalism Compatible with Democracy?" *Zeitschrift für Vergleichende Politikwissenschaft* 8, no. 2 (2014): 109–128.

17. Sheldon S. Wolin, *Democracy Incorporated: Managed Democracy and the Specter of Inverted Totalitarianism* (Princeton, NJ: Princeton University Press, 2008); Wendy Brown, *Undoing the Demos: Neoliberalism's Stealth Revolution* (New York: Zone Books, 2015).

18. Pippa Norris, *Democratic Phoenix: Reinventing Democratic Activism* (New York: Cambridge University Press, 2002); Russell J. Dalton, *The Good Citizen: How a Younger Generation Is Reshaping American Politics* (Thousand Oaks, CA: CQ Press, 2016).

19. Pierre Rosanvallon, *Counter-Democracy: Politics in an Age of Distrust* (New York: Cambridge University Press, 2008).

20. Despite its internal divergences, the theory of deliberative democracy generally falls within this line of inquiry. Its basic proposition is that law is legitimate only when it emerges from a deliberative setting in which citizens persuade each other of the desirability or reasonableness of that law. The focus on the question of legitimacy is especially pronounced in the "liberal" variant of deliberative democracy, represented most notably by John Rawls. John Rawls, *Political Liberalism* (1993; New York: Columbia University Press, 2007). See also Bernard Manin, "On Legitimacy and Political Deliberation," *Political Theory* 15, no. 3 (1987): 338–368; Thomas Nagel, "Moral Conflict and Political Legitimacy," *Philosophy and Public Affairs* 16, no. 3 (1987): 215–240.

A more "democratic" iteration of deliberative democracy, advanced most notably by Jürgen Habermas, places more emphasis on the formation of public opinion in civil society.See the exchange between Rawls and Habermas: Jürgen Habermas, "Reconciliation through the Public Use of Reason: Remarks on John Rawls's Political Liberalism," and John Rawls, "Political Liberalism: Reply to Habermas," *Journal of Philosophy* 92, no. 3 (1995): 109–131, 132–180, respectively. But in his later works, Habermas, too, paid greater attention to establishing an institutional framework for deliberation in the form of legitimate laws, while glossing over the question of how deliberation might actually happen in that institutional space. Jürgen Habermas, *Between Facts and Norms* (Cambridge, MA: MIT Press, 1996). For a critique that proposes that the idealization of orderly deliberation—as opposed to allegedly unruly participation—too quickly concedes the charge, made by advocates of Cold War democracy, that too much or unregulated popular participation may not deepen but actually imperil democracy, see Emily Hauptmann, "Can Less Be More? Leftist Deliberative Democrats' Critique of Participatory Democracy," *Polity* 33, no. 3 (2001): 397–421.

21. Carole Pateman, *Participation and Democratic Theory* (Cambridge: Cambridge University Press, 1970); Peter Bachrach and Aryeh Botwinick, *Power and Empowerment: A Radical Theory of Participatory Democracy* (Philadelphia: Temple University Press, 1992); Benjamin Barber, *Strong Democracy: Participatory Politics for a New Age* (1984; Berkeley: University of California Press, 2003).
22. Anne Phillips, *The Politics of Presence* (Oxford: Oxford University Press, 1995); Iris Marion Young, *Inclusion and Democracy* (Oxford: Oxford University Press, 2000).
23. Sheldon S. Wolin, "Fugitive Democracy," *Constellations* 1, no. 1 (1994): 11–25.
24. Michel Crozier, Samuel P. Huntington, and Joji Watanuki, *The Crisis of Democracy* (New York: New York University Press, 1975).
25. Sheldon Wolin is perhaps the most radical advocate of this position. He proposes to associate democracy exclusively with the spontaneous emergence of popular movements, detaching it from institutionalization as such. "I propose accepting the familiar charges that democracy is inherently unstable, inclined toward anarchy, and identified with revolution and using these traits as the basis for a different, *a*constitutional conception of democracy.... This democracy might be summed up as the idea and practice of rational disorganization." Sheldon S. Wolin, "Norm and Form: The Constitutionalizing of Democracy," in *Athenian Political Thought and the Reconstruction of American Democracy,* ed. J. Peter Euben, Josiah Ober, and John R. Wallach (Ithaca, NY: Cornell University Press, 1994), 37. See also Jacques Rancière, *Disagreement: Politics and Philosophy* (Minneapolis: University of Minnesota Press, 2008).
26. The "directness" of Greek democracy, Manin writes, "consisted more in the way their members were recruited, which was by lot, than from being identical to or identified with the people." Bernard Manin, *The Principles of Representative Government* (New York: Cambridge University Press, 1997), 25.
27. David Plotke, "Representation Is Democracy," *Constellations* 4, no. 1 (1997): 19–34; Nadia Urbinati, "Representation as Advocacy: A Study of Democratic Deliberation," *Political Theory* 28, no. 6 (2000): 758–786; Urbinati, "Continuity and Rupture: The Power of Judgment in Democratic Representation," *Constellations* 12, no. 2 (2005): 194–222; Lisa Disch, "Toward a Mobilization Conception of Democratic Representation," *American Political Science Review* 105, no. 1 (2011): 100–114. For a useful review of this emerging literature, see Nadia Urbinati and Mark E. Warren, "The Concept of Representation in Contemporary Democratic Theory," *Annual Review of Political Science* 11, no. 1 (2008): 387–412.
28. Inspired by the challenges to the concept of the rational, independent, sovereign subject, mounted by thinkers such as Michel Foucault and Emmanuel

Levinas, several political theorists have suggested that we acknowledge the inherent ambiguity, corporeality, and vulnerability of our identity and attend to differences that may unsettle our habitual ways of being. William E. Connolly, *Why I Am Not a Secularist* (Minneapolis: University of Minnesota Press, 1999); Judith Butler, *Giving an Account of Oneself* (New York: Fordham University Press, 2005); Stephen K. White, *Sustaining Affirmation: The Strengths of Weak Ontology in Political Theory* (Princeton, NJ: Princeton University Press, 2000); Romand Coles, *Rethinking Generosity: Critical Theory and the Politics of Caritas* (Ithaca, NY: Cornell University Press, 1997); Ella Myers, *Worldly Ethics: Democratic Politics and Care for the World* (Durham, NC: Duke University Press, 2013).

29. Wendy Brown, "Moralism as Anti-Politics," in *Politics Out of History* (Princeton, NJ: Princeton University Press, 2001), 18–44; Jodi Dean, "The Politics of Avoidance: The Limits of Weak Ontology," *Hedgehog Review* 7, no. 2 (2005): 55–65; Bonnie Honig, "The Politics of Ethos," *European Journal of Political Theory* 10, no. 3 (2011): 422–429; Antonio Y. Vázquez-Arroyo, *Political Responsibility* (New York: Columbia University Press, 2016).

30. Danielle S. Allen, *Talking to Strangers: Anxieties of Citizenship since* Brown v. Board of Education (Chicago: University of Chicago Press, 2004), 29.

31. For "elitist democracy," see Peter Bachrach and Morton S. Baratz, "Two Faces of Power," *American Political Science Review* 56, no. 4 (1962): 947–952; Jack L. Walker, "A Critique of the Elitist Theory of Democracy," *American Political Science Review* 60, no. 2 (1966): 285–295. For "competitive democracy," see Graeme Duncan and Steven Lukes, "The New Democracy," *Political Studies* 11, no. 2 (1963): 156–177. For the "procedural" or "process" theory of democracy, see David M. Ricci, "Democracy Attenuated: Schumpeter, the Process Theory, and American Democratic Thought," *Journal of Politics* 32, no. 2 (1970): 239–267. The "minimalist" conception of democracy became, and still is, a concept widely used by political scientists, especially by those who seek to categorize different countries' regime type. See Samuel Huntington's influential work on democratic transition, *The Third Wave: Democratization in the Late Twentieth Century* (Norman: University of Oklahoma Press, 1993). For a normative argument in favor of the minimalist conception, see William H. Riker, *Liberalism against Populism: A Confrontation between the Theory of Democracy and the Theory of Social Choice* (Prospect Heights, IL: Waveland Press, 1982); Adam Przeworski, "Minimalist Conception of Democracy: A Defense," in *Democracy's Values,* ed. Ian Shapiro and Casiano Hacker-Cordon (New York: Cambridge University Press, 1999), 23–55. Although these terms capture slightly different aspects of Cold War democratic theory, they overlap with one another and are often used interchangeably. See Pateman, *Participation and Democratic Theory,* 1–21.

32. James Madison, Alexander Hamilton, and John Jay, *The Federalist Papers,* ed. Isaac Kramnick (New York: Penguin, 1987), no. 51, 320.

33. Crouch, *Post-Democracy,* 85–102; Colin Hay, "Re-Stating Politics, Re-Politicising the State: Neo-Liberalism, Economic Imperatives and the Rise of the Competition State," *Political Quarterly* 75, no. 1 (2004): 38–50; Colin Leys, *Market-Driven Politics: Neoliberal Democracy and the Public Interest* (London: Verso, 2003); Wendy Brown, "Neo-Liberalism and the End of Liberal Democracy,"

Theory and Event 7, no. 1 (2003); Brown, *Undoing the Demos*; Wolin, *Democracy Incorporated*; Merkel, "Is Capitalism Compatible with Democracy?"

34. Brown, *Undoing the Demos,* 221.

35. George A. Reisch, *How the Cold War Transformed Philosophy of Science* (New York: Cambridge University Press, 2005); Philip Mirowski, *Machine Dreams: Economics Becomes a Cyborg Science* (New York: Cambridge University Press, 2002); Ellen Herman, *The Romance of American Psychology: Political Culture in the Age of Experts, 1940–1970* (Berkeley: University of California Press, 1995); Christopher Simpson, *Science of Coercion: Communication Research and Psychological Warfare, 1945–1960* (New York: Oxford University Press, 1996); S. M. Amadae, *Rationalizing Capitalist Democracy: The Cold War Origins of Rational Choice Liberalism* (Chicago: University of Chicago Press, 2003).

36. Christopher Simpson, ed., *Universities and Empire: Money and Politics in the Social Sciences during the Cold War* (New York: New Press, 1998); Emily Hauptmann, "From Opposition to Accommodation: How Rockefeller Foundation Grants Redefined Relations between Political Theory and Social Science in the 1950s," *American Political Science Review* 100, no. 4 (2006): 643–649; Hauptmann, "The Ford Foundation and the Rise of Behavioralism in Political Science," *Journal of the History of the Behavioral Sciences* 48, no. 2 (2012): 154–173; Mark Solevey, *Shaky Foundations: The Politics-Patronage–Social Science Nexus in Cold War America* (New Brunswick, NJ: Rutgers University Press, 2013); Hunter Heyck, *Age of System: Understanding the Rise of Modern Social Science* (Baltimore, MD: Johns Hopkins University Press, 2015), 51–80.

37. John G. Gunnell, *The Descent of Political Theory: A Genealogy of an American Vocation* (Chicago: University of Chicago Press, 1993); David Ricci, *The Tragedy of American Political Science: Politics, Scholarship, and Democracy* (New Haven, CT: Yale University Press, 1984), 133–175; Raymond Seidelman, with the assistance of Edward J. Harpham, *Disenchanted Realists: Political Science and the American Crisis, 1884–1984* (Albany: State University of New York Press, 1985), 159–186; Emily Hauptmann, *Putting Choice before Democracy: A Critique of Rational Choice Theory* (Albany: State University of New York Press, 1996); Amadae, *Rationalizing Capitalist Democracy.*

38. John G. Gunnell, *Imagining the American Polity* (University Park: Pennsylvania State University Press, 2004); Avigail I. Eisenberg, *Reconstructing Political Pluralism* (Albany: State University of New York Press, 1995).

39. Recently, a number of scholars cautioned against drawing too strong a causal connection between the national security state and the social sciences during the Cold War, suggesting that some of the major tenets of the postwar social sciences were not invented to cater to national security needs but inherited from the academic work of the scholars of the preceding generations, and the content of those studies did not always reinforce or justify the state's preconceptions and actions. Joel Isaac, "The Human Sciences in Cold War America," *Historical Journal* 50, no. 3 (2007): 725–746; David C. Engerman, "Social Science in the Cold War," *Isis* 101, no. 2 (2010): 393–400; Peter Mandler, "Deconstructing 'Cold War Anthropology,'" in *Uncertain Empire: American History and the Idea of the Cold War,* ed. Joel Isaac and Duncan Bell (New York: Oxford University Press, 2012), 245–266. Cf. Philip Mirowski, "A History Best Served Cold," in *Uncertain Empire,* 61–74.

This is an important caveat, and I remain sensitive to the internal dynamics of different intellectual discourses and scholarly disciplines.But in some sense my approach is the opposite of what Isaac and Engerman propose. While they call for widening the temporal horizon and narrowing disciplinary focus, I focus on the Cold War while broadening the purview as to its impact. Viewed from the perspective of a particular theme or idea, such as democracy, the Cold War did effect a transformation, in the sense of fortifying, justifying, and bringing together particular strands of thought. However, this does not mean—and I think I agree with Isaac and Engerman here—that this transformation can be reduced to national security concerns and strategies alone. My discussion in the following chapters should make clear the heterogeneity of the Cold War intellectual universe.

40. The relevant literature on the history of particular branches of science is cited in the individual chapters that follow. Major intellectual histories of postwar political thought (some of which cover a longer time period) include Edward A. Purcell Jr., *The Crisis of Democratic Theory: Scientific Naturalism and the Problem of Value* (Lexington: University Press of Kentucky, 1973); Robert Booth Fowler, *Believing Skeptics: American Political Intellectuals, 1945–1964* (Westport, CT: Greenwood Press, 1978); Richard H. Pells, *The Liberal Mind in a Conservative Age: American Intellectuals in the 1940s and 1950s* (New York: Harper & Row, 1985); Russell L. Hanson, *The Democratic Imagination in America: Conversations with Our Past* (Princeton, NJ: Princeton University Press, 1985); Wilfred M. McClay, *The Masterless: Self and Society in Modern America* (Chapel Hill: University of North Carolina Press, 1994); Howard Brick, *Age of Contradiction: American Thought and Culture in the 1960s* (Ithaca, NY: Cornell University Press, 1998); Udi Greenberg, *The Weimar Century: German Émigrés and the Ideological Foundations of the Cold War* (Princeton, NJ: Princeton University Press, 2014); Marc Stears, *Demanding Democracy: American Radicals in Search of a New Politics* (Princeton, NJ: Princeton University Press, 2010).

41. David Ciepley, *Liberalism in the Shadow of Totalitarianism* (Cambridge, MA: Harvard University Press, 2006).

42. For an excellent discussion of similar themes in the European context, see Jan-Werner Müller, *Contesting Democracy: Political Thought in Twentieth-Century Europe* (New Haven, CT: Yale University Press, 2011).

43. For a survey of the postwar development of conservatism, see George H. Nash, *The Conservative Intellectual Movement in America, since 1945* (New York: Basic Books, 1976).

44. John Dewey, *The Public and Its Problems* (New York: Holt, 1927), 144.

Chapter 2. Locating the Demos

1. For the diversity of ideas held by progressive thinkers, see Daniel T. Rodgers, "In Search of Progressivism," *Reviews in American History* 10, no. 4 (1982): 113–132.

2. In an impressive recent work, Jeffrey Green also called attention to the problem of reception in democratic politics. Jeffrey E. Green, *The Eyes of the People: Democracy in an Age of Spectatorship* (New York: Oxford University

Press, 2010). Stressing that ordinary citizens experience politics most often as spectators rather than decision makers, Green proposes to shift the normative focus of democracy from the "vocal model," which tries to make the decision-making process directly reflect citizens' voice, to the "ocular model," which focuses on regulating the public appearance of leaders as a primary means of popular empowerment. Because ordinary citizens cannot be expected to possess the knowledge, opinions, or will required for decision-making, Green contends, they can be empowered not by facilitating their involvement in decision-making but by "a maximization of leaders' subjection to public contestation above and beyond election day" (177).

I depart from Green in conceptualizing citizens' responsiveness in explicit connection with the normative criteria of the common good and political equality. I also approach ordinary citizens' apparent ignorance or indifference as a product of institutional and structural arrangements rather than an ontological condition. I examine the danger of the ontological approach in chapter 3, where I discuss Joseph Schumpeter's juxtaposition of allegedly "idealistic" classical democratic theory and his purportedly "realistic" alternative—the juxtaposition Green updates with his vocal and ocular models of democracy.

3. John Rawls, *Political Liberalism,* expanded ed. (1993; New York: Columbia University Press, 2007), 22.
4. Rawls, *Political Liberalism,* 26.
5. Rawls, 27.
6. For a discussion of the problem of "motivational deficit" in Rawls's and Habermas's theories of deliberative democracy, see Sharon R. Krause, "Desiring Justice: Motivation and Justification in Rawls and Habermas," *Contemporary Political Theory* 4, no. 4 (2005): 365–385.
7. John Rawls, *A Theory of Justice* (Cambridge, MA: Harvard University Press, 1971), 118, 127.
8. Rawls, *A Theory of Justice,* 14.
9. Rawls, 148.
10. Rawls, 121, 129.
11. John Rawls, "Justice as Fairness: Political, Not Metaphysical," *Philosophy and Public Affairs* 14, no. 3 (1985): 237n20.
12. Rawls, *Political Liberalism,* 49.
13. Rawls, 52.
14. John Rawls, *Justice as Fairness: A Restatement,* ed. Erin Kelly (Cambridge, MA: Harvard University Press, 2001), 81–82.
15. Rawls, *Political Liberalism,* 51; emphasis added.
16. Rawls sketches various stages of moral development through which a person might acquire this moral sensibility. Although Rawls insists that his moral psychology does not have to be supported by psychology, he draws on the psychological theory of Lawrence Kohlberg (who is inspired by Jean Piaget), which identifies the inclination toward universal moral principles as the highest stage of moral development. Rawls, *A Theory of Justice,* 461n8. But Kohlberg's Kantian theory has been challenged by many feminist scholars, most notably Carol Gilligan, who argues that Kohlberg's theory marginalizes feminine virtues such as care and sympathy. Lawrence Kohlberg, *The Psychology of Moral Development: Moral Stages and the Idea of Justice* (San Francisco:

Harper and Row, 1981); Carol Gilligan, *In a Different Voice: Psychological Theory and Women's Development* (Cambridge, MA: Harvard University Press, 1982).

17. For example, Amy Gutmann and Dennis Thompson, two prominent advocates of deliberative democracy, distinguish their theory from what they call "aggregative theories of democracy." According to Gutmann and Thompson's description, aggregative theories reduce democracy to voting or calculating mechanisms that question neither people's preferences nor the methods of aggregation. Amy Gutmann and Dennis Thompson, *Why Deliberative Democracy?* (Princeton, NJ: Princeton University Press, 2004), 13–21.

18. In philosophy, various approaches emphasize different aspects of affect. Some highlight cognitive capacities of affect: Martha Nussbaum, *Love's Knowledge* (Oxford: Oxford University Press, 1990); Nussbaum, *Upheavals of Thought: The Intelligence of Emotions* (Cambridge: Cambridge University Press, 2000); Robert C. Solomon, *The Passions: The Myth and Nature of Human Emotion* (Garden City, NY: Anchor Press, 1976); Jerome Neu, *A Tear Is an Intelligent Thing: The Meaning of Emotion* (New York: Oxford University Press, 2000). Others focus on how affect shapes our perception: Ronald de Sousa, *The Rationality of Emotion* (Cambridge, MA: MIT Press, 1987); Amélie Rorty, "Explaining Emotions," in *Explaining Emotions,* ed. Amélie Rorty (Berkeley: University of California Press, 1980), 139–161. Still others emphasize the visceral aspect of affect: Silvan Tomkins, "What Are Affects?" in *Shame and Its Sisters: A Silvan Tomkins Reader,* ed. Eve Kosofsky Sedgwick and Adam Frank (Durham, NC: Duke University Press, 1995), 33–74; Robert Zajonc, "On the Primacy of Affect," in *Approaches to Emotion,* ed. Klaus R. Scherer and Paul Ekman (Hillsdale, NJ: L. Erlbaum Associates, 1984), 259–270. In neuroscience, Antonio Damasio's pioneering work has brought to light the affective dimension of consciousness. Antonio R. Damasio, *Descartes' Error: Emotion, Reason, and the Human Brain* (New York: HarperCollins, 2000); Damasio, *The Feeling of What Happens: Body and Emotion in the Making of Consciousness* (New York: Harcourt, 2003); see also Joseph LeDoux, *The Emotional Brain: The Mysterious Underpinnings of Emotional Life* (New York: Simon and Schuster, 1996). In political science, scholars have attempted to incorporate affect into the theory of political judgment. Most notable is the collaborative work of George Marcus, W. Russell Neuman, and Michael Mackuen. See their two edited volumes: *The Affective Intelligence and Political Judgment* (Chicago: University of Chicago Press, 2000); *The Affect Effect: Dynamics of Emotion in Political Thinking and Behavior* (Chicago: University of Chicago Press, 2007). In the humanities, notable works include, among many others, Brian Massumi, *Parables of the Virtual* (Durham, NC: Duke University Press, 2002), esp. 23–45; Sianne Ngai, *Ugly Feelings* (Cambridge, MA: Harvard University Press, 2005); Charles Altieri, *The Particulars of Rapture: The Aesthetics of the Affects* (Ithaca, NY: Cornell University Press, 2003); William Reddy, *The Navigation of Feeling: A Framework for the History of Emotions* (Cambridge: Cambridge University Press, 2001); Rei Terada, *Feeling in Theory* (Cambridge, MA: Harvard University Press, 2001); Sara Ahmed, *The Cultural Politics of Emotion* (New York: Routledge, 2004); Jonathan Flatley, *Affective Mapping: Melancholia and the Politics of Modernism* (Cambridge, MA: Harvard University Press, 2008).

19. William E. Connolly, *Neuropolitics: Thinking, Culture, Speed* (Minneapolis:

University of Minnesota Press, 2002); Leslie Paul Thiele, *The Heart of Judgment: Practical Wisdom, Neuroscience, and Narrative* (New York: Cambridge University Press, 2006); and John Protevi, *Political Affect: Connecting the Social and the Somatic* (Minneapolis: University of Minnesota Press, 2009). For a critique, see John G. Gunnell, "Are We Losing Our Minds? Cognitive Science and the Study of Politics," *Political Theory* 35, no. 6 (2007): 704–731.

20. Tomkins, "What Are Affects?"

21. Tomkins identified nine basic affects: shame, disgust, excitement, joy, fear, anger, surprise, distress, and contempt. Silvan S. Tomkins, "Affect Theory," in *Approaches to Emotion*, 167–168.

22. The social constructivist approach in social psychology and anthropology highlights this aspect of affect. For notable accounts, see James R. Averill, "A Constructivist View of Emotion," in *Emotion: Theory, Research, and Experience*, vol. 1, *Theories of Emotion*, ed. Robert Plutchik and Henry Kellerman (New York: Academic Press, 1980), 305–339; Rom Harré, ed., *The Social Construction of Emotions* (Oxford: Blackwell, 1986); Arlie Russell Hochschild, "Emotion Work, Feeling Rules, and Social Structures," *American Journal of Sociology* 85, no. 3 (1979): 551–575; Catherine Lutz, *Unnatural Emotions* (Chicago: University Chicago Press, 1988); Richard A. Shweder and Robert Alan LeVine, eds., *Culture Theory: Essays on Mind, Self, and Emotion* (New York: Cambridge University Press, 1984). Tomkins, too, suggested that the experience of affect may be socialized, though he did not develop the idea. Tomkins, "The Socialization of Affect and the Resultant Ideo-Affective Postures Which Evoke Resonance to the Ideological Polarity," in *Exploring Affect: The Selected Writings of Silvan S. Tomkins*, ed. E. Virginia Demos (Cambridge: Cambridge University Press, 1995), 168–195.

23. Some scholars trace this ademocratic or antidemocratic subjectivity to the tradition of liberalism itself. For an insightful study that analyzes how liberalism cultivates a particular orientation toward power in citizens, turning them into clients or consumers, see Stephen L. Esquith, *Intimacy and Spectacle: Liberal Theory as Political Education* (Ithaca, NY: Cornell University Press, 1994).

24. Jean-Jacques Rousseau, *The Social Contract and Discourses*, trans. G. D. H. Cole (London: Everyman Library, 1993), 195.

25. John Stuart Mill, *On Liberty and Other Essays* (New York: Oxford University Press, 2008), 148.

26. I focus exclusively on intellectuals and their ideas. Although I switch between "progressive thinkers" and "the progressives" in the following discussion, I do not mean the Progressives—individuals who were involved with the Progressive Party and supported Theodore Roosevelt for presidency in 1912. On progressivism, see, among many others, Morton G. White, *Social Thought in America: Revolt against Formalism* (New York: Viking, 1949); Richard H. Hofstadter, *The Age of Reform* (New York: Vintage, 1955); Robert H. Wiebe, *The Search for Order, 1877–1920* (New York: Hill and Wang, 1967); James T. Kloppenberg, *Uncertain Victory: Social Democracy and Progressivism in European and American Thought, 1870–1920* (New York: Oxford University Press, 1986); Eldon J. Eisenach, *The Lost Promise of Progressivism* (Lawrence: University Press of Kansas, 1994); Daniel T. Rogers, *Atlantic Crossings: Social*

Politics in a Progressive Age (Cambridge, MA: Harvard University Press, 1998); Kevin Mattson, *Creating a Democratic Public: The Struggle for Urban Participatory Democracy during the Progressive Era* (University Park: Pennsylvania State University Press, 1998); Sidney M. Milkins and Jerome M. Mileur, eds., *Progressivism and the New Democracy* (Amherst: University of Massachusetts Press, 1999).

27. Wilfred M. McClay, *The Masterless: Self and Society in Modern America* (Chapel Hill: University of North Carolina Press, 1994), 150. See also Kloppenberg, *Uncertain Victory,* 96–99; Eisenach, *Lost Promise,* 187–193; James Livingston, "The Strange Career of the 'Social Self,'" *Radical History Review* 76 (2000): 53–79.

28. John Dewey, "The Reflex Arc Concept in Psychology," *Psychological Review* 3, no. 4 (1896): 368.

29. John Dewey, *Human Nature and Conduct* (New York: Holt, 1922), 14–15; emphasis in original.

30. Dewey, *Human Nature,* 52–53.

31. John Dewey, *Reconstruction in Philosophy* (1920; New York: Beacon Press, 1948), 30.

32. Dewey, *Human Nature,* 305.

33. Dewey, 305.

34. Dewey, 305.

35. Dewey, 305; emphasis in original.

36. Dewey, 9.

37. John Dewey, "The Lost Individual," in *Individualism Old and New* (1930; New York: Prometheus, 1999), 27, 29.

38. Dewey, "The Lost Individual," 27.

39. Dewey, 31.

40. John Dewey, *The Public and Its Problems* (New York: Holt, 1927), 207.

41. Dewey, *The Public and Its Problems,* 157.

42. Dewey, 158.

43. Dewey, 151; see also 152, 188, 197.

44. Edward A. Purcell Jr., *The Crisis of Democratic Theory: Scientific Naturalism and the Problem of Value* (Lexington: University Press of Kentucky, 1973), 197–217.

45. Purcell, *Crisis of Democratic Theory,* 201.

46. Purcell, 236.

47. The most comprehensive account of this perspective is found in Dewey, *Reconstruction in Philosophy.* For discussion, see Robert B. Westbrook, *John Dewey and American Democracy* (Ithaca, NY: Cornell University Press, 1999), 117–149.

48. Aziz Rana, "Progressivism and the Constitution," in *The Progressives' Century,* ed. Stephen Skowronek, Stephen M. Engel, and Bruce Ackerman (New Haven, CT: Yale University Press, 2016), 46.

49. This perspective was articulated most influentially in Charles A. Beard, *An Economic Interpretation of the Constitution of the United States* (New York: Macmillan, 1935).

50. This vision is encapsulated in the following remark, made by Herbert Croly, a cofounder of the *New Republic* and one of the most influential progressives.

"The new [democratic] organization will be intended first, last and always to promote political education. It must be adapted to action, but the action must merely be the decisive temporary result of widespread popular fermentation. It must have the chance to be efficient, but only for the purpose of being educational. It must be able to educate, but primarily by the road of efficient action. The new system can accomplish nothing without human energy, intelligence, sacrifice and faith, but if those qualities are present, it will make the best use of them." Herbert Croly, *Progressive Democracy* (New York: Macmillan, 1914), 283.

51. In *The Crowd,* Le Bon argued that the crowd was characterized by "impulsiveness, irritability, incapacity to reason, the absence of judgment and of the critical spirit, the exaggerations of the sentiments." He also contended that the crowd was a particular mentality that did not "always involve the simultaneous presence of a number of individuals on one spot." Gustave Le Bon, *The Crowd: A Study of the Popular Mind,* 2nd ed. (London: T. F. Unwin, 1897), 16, 2–3. For an excellent discussion of Le Bon's theory and its impact, see Robert A. Nye, *The Origins of Crowd Psychology: Gustave Le Bon and the Crisis of Mass Democracy in the Third Republic* (London: Sage, 1975).

52. Daria Frezza, *The Leader and the Crowd: Democracy in American Public Discourse, 1880–1941* (Athens: University of Georgia Press, 2007), 56–60. See also Christian Borch, *The Politics of Crowds: An Alternative History of Sociology* (Cambridge: Cambridge University Press, 2012), chap. 4; Erica G. King, "Reconciling Democracy and the Crowd in Turn-of-the-Century American Social-Psychological Thought," *Journal of the History of the Behavioral Sciences* 26, no. 4 (1990): 334–344.

53. Dewey, *Human Nature,* 61.

54. John Dewey, *Lectures in China, 1919–1920* (Honolulu: University of Hawaii Press, 1973), 96–97.

55. John Dewey, "The Crisis of Culture" (1930), in *Individualism Old and New,* 59.

56. Dewey, *The Public and Its Problems,* 146–147; see also 126.

57. John Dewey, *Freedom and Culture* (1939; New York: Prometheus, 1989), 113, 114.

58. Some asserted that Dewey's pragmatism justifies technocratic elitism, while others complained that it lacks normative criteria and is unable to guide particular political decisions. For the former view, see R. Jeffrey Lustig, *Corporate Liberalism: The Origins of Modern American Political Theory, 1890–1920* (Berkeley: University of California Press, 1982); James Neuchterlein, "The Dream of Scientific Liberalism: The New Republic and American Progressive Thought, 1914–1920," *Review of Politics* 42, no. 2 (1980): 167–190. The latter view is traced to Lewis Mumford's famous charge of "pragmatic acquiescence," in *The Golden Day* (New York: Boni and Liveright, 1926). Since then this line of criticism has been repeated in one form or another. Max Horkheimer, *Eclipse of Reason* (New York: Oxford University Press, 1947); C. Wright Mills, *Sociology and Pragmatism: The Higher Learning in America* (New York: Paine-Whitman, 1964); John Patrick Diggins, "Pragmatism and Its Limits," in *The Revival of Pragmatism,* ed. Morris Dickstein (Durham, NC: Duke University Press, 1999), 207–234.

59. Niebuhr complained that in identifying social intelligence as an engine of social change, Dewey glossed over the fact that social injustice is not an innocent by-product of ignorance but a situation deliberately created by "the economic interests of the owning class." Arguing that the impulse to further one's interests always takes precedence over reason, Niebuhr insisted that "social injustice cannot be resolved by moral and rational suasion alone." "Conflict is inevitable," he wrote, "and in this conflict power must be challenged by power." Reinhold Niebuhr, *Moral Man and Immoral Society* (1932; Louisville, KY: Westminster John Knox Press, 2001), xxvi, xxvii.

60. Jane Addams, "A Modern Lear," in *The Jane Addams Reader,* ed. Jean Bethke Elshtain (New York: Basic Books, 2002), 171; emphasis in original.

61. To be clear, this is not to uncritically endorse the progressives' vision of democracy. Numerous, though not all, progressives held deep-seated racial biases and worried that immigration might weaken the supposedly superior Anglo-Saxon traits of the American race—a scenario the sociologist Edward Ross hyperbolically called "race suicide." A large number of progressives supported the restriction on immigration, insisted on the "assimilation" of immigrants into American culture, and endorsed the continued denial of suffrage to African Americans in the South. See Frezza, *The Leader and the Crowd,* 41–51; John Higham, *Strangers in the Land: Patterns of American Nativism, 1860–1925,* 2nd ed. (New Brunswick, NJ: Rutgers University Press, 1988). Moreover, the progressives' racism intersected with gender biases in that they assigned the duty to maintain the racial stability of the Anglo-Saxon species exclusively to women, silently suppressing their political demands. Louise Michele Newman, *White Women's Rights: The Racial Origins of Feminism in the United States* (New York: Oxford University Press, 1999), chap. 2.

Chapter 3. Democracy against the Demos

1. Harry S. Truman, "Radio Report to the American People on the Potsdam Conference," August 9, 1945, in *Public Papers of the Presidents of the United States, 1945* (Washington, DC: Office of the Federal Register), 213.

2. Harry S. Truman, "Special Message to the Congress on Greece and Turkey: The Truman Doctrine," March 12, 1947, in *Public Papers of the Presidents of the United States, 1947* (Washington, DC: Office of the Federal Register), 178.

3. Abbott Gleason, *Totalitarianism: The Inner History of the Cold War* (New York: Oxford University Press, 1995), 72–88; Benjamin L. Alpers, *Dictators, Democracy, and American Public Culture: Envisioning the Totalitarian Enemy, 1920s–1950s* (Chapel Hill: University of North Carolina Press, 2003), 129–156; Udi Greenberg, *The Weimar Century: German Émigrés and the Ideological Foundations of the Cold War* (Princeton, NJ: Princeton University Press, 2014); Edward A. Purcell Jr., *The Crisis of Democratic Theory: Scientific Naturalism and the Problem of Value* (Lexington: University Press of Kentucky, 1973), 238–240; David Ciepley, *Liberalism in the Shadow of Totalitarianism* (Cambridge, MA: Harvard University Press, 2006), 183–228.

4. Carl J. Friedrich and Zbigniew K. Brzezinski, *Totalitarian Dictatorship and Democracy* (Cambridge, MA: Harvard University Press, 1956), vii.

5. As a concept, totalitarianism was subject to skepticism from the beginning, and it was widely repudiated by later scholars as an ideologically driven conceptual device to shore up liberal democracy and to vilify the Soviet Union. For earlier skepticism, see George Kennan's following remark: "When I try to picture totalitarianism to myself as a general phenomenon, what comes into my mind most prominently is neither the Nazi picture nor the Soviet picture as I have known them in the flesh, but rather the fictional and symbolic images created by such people as Orwell or Kafka or Koestler or the early Soviet satirists.... [Totalitarianism] is both a reality and a bad dream.... Its deepest reality lies strangely enough in its manifestation as a dream." George F. Kennan, "Totalitarianism in the Modern World," in *Totalitarianism: Proceedings of a Conference Held at the American Academy of Arts and Sciences, March 1953*, ed. Carl Friedrich (Cambridge, MA: Harvard University Press, 1954), 19–20. For later criticisms, see Herbert Spiro and Benjamin R. Barber, "Counter-Ideological Uses of 'Totalitarianism,'" *Political Society* 1, no. 1 (1970): 3–21; Ernest A. Menze, ed., *Totalitarianism Reconsidered* (Port Washington, NY: Kennikat Press, 1981).

6. Friedrich and Brzezinski, *Totalitarian Dictatorship and Democracy*, 13.

7. Friedrich and Brzezinski, 12.

8. Hans Kohn, *The Mind of Germany* (New York: Charles Scribner's Sons, 1960); George L. Mosse, *The Crisis of German Ideology: Intellectual Origins of the Third Reich* (New York: Grosset & Dunlap, 1964).

9. Friedrich Pollock, "State Capitalism: Its Possibilities and Limitations," *Studies in Philosophy and Social Science* 9, no. 2 (1941): 200–225; Franz Neumann, *Behemoth: The Structure and Practice of National Socialism* (New York: Oxford University Press, 1942); and a helpful discussion in William David Jones, *The Lost Debate: German Socialist Intellectuals and Totalitarianism* (Urbana: University of Illinois Press, 1999), 134–144. Cf. Friedrich A. Hayek, *The Road to Serfdom* (1944; Chicago: University of Chicago Press, 1994).

10. Eric Voegelin, "The New Science of Politics" (1952), in *Modernity without Restraint* (Columbia: University of Missouri Press, 2000), 75–242; Waldemar Gurian, "Totalitarianism as Political Religion," in *Totalitarianism,* ed. Carl J. Friedrich (New York: Grosset & Dunlap, 1964), 119–138. For a helpful discussion of Gurian, see Greenberg, *The Weimar Century,* chap. 3.

11. John H. Hallowell, *The Decline of Liberalism as an Ideology* (Berkeley and Los Angeles: University of California Press, 1943); Max Horkheimer and Theodor W. Adorno, *Dialectic of Enlightenment* (1944; Stanford, CA: Stanford University Press, 2002).

12. In his so-called long telegram, first published under a pseudonym in *Foreign Affairs* in July 1947, George Kennan identified a common tendency of totalitarianism and communism toward expansionism, catalyzing the rise of Cold War containment policies. George F. Kennan, "The Sources of Soviet Conduct," in *Foreign Relations of the United States,* vol. 6, *1946: Eastern Europe; the Soviet Union* (Washington, DC: Government Printing Office, 1969), 696–709. Later, however, Kennan became a critic of the "militarization" of Cold War foreign policy. See his "Overdue Changes in Our Foreign Policy," *Harper's,* August 1956, 27–33.

13. Graeme Duncan and Steven Lukes, "The New Democracy," *Political Studies* 11, no. 2 (1963): 156–177.

14. Joseph A. Schumpeter, *Capitalism, Socialism and Democracy* (New York: Harper, 1942), 269.

15. Robert A. Dahl, *A Preface to Democratic Theory* (Chicago: University of Chicago Press, 1956); Bernard R. Berelson, Paul F. Lazarsfeld, and William N. McPhee, *Voting: A Study of Opinion Formation in a Presidential Campaign* (Chicago: University of Chicago Press, 1954); Seymour Martin Lipset, *Political Man: The Social Bases of Politics* (Garden City, NY: Doubleday, 1960); Gabriel Almond and Sidney Verba, *The Civic Culture: Political Attitudes and Democracy in Five Nations* (Princeton, NJ: Princeton University Press, 1963); Henry Mayo, *An Introduction to Democratic Theory* (New York: Oxford University Press, 1960).

16. Sidney Hook, *Political Power and Personal Freedom* (New York: Criterion, 1959), 4, 5, 6; see also 122–123.

17. Daniel Boorstin, *The Genius of American Politics* (Chicago: University of Chicago Press, 1953), 3, 37.

18. Daniel Bell, "The End of Ideology in the West," in *The End of Ideology: On the Exhaustion of Political Ideas in the Fifties* (Cambridge, MA: Harvard University Press, 1960), 400, 405.

19. Arthur M. Schlesinger Jr., *The Vital Center: The Politics of Freedom* (1949; Boston: Houghton Mifflin, 1962), 159, 160.

20. Edward A. Purcell Jr., *The Crisis of Democratic Theory: Scientific Naturalism and the Problem of Value* (Lexington: University Press of Kentucky, 1973), 197–217; Robert Booth Fowler, *Believing Skeptics: American Political Intellectuals, 1945–1964* (Westport, CT: Greenwood Press, 1978), 121–128; John G. Gunnell, *Imagining the American Polity* (University Park: Pennsylvania State University Press, 2004), 183–217.

21. Mayo, *An Introduction to Democratic Theory*, 58.

22. Berelson et al., *Voting*, 306.

23. Almond and Verba, *The Civic Culture*, 474.

24. Dahl, *Preface*, 133. For major statements of methodological behavioralism, see Robert A. Dahl, "The Behavioral Approach in Political Science: Epitaph for a Monument to a Successful Protest," *American Political Science Review* 55, no. 4 (1961): 763–772; David Easton, *A Framework for Political Analysis* (Englewood Cliffs, NJ: Prentice Hall, 1965); Austin Ranney, ed., *Essays on the Behavioral Study of Politics* (Urbana: University of Illinois Press, 1962); Heinz Eulau, *The Behavioral Persuasion in Politics* (New York: Random House, 1963).

25. Lane Davis, "The Cost of Realism: Contemporary Restatements of Democracy," *Western Political Quarterly* 17, no. 1 (1964): 37–46; Jack L. Walker, "A Critique of Elitist Theory of Democracy," *American Political Science Review* 60, no. 2 (1966): 285–295; Christian Bay, "Politics and Pseudopolitics: A Critical Evaluation of Some Behavioral Literature," *American Political Science Review* 54, no. 1 (1965): 39–51; Charles A. McCoy and John Playford, eds., *Apolitical Politics: A Critique of Behavioralism* (New York: Thomas Y. Crowell, 1967). For discussion of the debate over behavioralism, see David Ricci, *The Tragedy of American Political Science: Politics, Scholarship, and Democracy* (New Haven, CT: Yale University Press, 1984), 133–175, 188–199; John G. Gunnell, *The Descent of Political Theory: A Genealogy of an American Vocation* (Chicago: University of Chicago Press, 1993), 221–250.

26. For an excellent discussion that traces the evolution of the theme of the

masses in twentieth-century political thought, see Richard Bellamy, "The Advent of the Masses," in *The Cambridge History of Twentieth-Century Political Thought,* ed. Terence Ball and Richard Bellamy (Cambridge: Cambridge University Press, 2003), 70–103.

27. Notable surveys of this theme include J. S. McClelland, *The Crowd and the Mob: From Plato to Canetti* (London: Routledge, 2011); Joseph V. Femia, *Against the Masses: Varieties of Anti-Democratic Thought since the French Revolution* (Oxford: Oxford University Press, 2001); Frezza, *The Leader and the Crowd;* Christian Borch, *The Politics of Crowds: An Alternative History of Sociology* (Cambridge: Cambridge University Press, 2012); Stefan Jonsson, *Crowds and Democracy: The Idea and Image of the Masses from Revolution to Fascism* (New York: Columbia University Press, 2013).

28. Schumpeter, *Capitalism, Socialism and Democracy,* 250.

29. Postwar political scientists' uncritical reception of Schumpeter provoked impassioned responses. John Plamenatz characterized Schumpeter's attack on classical democratic theory as "ignorant and inept." Schumpeter's theory is "worth discussing," fumed Plamenatz, "only because it has been taken seriously.... I suspect that not a few American political scientists, immersed in their studies of political behaviour in the largest of the Western democracies, gladly took [Schumpeter's] word for it that the theories of the past, which they were too busy to read, were so unrealistic as not to be worth reading." John P. Plamenatz, *Democracy and Illusion* (London: Longman, 1973), 96, 99.

30. Schumpeter, *Capitalism, Socialism and Democracy,* 248–249.

31. Carole Pateman, *Participation and Democratic Theory* (Cambridge: Cambridge University Press, 1970), 22–44.

32. Schumpeter, *Capitalism, Socialism and Democracy,* 121–142. For Schumpeter's intellectual debts to Weber, see Richard Swedberg, *Schumpeter: A Biography* (Princeton, NJ: Princeton University Press, 1991), 88–93.

33. Schumpeter is reported to have intimate knowledge of, and keen interest in, the so-called elite theories of democracy. "Anyone who knew Schumpeter personally can testify that he had a thorough knowledge of the theories of the elite of the late nineteenth century (Nietzsche, Pareto, Mosca, Michels, Le Bon) and took pleasure in flirting with such ideas." Eduard März, *Joseph Schumpeter: Scholar, Teacher, and Politician* (New Haven, CT: Yale University Press, 1991), 58. For an analysis of Schumpeter's economic theory through the lens of elite theory, see Esben Sloth Andersen, *Schumpeter's Evolutionary Economics: A Theoretical, Historical and Statistical Analysis of the Engine of Capitalism* (New York: Anthem, 2009), 67–97. März's remarks are quoted by Andersen at 67.

34. Schumpeter, *Capitalism, Socialism, and Democracy,* 127.

35. Schumpeter, 135.

36. Schumpeter, 214.

37. For a detailed discussion that situates Schumpeter's democratic theory in his socioeconomic thought, see John Medearis, *Joseph Schumpeter's Two Theories of Democracy* (Cambridge, MA: Harvard University Press, 2001), chaps. 3–4.

38. He also mentions Pareto, but only briefly as a way of referencing the broader trend in social sciences that stresses the importance of irrational elements in human behavior, and Graham Wallace, but only to assign him to a footnote for the reason that Wallace "fails to draw the obvious conclusion [that democracy

must radically reduce popular influence]" from his correct insight into human nature. Schumpeter, *Capitalism, Socialism, and Democracy,* 256.

39. Schumpeter, 257.
40. Schumpeter, 258.
41. Schumpeter, 260.
42. Schumpeter, 259, 260–261.
43. Schumpeter, 262.
44. Schumpeter, 283.
45. Schumpeter, 271.
46. Schumpeter, 272.
47. Schumpeter, 263.
48. Schumpeter, 270; emphasis added.
49. Berelson et al., *Voting*; Angus Campbell et al., *The American Voter* (New York: Wiley, 1960).
50. Robert A. Dahl and Charles Lindblom, *Politics, Economics and Welfare* (New York: Harper & Row, 1953), 309.
51. Mayo, *An Introduction to Democratic Theory,* 93.
52. Almond and Verba, *Civic Culture,* 474.
53. Charles E. Merriam and Harold F. Gosnell, *Non-Voting: Causes and Methods of Control* (Chicago: University of Chicago Press, 1924). See the discussion in Dorothy Ross, *The Origins of American Social Science* (New York: Cambridge University Press, 1991), 457–458. Even among postwar political scientists, a dissenting voice was not entirely absent. Criticizing the concept of rationality widely used in voting studies as too demanding, V. O. Key challenged the tendency to blame the people: "The masses do not corrupt themselves; if they are corrupt, they have been corrupted.... If a democracy tends toward indecision, decay, and disaster, the responsibility rests here, not in the mass of the people." V. O. Key, *Public Opinion and American Democracy* (New York: Alfred A. Knopf, 1961), 558.
54. Bruno Bettelheim, "Individual and Mass Behavior in Extreme Situations," *Journal of Abnormal and Social Psychology* 38, no. 4 (1943): 417–452; Leo Lowenthal, "Terror's Atomization of Man," *Commentary* 1 (January 1946): 1–8. For discussion, see Wilfred M. McClay, *The Masterless: Self and Society in Modern America* (Chapel Hill: University of North Carolina Press, 1994), 229–231; Mark Grief, *The Age of the Crisis of Man: Thought and Fiction in America, 1933–1973* (Princeton, NJ: Princeton University Press, 2015), 83–85.
55. Hannah Arendt, *The Origins of Totalitarianism* (1951; New York: Harcourt Brace Jovanovich, 1973), 315.
56. Arendt, *The Origins of Totalitarianism,* 315–316, 323–326, 329, 351–353.
57. Arendt, 437, 455.
58. Reinhold Niebuhr, *The Children of Light and the Children of Darkness: A Vindication of Democracy and a Critique of Its Traditional Defenders* (New York: Charles Scribner's Sons, 1944). For Niebuhr's impact on postwar political thought, see Arthur M. Schlesinger Jr., "Reinhold Niebuhr's Role in American Political Thought and Life," in *Reinhold Niebuhr: His Religious, Social, and Political Thought,* ed. Charles W. Kegley and Robert W. Bretall (New York: Macmillan, 1956), 126–150.
59. Daniel Bell, "America as a Mass Society: A Critique," in *The End of Ideology,* 21.
60. Mary McCarthy's response, in 1952, to Simone de Beauvoir's harsh critique of American society most vividly illustrates this view, with perhaps deliberate

flair. "The society characterized by Mlle. De Beauvoir as 'rigid,' 'frozen,' 'closed,' is in the process of great change. The mansions are torn down and the real estate 'development' takes their place: serried ranch houses, painted in pastel colors, each with its own picture window, and its garden, each equipped with deep freeze, oil furnace, and automatic washer, spring up in the wilderness. Class barriers disappear or become porous; the factory worker is an economic aristocrat in comparison with the middle-class clerk; even segregation is diminishing; consumption replaces acquisition as an incentive. The America invoked by Mlle. De Beauvoir as a country of vast inequalities and dramatic contrasts is ceasing to exist." Mary McCarthy, "Mlle. Gulliver en Amerique," *Reporter,* January 22, 1952, 36; quoted in Jackson Lears, "A Matter of Taste: Corporate Cultural Hegemony in a Mass-Consumption Society," in *Recasting America: Culture and Politics in the Age of Cold War,* ed. Lary May (Chicago: University of Chicago Press, 1989), 38.

61. Erich Fromm, *Escape from Freedom* (New York: Farrar & Rinehart, 1941), 24.
62. Fromm, *Escape from Freedom,* 36.
63. Fromm, 141.
64. Fromm, 164, 221–237.
65. Schlesinger, *The Vital Center,* 53.
66. Schlesinger, 170.
67. Schlesinger, 255, 272, 272–276. See also Erich Fromm, *The Sane Society* (New York: Rinehart & Company, 1955).
68. Schlesinger, *The Vital Center,* 56–57, quote at 56.
69. In his highly influential essay, Robert Nisbet attributed the popularity of this idea to a sudden resurgence of interest in Tocqueville in the postwar era as the foremost critic of mass democracy. Robert Nisbet, "Many Tocquevilles," *American Scholar* 46 (1976–1977): 59–75. Although Nisbet's claim was repeated by many later historians, it entirely lacked evidence and was largely a projection of his own political views. See Matthew J. Mancini, "Too Many Tocquevilles: The Fable of Tocqueville's American Reception," *Journal of the History of Ideas* 69, no. 2 (2008): 245–268.
70. Jan-Werner Müller, *Contesting Democracy: Political Thought in Twentieth-Century Europe* (New Haven, CT: Yale University Press, 2011), 126.
71. Bell, "America as a Mass Society."
72. Judith N. Shklar, *After Utopia: The Decline of Political Faith* (Princeton, NJ: Princeton University Press, 1957), 132. While Shklar is often considered a representative of postwar liberalism who shares a preoccupation with totalitarianism and a pessimistic and defensive political outlook, she was actually more skeptical about the dismissive description of the masses and more optimistic about the possibility of change than, say, Isaiah Berlin. For a nuanced reading of Shklar's political thought, see Katrina Forrester, "Hope and Memory in the Thought of Judith Shklar," *Modern Intellectual History* 8, no. 3 (2011): 591–602.
73. José Ortega y Gasset, *The Revolt of the Masses* (New York: W. W. Norton, 1932), 14, 11.
74. Ortega y Gasset, *The Revolt of the Masses,* 62.
75. Ortega y Gasset, 54.
76. Ortega y Gasset, 56.

77. Ortega y Gasset, 57.
78. Ortega y Gasset, 57–58.
79. Ortega y Gasset, 58, 63.
80. Ortega y Gasset, 76.
81. Ortega y Gasset, 73.
82. Ortega y Gasset, 17–18.
83. Karl Mannheim, "The Democratization of Culture" (1933), in *Essays on the Sociology of Culture* (London: Routledge, 1992), 173; see also Mannheim, "The Crisis of Culture in the Era of Mass-Democracies and Autarchies," *Sociological Review* 26, no. 2 (1934): 105–129.
84. Karl Loewenstein, "Militant Democracy and Fundamental Right I," *American Political Science Review* 31, no. 3 (1937): 418.
85. Theodor W. Adorno, with Else Frenkel-Brunswik, Daniel J. Levinson, and R. Nevitt Sanford, *The Authoritarian Personality* (New York: Harper, 1950), ix, x.
86. It would be more accurate to say that Adorno alerted his collaborators to this danger. *The Authoritarian Personality* was not a coherent work but a collection of individual chapters, written by different authors, with a thematic focus but without theoretical and methodological agreement. For an illuminating discussion of this background, specifically the tension between Adorno's and the other authors' theoretical approaches, see Peter E. Gordon, "The Authoritarian Personality Revisited: Reading Adorno in the Age of Trump," *boundary 2* 44, no. 2 (2017): 31–56.
87. Adorno et al., *The Authoritarian Personality*, 975.
88. Adorno et al., 1.
89. The full list of the character traits that the authors used to construct the so-called F-scale (designed to measure "implicit prefascist tendencies") included the following: conventionalism, authoritarian submission, authoritarian aggression, anti-intraception ("opposition to the subjective, the imaginative, the tender-minded"), superstition and stereotype, power and "toughness," destructiveness and cynicism, projectivity, and sex ("exaggerated concern with sexual 'goings-on'"). Adorno et al., *The Authoritarian Personality*, 226, 228.
90. Adorno et al., 457–459.
91. On how postwar social scientists widely used the psychopolitical frame and the methodology of *The Authoritarian Personality* to effectively dismiss political positions other than the centrist one, see Jamie Cohen-Cole, *The Open Mind: Cold War Politics and the Sciences of Human Nature* (Chicago: University of Chicago Press, 2014), 47–54.
92. Edward Shils, "Authoritarianism: 'Right' and 'Left,'" in *Studies in the Scope and Method of the "The Authoritarian Personality,"* ed. Richard Christie and Marie Jahoda (Glencoe, IL: Free Press, 1954), 24–49.
93. Lipset, *Political Man*, 223n5.
94. Lipset, 120.
95. Lipset, 120–121.
96. Lipset, 122.
97. Lipset, 133.
98. Lipset, 136, 137.
99. Lipset, 140.
100. Lipset, 406.

101. Lipset, 408.
102. Lipset, 408.
103. Mayo, *An Introduction to Democratic Theory*, 123.
104. Lipset, *Political Man*, 32.
105. Robert A. Dahl, "Further Reflections on the 'Elitist Theory of Democracy,'" *American Political Science Review* 60, no. 2 (1966): 301n12.
106. Berelson et al., *Voting*, 314.
107. Mayo, *An Introduction to Democratic Theory*, 123.
108. Herbert McClosky, "Consensus and Ideology in American Politics," *American Political Science Review* 58, no. 2 (1964): 376.
109. Dahl, "Further Reflections," 298.
110. Quentin Skinner, "The Empirical Theorists of Democracy and Their Critics: A Plague on Both Their Houses," *Political Theory* 1, no. 3 (1973): 298–299, 302–303.
111. Skinner, "Empirical Theorists," 302.
112. Chiding Dahl for failing to produce an alternative to classical democratic theory in his early work, Duncan and Lukes noted that the *Preface* was a "more sophisticated formulation." Duncan and Lukes, "New Democracy," 163n3. Lane Davis simply remarked that the *Preface* provided "an excellent discussion" of the deficiencies of classical democratic theory and did not make it a target of his critique. Lane Davis, "The Cost of Realism," 38n4. See also Skinner, "Empirical Theorists," 289.
113. Mark Wenman, "William E. Connolly: Resuming the Pluralist Tradition in American Political Science," *Political Theory* 43, no. 1 (2015): 54–79. Some material in the following discussion appeared in my critique of Wenman. Kyong-Min Son, "A Discordant Universe of Pluralisms: Response to Wenman," *Political Theory* 43, no. 4 (2015): 533–540.
114. Dahl, *Preface,* 3; see also 131.
115. Dahl, 48–50.
116. Dahl, 127–128, quote at 128; emphasis in original.
117. Dahl, 131.
118. Dahl, 132.
119. Dahl, 150–151.
120. Edward Shils, "Ideology and Civility: On the Politics of the Intellectual," *Sewanee Review* 66, no. 3 (1958): 472.
121. Schlesinger, *The Vital Center,* 157, 153–154, 174.
122. Bell, "Status Politics and New Anxieties: On the 'Radical Right' and Ideologies of the Fifties," in *The End of Ideology,* 112.
123. "A favorite counsel of the social scientists is that of accommodation. If two parties are in a conflict, let them, by conferring together, moderate their demands and arrive at a *modus vivendi.*... Undoubtedly there are innumerable conflicts which must be resolved in this fashion. But will a disinherited group, such as the Negroes for instance, ever win full justice in society in this fashion? Will not even its most minimum demands seem exorbitant to the dominant whites, among whom only a very small minority will regard the inter-racial problem from the perspective of objective justice? Or how are the industrial workers to [negotiate] with industrial owners, when the owners possess so much power that they can win the debate with the workers,

no matter how unconvincing their arguments? Only a very few sociologists seem to have learned [that] an adjustment of a social conflict, caused by the disproportion of power in society, will hardly result in justice as long as the disproportion of power remains." Reinhold Niebuhr, *Moral Man and Immoral Society* (1932; Louisville, KY: Westminster John Knox Press, 2001), xxviii.

124. Reinhold Niebuhr, *The Irony of American History* (New York: Scribner's Sons, 1952), 31.

125. Peter Bachrach and Morton Baratz, "Two Faces of Power," *American Political Science Review* 56, no. 4 (1962): 947–952; Bachrach and Baratz, "Decisions and Non-Decisions: An Analytical Framework," *American Political Science Review* 57, no. 3 (1963): 632–642.

126. Steven Lukes, *Power: A Radical View* (London: Macmillan, 1974).

127. Dahl, *Preface,* 89.

128. Dahl, "Further Reflections," 303.

129. Seymour Martin Lipset makes the same point: "Increased participation is un-doubtedly a good thing for democracy," he writes, but only when "the lower strata [are] brought into [the] electoral process *gradually.*" Lipset, *Political Man,* 219.

130. The line of critique I draw from Lowi and Wolff does not exclude the concerns about inclusion. Both Lowi and Wolff are explicit that postwar pluralism is not nearly as inclusive as it claims to be. Lowi points out that political plural-ism reduces "the role of government" to "one of insuring access to the most effectively organized" and "transforms the situation from one of potential competition to one of potential oligopoly." Theodore J. Lowi, *The End of Liberalism: The Second Republic of the United States* (1969; New York: W. W. Norton, 1979), 51, 58. Similarly, Wolff distinguishes "interest-conflict" and "power-conflict," arguing that in political pluralism the government "quite successfully referees the conflict among competing *powers*—any group which has already managed to accumulate a significant quantum of power.... But legitimate *interests* which have been ignored, suppressed, defeated, or which have not yet succeeded in organizing themselves for effective action, will find their disadvantageous position perpetuated through the decisions of the government." Robert Paul Wolff, "Beyond Tolerance," in *A Critique of Pure Tolerance,* by Robert Paul Wolff, Barrington Moore Jr., and Herbert Marcuse (Boston: Beacon Press, 1965), 47; emphasis in original.

131. Lowi, *The End of Liberalism,* 51.

132. David Truman, *The Governmental Process: Political Interests and Public Opinion* (New York: Knopf, 1951), chap. 16.

133. Its speculative character was noted by even the most sympathetic readers. Dahl observed that the overlapping membership theory was "popular among American political scientists" and said it was "highly plausible," but he admit-ted that "nothing except the most fragmentary evidence exists" to support it. Dahl, *Preface,* 104, 105. Similarly, Sidney Verba referred to "the widespread use of the overlapping membership theory and the paucity of empirical test-ing of it" and reported that his data "do not support the hypotheses." Sidney Verba, "Organizational Membership and Democratic Consensus," *Journal of Politics* 27, no. 3 (1965): 497.

134. Wolff, "Beyond Tolerance," 49–50.

135. Lowi, *The End of Liberalism,* 279, 291; emphasis in original.

136. Dahl, *Preface*, 51.
137. Robert A. Dahl, *Who Governs? Democracy and Power in an American City* (New Haven, CT: Yale University Press, 1961), 316.
138. Dahl, *Who Governs?*, 317.
139. Dahl, *Preface*, 132.
140. Dahl, *Preface*, 133; emphasis added.
141. Graeme Duncan and Steven Lukes, "The New Democracy," *Political Studies* 11, no. 2 (1963): 173. See also Davis, "The Cost of Realism," 39; Walker, "A Critique of Elitist Theory," 287.
142. Davis, "The Cost of Realism," 39. See also Walker, "A Critique of Elitist Theory," 288; Duncan and Lukes, "The New Democracy," 158–161.

Chapter 4. The Search for Dynamic Stability

1. David Easton, *The Political System: An Inquiry into the State of Political Science* (New York: Knopf, 1953), 303.
2. David Easton, *A Systems Analysis of Political Life* (New York: John Wiley and Sons, 1965), 427.
3. David Easton, *A Framework for Political Analysis* (Englewood Cliffs, NJ: Prentice Hall, 1965), 7. For the literature on methodological behavioralism, see chap. 3, note 24.
4. David Easton, "Walter Bagehot and Liberal Realism," *American Political Science Review* 43, no. 1 (1949): 37.
5. Easton, *Systems Analysis*, 428.
6. Ludwig von Bertalanffy, *General Systems Theory* (New York: Braziller, 1968); Talcott Parsons, "On Building Social System Theory: A Personal History," *Daedalus* 99, no. 4 (1970): 830–831, 849–851.
7. John D. Astin, "Easton I and Easton II," *Western Political Quarterly* 25, no. 4 (1972): 727.
8. William C. Mitchell, "Politics as the Allocation of Values: A Critique," *Ethics* 71, no. 2 (1961): 79–89; J. S. Sorzano, "David Easton and the Invisible Hand," *American Political Science Review* 69, no. 1 (1975): 91–106.
9. John G. Gunnell, "The Reconstitution of Political Theory: David Easton, Behavioralism, and the Long Road to System," *Journal of the History of the Behavioral Sciences* 49, no. 2 (2013): 193.
10. David Easton, "The Relevance of Biopolitics to Political Theory," in *Biology and Politics: Recent Explorations,* ed. Albert Somit (The Hague: Mouton, 1976), 237–247.
11. Easton, *Framework*, xi–xii.
12. Easton, *The Political System,* 132.
13. Easton, *Framework*, 99.
14. Easton, 100.
15. Easton, xi.
16. Easton, 128n6, 130n7. A longtime colleague and sometime collaborator of Wiener's at MIT (1941–1957), Deutsch was one of the earliest advocates of applying cybernetic frameworks to political science. He propounded his views beginning in the late 1940s. On Deutsch, see Richard L. Merritt, Bruce M.

Russett, and Robert A. Dahl, "Karl Wolfgang Deutsch," *Biographical Memoirs of the National Academy of Sciences* 80 (2001): 58–79; Karl W. Deutsch, "Some Memories of Norbert Wiener: The Man and His Thought," *IEEE Transactions on Systems, Man, and Cybernetics* 5, no. 3 (1975): 368–372. See also Ronald R. Kline, *The Cybernetics Moment* (Baltimore, MD: Johns Hopkins University Press, 2015), 143–148.

17. Robert Lilienfeld, *The Rise of Systems Theory: An Ideological Analysis* (New York: Wiley, 1978); Andrew Pickering, "Cyborg History and the World War II Regime," *Perspectives on Science* 3 (1995): 1–45; Stephen P. Waring, "Cold Calculus: The Cold War and Operations Research," *Radical History Review* 63 (1995): 29–51; Philip Mirowski, *Machine Dreams: Economics Becomes a Cyborg Science* (New York: Cambridge University Press, 2002); E. Roy Weintraub, *How Economics Became a Mathematical Science* (Durham, NC: Duke University Press, 2002); S. M. Amadae, *Rationalizing Capitalist Democracy: The Cold War Origins of Rational Choice Liberalism* (Chicago: University of Chicago Press, 2003); Paul Erickson et al., *How Reason Almost Lost Its Mind: The Strange Career of Cold War Rationality* (Chicago: University of Chicago Press, 2013); Hunter Heyck, *Age of System: Understanding the Rise of Modern Social Science* (Baltimore, MD: Johns Hopkins University Press, 2015), chaps. 3–6.

18. David F. Noble, *America by Design: Science, Technology, and the Rise of Corporate Capitalism* (New York: Alfred A. Knopf, 1977); William Thomas, *Rational Action: The Sciences of Policy in Britain and America, 1940–1960* (Cambridge, MA: MIT Press, 2015), 177–194, 243–255.

19. Ida Hoos, *Systems Analysis in Public Policy* (Berkeley: University of California Press, 1972).

20. Stuart A. Umpleby and Eric B. Dent, "The Origins and Purposes of Several Traditions in Systems Theory and Cybernetics," *Cybernetics and Systems* 30, no. 2 (1999): 79–103; George P. Richardson, *Feedback Thought in Social Science and Systems Theory* (Philadelphia: University of Pennsylvania Press, 1991), 92–317.

21. Mirowski, *Machine Dreams*; Amadae, *Rationalizing Capitalist Democracy.*

22. Donna J. Haraway, "A Cyborg Manifesto: Science, Technology, and Socialist-Feminism in the Late Twentieth Century," in *Simians, Cyborgs, and Women: The Reinvention of Nature* (New York: Routledge, 1991), 149–181; Andrew Pickering, *The Cybernetic Brain* (Chicago: University of Chicago Press, 2010).

23. Easton, *Framework*, 120.

24. Easton, 128.

25. Easton, 78.

26. Easton, 25.

27. Easton, 128.

28. Henrik P. Bang, "David Easton's Postmodern Images," *Political Theory* 26, no. 3 (1998): 281–316.

29. Easton, *Framework*, 77.

30. Easton, *Systems Analysis*, 163.

31. Easton, 224.

32. Easton, 224.

33. Easton, 269.

34. Easton, 273.

35. Easton, 279.

36. Easton, 278, 272.

37. Easton, 293–294, 320–321.

38. Easton, 316.

39. Easton, 278–342.

40. It may be worth repeating that I am focusing on the application of Easton's theory to democracy. His general theory is intended to account for all systems, from dictatorship to democracy, so various factors contributing to the persistence of a system—including not just feedback and response but also suppression of opposition, socialization, and technological innovations—should be present, though in varying degrees, in all regime types. As noted at the outset, however, Easton distinguishes democracy from dictatorship by highlighting its decentralized power structure and the authorities' responsiveness to its members' demands, so the democratic nature of a political system rests on the degree to which it maintains its stability while facilitating the political expression of its members' concerns and responding to their demands. Conversely, the more it relies on the factors that allow it to persist without being inclusive and responsive, the more suspect its democratic credentials become. The invention of railways, for example, might raise people's standard of living, but that holds true in both dictatorship and democracy; unless it directly causes a political system to be more inclusive and responsive, it is extraneous to the system's claim to be democratic.

41. Easton, *Systems Analysis,* 330.

42. Easton, 330–331.

43. Easton, 331.

44. Easton, *Framework,* 132.

45. Easton, 132.

46. Easton, 133; see also 82, 84, 87.

47. Easton, 88; emphasis added.

48. Easton, *Systems Analysis,* 330.

49. C. West Churchman, Russell L. Ackoff, and E. Leonard Arnoff, *Introduction to Operations Research* (New York: John Wiley, 1957); James Digby, "Operations Research and Systems Analysis at RAND, 1948–1967," reprinted from *OR/MS Today* 15 (December 1988), Rand N-2936-RC, http://www.rand.org/pubs/notes/N2936.html; M. Fortun and S. S. Schweber, "Scientists and the Legacy of World War II: The Case of Operations Research," *Social Studies of Science* 23, no. 4 (1993): 595–642; Maurice W. Kirby, "Operations Research Trajectories: The Anglo-American Experience from the 1940s to the 1990s," *Operations Research* 48 (2000): 661–670; Erickson et al., *How Reason Almost Lost Its Mind,* chap. 2; Thomas, *Rational Action,* 199–209.

50. Paul N. Edwards, *The Closed World: Computers and the Politics of Discourse in Cold War America* (Cambridge, MA: MIT Press, 1996), 106; emphasis in original.

51. The historian Paul Bracken reports that since the 1950s the Soviet Union has had the ability to launch nuclear cruise missiles from submarines off the Atlantic coast of the United States. That ability was dramatically enhanced by the deployment of the Yankee class of Soviet submarines in 1969, which reduced the flight time of missiles to the range of four to fifteen minutes. Paul Bracken, *The Command and Control of Nuclear Forces* (New Haven, CT: Yale University Press, 1984), 34.

52. Heyck, *Age of System,* 127–128, 132–134, quote at 128.

53. For Simon's early discussion of the "limits of rationality," see Herbert A. Simon, *Administrative Behavior: A Study of Decision-Making Processes in Administrative Organizations,* 4th ed. (1947; New York: Free Press, 1997), 93. Simon was deeply inspired by Ashby's *Design for a Brain* (1952) and declared, in a letter to Ashby, that it was "the most exciting book I have read in a decade." As early as 1952, Simon applied cybernetic or servomechanic theory to inventory control. Herbert A. Simon, "On the Application of Servomechanism Theory in the Study of Production Control," *Econometrica* 20, no. 2 (1952): 247–268. Hunter Crowther-Heyck, *Herbert A. Simon: The Bounds of Reason in Modern America* (Baltimore, MD: Johns Hopkins University Press, 2005), 186–194, Simon's letter to Ashby quoted at 189.

54. Herbert A. Simon, "A Behavioral Model of Rational Choice," *Quarterly Journal of Economics* 69, no. 1 (1955): 99.

55. Simon, "Behavioral Model," 104–106.

56. Simon, *Administrative Behavior,* 92.

57. Simon, 92.

58. Simon, 106–107.

59. For primary accounts, see David Novick, "The Department of Defense," in *Program Budgeting: Program Analysis and the Federal Budget,* ed. David Novick (Cambridge, MA: Harvard University Press, 1965), 81–117; Alain C. Enthoven and K. Wayne Smith, *How Much Is Enough? Shaping the Defense Program, 1961–1969* (New York: Harper & Row, 1971). For accounts by historians, see Gregory Palmer, *The McNamara Strategy and the Vietnam War: Program Budgeting in the Pentagon, 1960–1968* (Westport, CT: Greenwood Press, 1978); Hoos, *Systems Analysis in Public Policy,* 44–63; Amadae, *Rationalizing Capitalist Democracy,* 57–71; Stephanie Caroline Young, "Power and the Purse: Defense Budgeting and American Politics, 1947–1972" (PhD diss., University of California, Berkeley, 2010).

60. Robert T. Golembiewski and Patrick Scott, "A Micropolitical Perspective on Rational Budgeting: A Conjectural Footnote on the Dissemination of PPBS," *Public Budgeting and Financial Management* 1, no. 3 (1989): 327–370; David R. Jardini, "Out of the Blue Yonder: The Transfer of Systems Thinking from the Pentagon to the Great Society, 1961–1965," in *Systems, Experts, and Computers: The Systems Approach in Management and Engineering, World War II and After,* ed. Agatha C. Hughes and Thomas P. Hughes (Cambridge, MA: MIT Press, 2000), 320–327. This extension is widely considered a failure. Long dysfunctional, the PPBS was quietly terminated in 1971. For an early critique of the PPBS that identified its centralizing tendencies, see Aaron Wildavsky, "The Political Economy of Efficiency: Cost-Benefit Analysis, Systems Analysis, and Program Budgeting," *Public Administration Review* 26, no. 4 (1966): 292–310. For an alternative account, see Allen Schick, "A Death in the Bureaucracy: The Demise of Federal PPB," *Public Administration Review* 33, no. 2 (1973): 146–156.

61. The story of McNamara's ascent to the position of US secretary of defense is told by numerous historians. David Halberstam, *The Best and the Brightest* (New York: Ballantine Books, 1993); Fred M. Kaplan, *The Wizards of Armageddon* (New York: Simon & Schuster, 1983); Gregg F. Herken, *Counsels of War*

(New York: Knopf, 1985); Deborah Shapley, *Promise and Power: The Life and Times of Robert McNamara* (Boston: Little, Brown, 1993).

62. In an influential defense of the economic management of the military that served as a blueprint for the DoD restructuring, *The Economics of Defense in the Nuclear Age* (1960), Charles J. Hitch (whom McNamara would soon bring in as DoD comptroller) and Roland N. McKean identified this as "by far the most important reform." As they put it, "Economic analysis is concerned with objectives, not objects; it can identify efficient programs for achieving objectives only if it can relate costs to such programs." Charles J. Hitch and Roland N. McKean, *The Economics of Defense in the Nuclear Age,* RAND report R-346 (Cambridge, MA: Harvard University Press, 1960), 233. On McNamara's enthusiastic reaction to the Hitch-McKean report, see Kaplan, *The Wizards of Armageddon,* 252–53; Shapley, *Promise and Power,* 100–101.

63. Novick, "The Department of Defense"; Allen Schick, "The Road to PPB: The Stages of Budget Reform," *Public Administration Review* 26, no. 4 (1966): 243–258.

64. Enthoven and Smith, *How Much Is Enough?,* 75; Hoos, *Systems Analysis in Public Policy,* 45–46.

65. Amadae, *Rationalizing Capitalist Democracy,* 65.

66. Albert Wohlstetter, "Analysis and Design of Conflict Systems," in *Analysis for Military Decisions,* RAND report R-387, ed. E. S. Quade (Santa Monica, CA: RAND, November 1964), 126.

67. McNamara's practice generated widespread resentment among military officers and provoked heated criticism. General Curtis Lemay, writing in 1968, bitterly complained that "the military profession has been invaded by pundits who set themselves up as popular oracles on military strategy." "Today's armchair strategists, glibly writing about military matters ... can do incalculable harm. 'Experts' in a field where they have no experience, they propose strategies based upon hopes and fears rather than upon facts and seasoned judgments." Quoted in Enthoven and Smith, *How Much Is Enough?,* 78.

68. Seizing on the perceived softness of the Eisenhower administration's foreign policy, John F. Kennedy and the Democrats successfully politicized the missile gap theory, even though it was based on little hard evidence and contradicted by army and navy sources. On the missile gap debate, see Kaplan, *The Wizards of Armageddon,* 155–173. Early in his tenure as secretary of defense, McNamara seemed to have reached an independent judgment that the missile gap did not exist. In his first press briefing, he stated that the intelligence he had seen so far showed that the United States had more operational missiles than the Soviets. After his remark caused an uproar, over which he offered to resign, McNamara quickly denied his initial statement. Shapley, *Promise and Power,* 97–99.

69. Amadae, *Rationalizing Capitalist Democracy,* 59.

70. Gregory A. Daddis, *No Sure Victory: Measuring U.S. Army Effectiveness and Progress in the Vietnam War* (New York: Oxford University Press, 2011), 10.

71. Hitch and McKean, *The Economics of Defense in the Nuclear Age,* 237, 236.

72. Hitch and McKean, 223, 220.

73. Gene I. Rochlin, *Trapped in the Net: The Unanticipated Consequences of*

Computerization (Princeton, NJ: Princeton University Press, 1998), 51–73, quote at 63.

74. Andrew Pickering challenges the view that associates cybernetics with a hierarchical command-and-control framework, insisting that especially the later development of cybernetics "adumbrates and argues for a performative form of democracy, within social organizations, between social organizations, and even between people and things." Pickering, *The Cybernetic Brain*, 383. Similarly, Debora Hammond criticizes the tendency to equate systems science with "systems analysis" as developed by "the RAND Corporation and other government-funded think tanks during the Cold War years," pointing out that "the dominant current of work within the group [the Society for General Systems Research] reflects a concern with more collaborative approaches to decisionmaking [sic] within social systems." Hammond, *The Science of Synthesis*, 3.

75. Notable attempts to apply systems science to facilitate decentralized social interaction include Fred Emery and Eric Trist's account of sociotechnical system, Kenneth Boulding's work on economic organization and conflict resolution, and Stafford Beer's participatory management theory. As I discuss with reference to Beer hereafter, however, some of these thinkers were not always fully sensitive to the perils of technological and bureaucratic integration. Fred E. Emery and Eric L. Trist, "Socio-Technical Systems," in *Management Science Models and Techniques*, vol. 2, ed. C. West Churchman and Michel M. Verhulst (New York: Pergamon, 1960), 83–97; Kenneth Boulding, *The Organizational Revolution: A Study in the Ethics of Economic Organization* (New York: Harper, 1953); Boulding, *Conflict and Defense: A General Theory* (New York: Harper, 1962); Stafford Beer, *The Heart of the Enterprise* (New York: Wiley, 1979).

76. It is possible that as a system reiterates its operation over time, its members learn its goals and rules, which they may initially have taken for granted, and challenge or change them. As far as I know, Easton did not directly consider this issue. But in light of his definition of democracy, Easton might say that the more delayed or thwarted learning is in a system, the less democratic that system is. So factors that suppress its members' learning—lack of transparency, manipulation, socialization, and so on—would cast doubt on the system's democratic credentials. Then, the centralizing tendencies of systems science I identified in this section, and the normalizing and disciplinary tendencies of cybernetics I discuss in the following section, are to be viewed as a barrier to learning.

77. Easton, *Framework*, 133.

78. Edwards, *The Closed World*, 139.

79. Antoine Bousquet, "Cyberneticizing the American War Machine: Science and Computers in the Cold War," *Cold War History* 8, no. 1 (2008): 91.

80. Cybernetics originated in Norbert Wiener's wartime work on the antiaircraft predictor and was further developed and widely circulated in a series of conferences sponsored by the Josiah Macy Jr. Foundation between 1946 and 1953. On the early development of cybernetics, see Peter Galison, "The Ontology of the Enemy: Norbert Wiener and the Cybernetic Vision," *Critical Inquiry* 21, no. 1 (1994): 228–266; Steve J. Heims, *Constructing a Social Science for Postwar America: The Cybernetics Group, 1946-1953* (Cambridge, MA: MIT Press, 1991); Edwards, *The Closed World*, 180–207; Hayles, *How We Became Posthuman*, 50–83.

For a useful study that seeks to decenter the focus on Wiener and the Macy conferences by tracing the origins of cybernetics to various technologies and theoretical approaches before World War II, see David A. Mindell, *Between Human and Machine: Feedback, Control, and Computing before Cybernetics* (Baltimore, MD: Johns Hopkins University Press, 2002).

81. Arturo Rosenblueth, Norbert Wiener, and Julian Bigelow, "Behavior, Purpose and Teleology," *Philosophy of Science* 10, no. 1 (1943): 22.

82. Rosenblueth et al., 19.

83. Rosenblueth et al., 19.

84. Rosenblueth et al., 19.

85. W. Ross Ashby, *Design for a Brain: The Origin of Adaptive Behaviour,* 2nd ed. (1952; New York: John Wiley and Sons, 1960), 76. Ashby uses the term "coupling" to describe the same phenomenon in W. Ross Ashby, *An Introduction to Cybernetics* (New York: John Wiley and Sons, 1956), 48–53.

86. Ashby, *Design for a Brain,* 71–74.

87. Ashby, *Design for a Brain,* 161; Ashby, *An Introduction to Cybernetics,* 53–54.

88. Pickering, *The Cybernetic Brain,* 106.

89. Ashby, *Design for a Brain,* 79; emphasis in original.

90. Ashby, *Design for a Brain,* 41–43; Ashby, *An Introduction to Cybernetics,* 197–201.

91. Herbert A. Simon, "Notes on the Observation and Measurement of Political Power," *Journal of Politics* 15, no. 4 (1953): 504. Instead of domination, Simon described this type of joining as "unilateral coupling"; see 503n6, 507.

92. Simon, "Notes on the Observation," 503.

93. Simon, 506.

94. Simon, 504–505.

95. Norbert Wiener, *I Am a Mathematician* (Garden City, NY: Doubleday, 1956), 242–256; Pesi R. Masani, *Norbert Wiener, 1894–1964* (Basel: Birkhaƅuser, 1990), chap. 14; Pesi R. Masani and R. S. Phillips, "Antiaircraft Fire Control and the Emergence of Cybernetics," in *Norbert Wiener: Collected Works, with Commentaries,* vol. 4, ed. Pesi R. Masani (Cambridge, MA: MIT Press, 1976), 141–179; Stuart Bennett, "Norbert Wiener and Control of Anti-Aircraft Guns," *IEEE Control Systems* 14, no. 6 (1994): 58–62; Kline, *The Cybernetic Moment,* 18–26; Mindell, *Between Human and Machine,* 276–283; Galison, "The Ontology of the Enemy."

96. Wiener, quoted in Galison, "The Ontology of the Enemy," 240.

97. Wiener, quoted in Galison, 236.

98. Easton, *Systems Analysis,* 367n1.

99. Stafford Beer, *Brain of the Firm,* 2nd ed. (1972; New York: John Wiley and Sons, 1981), 247.

100. Beer, *Brain of the Firm,* 124.

101. Beer, 167.

102. Beer, 145; emphasis in original. Beer's conceptualization of learning suggests that, like veto power, learning can have a distinct meaning in the world of cybernetics. We should carefully consider the extent to which the existence of a learning mechanism in a cybernetic organization, like the less overt hierarchy of command-and-control, can conceal the fact that "mutual learning" is actually geared to meeting the whole system's goals more efficiently

and reliably, rather than genuinely accommodating its members' needs and demands.

103. Stafford Beer, *Platform for Change* (New York: Wiley, 1975), 429.

104. Beer, *Brain of the Firm*, 132; emphasis in original.

105. Werner Ulrich, "A Critique of Pure Cybernetic Reason: The Chilean Experience with Cybernetics," *Journal of Applied Systems Analysis* 8 (1981): 55; emphasis in original.

106. Pickering, *The Cybernetic Brain*, 267.

107. Pickering, 288.

108. Pickering, 278–282.

109. Pickering, 283.

110. Edward A. Purcell Jr., *The Crisis of Democratic Theory: Scientific Naturalism and the Problem of Value* (Lexington: University Press of Kentucky, 1973), 261.

111. Graeme Duncan and Steven Lukes, "The New Democracy," *Political Studies* 11, no. 2 (1963): 157.

Chapter 5. Cold War Neoliberalism and the Capitalist Restructuring of Democracy

1. Jeremy Shearmur, "Hayek's Politics," in *The Cambridge Companion to Hayek*, ed. Edward Feser (Cambridge: Cambridge University Press, 2006), 148–170; Ben Jackson, "At the Origins of Neoliberalism: The Free Economy and the Strong State, 1930–1947," *Historical Journal* 53, no. 1 (2010): 129–151; Philip Mirowski and Dieter Plehwe, eds., *The Road from Mont Pèlerin: The Making of the Neoliberal Thought Collective* (Cambridge, MA: Harvard University Press, 2009); Angus Burgin, *The Great Persuasion: Reinventing Free Markets since the Great Depression* (Cambridge, MA: Harvard University Press, 2012); Daniel Stedman Jones, *Masters of the Universe: Hayek, Friedman, and the Birth of Neoliberal Politics* (Princeton, NJ: Princeton University Press, 2012).

2. Wendy Brown, *Undoing the Demos: Neoliberalism's Stealth Revolution* (New York: Zone Books, 2015), 18; see also Brown, "Neo-liberalism and the End of Liberalism," *Theory and Event* 7, no. 1 (2003).

3. Antonio Y. Vázquez-Arroyo, "Liberal Democracy and Neoliberalism: A Critical Juxtaposition," *New Political Science* 30, no. 2 (2008): 127–159.

4. Hayek first convened the society in 1947 and served as its first president between 1948 and 1960. For an inside history of the Mont Pèlerin Society, see R. M. Hartwell, *A History of the Mont Pelerin Society* (Indianapolis: Liberty Fund, 1995). For the powerful role the society played in the production and global dissemination of neoliberalism, see John L. Kelley, "The Revitalization of Market Liberalism," in *Bringing the Market Back In: The Political Revitalization of Market Liberalism* (Basingstoke: Palgrave Macmillan, 1997), 31–80; Dieter Plehwe and Bernhard Walpen, "Between Network and Complex Organization: The Making of Neoliberal Knowledge and Hegemony," in *Neoliberal Hegemony: A Global Critique*, ed. Dieter Plehwe, Bernhard Walpen, and Gisela Neunhöffer (New York: Routledge, 2006), 27–50.

5. F. A. Hayek, *Hayek on Hayek: An Autobiographical Dialogue*, ed. Stephen Kresge and Leif Wenar (Chicago: University of Chicago Press, 1994), 99, 102–103.

6. Alan Ebenstein, *Hayek's Journey: The Mind of Friedrich Hayek* (New York: Palgrave Macmillan, 2003), 141.

7. Ebenstein, *Hayek's Journey,* 187–190.

8. Hayek, quoted in Ebenstein, *Hayek's Journey,* 141.

9. Upon reading *Serfdom,* John Maynard Keynes made this criticism in his well-known letter to Hayek. Keynes wrote: "As soon as you admit that the extreme is not possible, and that a line has to be drawn, you are, on your own argument, done for, since you are trying to persuade us that so soon as one moves in the planned direction you are necessarily launched on the slippery path which will lead you in due course over the precipice." Quoted in Jones, *Masters of the Universe,* 67. Jeremy Shearmur persuasively argues that Hayek was indeed preoccupied with this issue in the period between *Serfdom* and *The Constitution of Liberty.* Jeremy Shearmur, "Hayek, Keynes, and the State," *History of Economics Review* 26, no. 1 (1997): 68–82.

10. Friedrich A. Hayek, *Law, Legislation, and Liberty,* vol. 3, *The Political Order of a Free People* (Chicago: University of Chicago Press, 1979), xii (hereafter cited as *Political Order*).

11. Friedrich A. Hayek, *Law, Legislation, and Liberty,* vol. 2, *The Mirage of Social Justice* (Chicago: University of Chicago, 1976), xi–xiii (hereafter cited as *The Mirage of Social Justice*); Hayek, *Political Order,* xi; Ebenstein, *Hayek's Journey,* 188–189.

12. Hayek, *The Road to Serfdom,* xlv. For the context of Hayek's political endeavor, see Jan-Werner Müller, *Contesting Democracy: Political Thought in Twentieth-Century Europe* (New Haven, CT: Yale University Press, 2011), 150–154; Perry Anderson, *Spectrum* (London: Verso, 2005), 3–28.

13. Hayek, *The Road to Serfdom,* 6.

14. Hayek, 63.

15. *The Road to Serfdom* made the front page of both the *New York Times* and the *New York Herald Tribune* immediately after its publication. *Reader's Digest* ran a condensed version in April 1945, and the Book of the Month Club distributed some 600,000 copies of the condensation. Milton Friedman, "Introduction," in *The Road to Serfdom,* by Friedrich A. Hayek, fiftieth anniversary edition (1944; Chicago: University of Chicago Press, 1994), xix. For Hayek's personal recollection, see Hayek, *Hayek on Hayek,* 102–105. For discussion, see Ebenstein, *Hayek's Journey,* 120–121; Burgin, *The Great Persuasion,* 87–93.

16. Hayek, *Hayek on Hayek,* 102–103; Hayek, *Law, Legislation, and Liberty,* vol. 1, *Rules and Order* (Chicago: University of Chicago Press, 1973), 58 (hereafter cited as *Rules and Order*); Hayek, "Preface to the 1976 Reprint Edition," in *The Road to Serfdom,* xxiv.

17. Hayek, *The Road to Serfdom,* 41.

18. Hayek, 42.

19. Hayek, 43.

20. Hayek, 44.

21. Hayek, 133, 133–134. Later, however, Hayek regretted these concessions. Writing in 1976, he said that "I had not wholly freed myself from all the current interventionist superstitions, and in consequence still made various concessions which I now think unwarranted." Hayek, "Preface to the 1976 Reprint Edition," in *The Road to Serfdom,* xxiv.

22. Hayek, "Preface," xlvi.
23. Hayek recalled that *Serfdom* was first conceived in a memorandum he wrote in 1933 for Lord Beveridge, when he was the director of LSE. Hayek, *Hayek on Hayek,* 102.
24. Hayek, *The Road to Serfdom,* 201–202.
25. Hayek, 35.
26. Hayek, 29, 31.
27. F. A. Hayek, *The Collected Works of F. A. Hayek,* vol. 9, *Contra Keynes and Cambridge,* ed. Bruce Caldwell (Chicago: University of Chicago Press, 1995), 127–128.
28. F. A. Hayek, ed., *Collectivist Economic Planning: Critical Studies of the Possibilities of Socialism* (London: Routledge and Kegan Paul, 1935). For a detailed discussion of this debate, see Bruce Caldwell, "Hayek and Socialism," *Journal of Economic Literature* 35, no. 4 (1997): 1858–1866.
29. F. A. Hayek, "Economics and Knowledge" (1936), in *Individualism and Economic Order* (Chicago: University of Chicago Press, 1948), 50–51; emphasis in original.
30. Friedrich A. Hayek, "The Use of Knowledge in Society" (1945), in *Individualism and Economic Order,* 77–78.
31. Hayek, *Hayek on Hayek,* 80.
32. A number of scholars have noted that "Economics and Knowledge" marked a turning point in the development of Hayek's ideas. Bruce Caldwell, "Hayek's Transformation," *History of Political Economy* 20, no. 4 (1988): 513–541; Meghnad Desai, "Equilibrium, Expectations, and Knowledge," in *Hayek, Co-Ordination, and Evolution: His Legacy in Philosophy, Politics, Economics, and the History of Ideas,* ed. Jack Birner and Rudy van Zijp (London: Routledge, 1994), 32–43; Andrew Gamble, "Hayek on Knowledge, Economics, and Society," in *The Cambridge Companion to Hayek,* 113–116; Burgin, *The Great Persuasion,* 50–51.
33. Hayek, *The Road to Serfdom,* 55.
34. Hayek, 56; see also 41.
35. Hayek, 45; see also 41, 43.
36. Hayek, 81; see also 89.
37. Hayek, 64.
38. Hayek, 69. Milton Friedman later reiterated this point almost verbatim in claiming that the capitalist market is more favorable to individual freedom and social stability than political institutions. "Fundamental differences in basic values can seldom if ever be resolved at the ballot box; ultimately they can only be decided, though not resolved, by conflict.... [Thus] Every extension of the range of issues for which explicit agreement is sought strains further the delicate threads that hold society together.... The strain is least if agreement for joint action need be reached only on a limited range of issues." Milton Friedman, *Capitalism and Freedom* (Chicago: University of Chicago Press, 1962), 23–24.
39. Hayek, *The Road to Serfdom,* 69, 75.
40. Hayek, 75.
41. Alvin H. Hansen, "The New Crusade against Planning," *New Republic* 112 (January 1, 1945): 11–12; Carl J. Friedrich, review of *The Road to Serfdom, American Political Science Review* 39, no. 3 (1945): 577–578; T. V. Smith, review of *The Road to Serfdom, Ethics* 55, no. 3 (1945): 224.

42. Hayek, *The Road to Serfdom*, 16.
43. Hayek, 77–78.
44. Hayek, 78.
45. Hayek, 152.
46. Hayek, 153.
47. Hayek, 166.
48. Hayek, 30n2.
49. John Dewey, "Toward a New Individualism," in *Individualism Old and New* (1930; New York: Prometheus, 1999), 40, 43; originally published in *New Republic* 62 (February 19, 1930).
50. Dewey, "Toward a New Individualism," 44.
51. John Dewey, "Capitalistic or Public Socialism?" in *Individualism Old and New*, 53–54, 55–56; Originally published in *New Republic* 62 (March 5, 1930).
52. See, e.g., George Soule (who became, along with Bruce Bliven, the *New Republic*'s editor in 1930 and was chiefly responsible for its economic view), "How Long Prosperity?" *New Republic* 45 (February 3, 1926): 289–291; "Are Depressions Avoidable?" *New Republic* 65 (February 11, 1931): 342–344; "The Boon of Falling Prices," *New Republic* 50 (May 11, 1927): 328–330; "Gold and the Industrial Depression," *New Republic* 64 (November 12, 1931): 339–343.
53. Hayek, *The Road to Serfdom*, 97.
54. Daniel Bell, *Marxian Socialism in the United States* (1952; Ithaca, NY: Cornell University Press, 1967), 134; Matthew Josephson, *Infidel in the Temple* (New York, 1967); James Burkhart Gilbert, *Writers and Partisans: A History of Literary Radicalism in America* (New York: Wiley, 1968); Arthur A. Ekirch Jr., *Ideologies and Utopias: The Impact of the New Deal on American Thought* (Chicago: Quadrangle, 1969); Richard H. Pells, *Radical Visions and American Dreams: Culture and Social Thought in the Depression Years* (New York: Harper & Row, 1973).
55. Stuart Chase, *A New Deal* (New York: Macmillan, 1933), 1.
56. Chase, *A New Deal*, 22–23.
57. Chase, 188.
58. Chase, 211.
59. Chase, 217.
60. On critiques of the New Deal, see Ekirch, *Ideologies and Utopia*, 177–207; Pells, *Radical Visions and American Dreams*, 78–86. On the Spanish Civil War's impact on intellectuals, see Ekirch, *Ideologies and Utopia*, 218–222; Josephson, *Infidel in the Temple*, 405–436. On the rediscovery of American values in the face of the looming war, see Pells, *Radical Visions and American Dreams*, 310–319.
61. Bell, *Marxian Socialism*, 150–152; Ekirch, *Ideologies and Utopia*, 230–235; Josephson, *Infidel in the Temple*, 456–463; Pells, *Radical Visions and American Dreams*, 347–351.
62. Thomas R. Maddux, "Red Fascism, Brown Bolshevism: The American Image of Totalitarianism in the 1930s," *Historian* 40, no. 1 (1977): 85–103; Les K. Adler and Thomas G. Paterson, "Red Fascism: The Merger of Nazi Germany and Soviet Russia in the American Image of Totalitarianism, 1930s–1950s," *American Historical Review* 75, no. 4 (1970): 1046–1064; Abbott Gleason, *Totalitarianism: The Inner History of the Cold War* (New York: Oxford University Press, 1995), 38–71.

63. "Manifesto," *Nation*, May 27, 1939, 626.

64. "Liberty and Common Sense," *New Republic* 99 (May 31, 1939): 89, 89–90.

65. "Correspondence," *New Republic* 100 (October 25, 1939): 344. I was directed to these exchanges by Gleason, *Totalitarianism*, 47.

66. Max Eastman, *Stalin's Russia and the Crisis of Socialism* (New York: W. W. Norton, 1940); Hayek, *The Road to Serfdom*, 31–32, 115–116.

67. James Burnham, *The Managerial Revolution* (New York: John Day, 1941); Hayek, *The Road to Serfdom*, 114n1.

68. Walter Lippmann, *An Inquiry into the Principles of the Good Society* (Boston: Little, Brown, 1937), 106.

69. Lippmann, *Inquiry into the Principles*, vii. Lippmann sent the proofs of *The Good Society* to Hayek, thanking him for his work. Lippmann's letter to Hayek, March 12, 1937, is quoted in Burgin, *The Great Persuasion*, 59.

70. Hayek claimed that the doctrine of individualism he espoused is rooted in the foundations of Western civilization laid by Christianity and Greek and Roman thoughts. But his primary reference was to modern liberalism, which he associated with John Locke, David Hume, Adam Smith, Lord Acton, and Alexis de Tocqueville. Hayek, *The Road to Serfdom*, 16–17.

71. Hayek, 48.

72. Perhaps anticipating the criticism that he makes individual liberty a "matter of expediency," Hayek inserted an apologetic note in the introduction of *The Constitution of Liberty*. Proclaiming that individual liberty is an "indisputable ethical presupposition," he insisted that to "convince those who do not already share our moral suppositions," a further defense is warranted. "We must show that individual liberty is the source and condition of most moral values. What a free society offers to the individual is much more than what he would be able to do if only he were free." F. A. Hayek, *The Constitution of Liberty* (1960; Chicago: University of Chicago, 2011), 52–53.

73. Friedrich A. Hayek, "Individualism: True and False" (1945), in *Individualism and Economic Order*, 6.

74. Hayek, "Individualism," 26.

75. Hayek, 25, 26; see also Hayek, *The Constitution of Liberty*, 213–214.

76. Hayek, *The Constitution of Liberty*, 199.

77. Hayek, 200–201.

78. Hayek, 221.

79. Hayek, 218.

80. Hayek, 220, 228.

81. Hayek, 210, 221.

82. Hayek, 223.

83. Bruno Leoni, *Freedom and the Law* (1961; Indianapolis: Liberty Fund, 1991); Ronald Hamowy, "Law and the Liberal Society: F. A. Hayek's Constitution of Liberty," *Journal of Libertarian Studies* 2, no. 4 (1978): 287–297.

84. Friedrich A. Hayek, "Freedom and Coercion: Some Comments on a Critique of Mr. Ronald Hamowy" (1961), in *Studies in Philosophy, Politics, and Economics* (Chicago: University of Chicago Press, 1967), 348–349. In *Law, Legislation, and Liberty*, Hayek more explicitly acknowledged a "defect" in his formulation of this issue. Hayek, *Rules and Order*, 110n10.

85. Hayek, *The Constitution of Liberty*, 216.

86. Hayek, *Rules and Order,* 37.
87. Hayek, 43–44.
88. Hayek, 44.
89. Hayek, 45.
90. Hayek, *The Mirage of Social Justice,* 109.
91. Hayek, 112.
92. Hayek, 112.
93. Hayek, 109.
94. Hayek, *The Road to Serfdom,* 42.
95. Hayek, *The Mirage of Social Justice,* 115–116.
96. Hayek, 166; see also 206–207.
97. Hayek, "Individualism: True and False," 29.
98. Hayek, *The Constitution of Liberty,* 167.
99. Hayek, *The Mirage of Social Justice,* 113.
100. Hayek, 4.
101. Hayek, 132. As Hayek acknowledges, there is an interesting parallel between Hayek's argument here and John Rawls's famous concept of the original position in *A Theory of Justice* (1971). Indeed, Hayek states that Rawls and he "agree on what is to me the essential point." To demonstrate that his *critique* of social justice aligns with Rawls's *defense* of it, Hayek cites Rawls's remark that the principles of justice "do not seek specific distributions of desired things as just" but rather "define the crucial constraints which institutions and joint activities must satisfy if persons engaging in them are to have no complaints against them" (xii, 38n19, 100). It is curious that Hayek does not consider the stark differences in their substantive argument equally essential. Although Rawls's original position requires individuals to extrapolate general rules concerning the basic structure of society independently of their particular positions, it results in a vigorous defense of equality and welfare measures. While I cannot go into detail here, an important source of difference is that Rawls and Hayek presuppose different political subjectivities and, as a result, envision a different kind of social cooperation. I discuss Rawls's conceptualization of subjectivity and its limitations in chapter 2.
102. Hayek, *The Constitution of Liberty,* 148–165; *The Mirage of Social Justice,* 62–85.
103. Hayek, *The Mirage of Social Justice,* 143.
104. Hayek, *Political Order,* 160.
105. Hayek, 161–162.
106. In his review of *The Road to Serfdom,* Joseph Schumpeter chided Hayek for neglecting that the very working of capitalism politically empowered the masses. Schumpeter pointed out that, without confronting the reality of mass democracy, Hayek's appeal to individual initiative and self-reliance had no chance of being realized. Joseph A. Schumpeter, review of *The Road to Serfdom, Journal of Political Economy* 54, no. 3 (1946): 270. As he developed a positive theory of neoliberalism in his later works, Hayek paid far more attention to the issue of democracy. While Schumpeter and Hayek approached capitalism with a different focus (heroic entrepreneurs versus the diffuse process of information processing), they converged in the view that democracy needs to be restrained for capitalism to work. As discussed in chapter 3, Schumpeter was more openly autocratic in his proposals, partly because he

placed more emphasis on capitalism's tendency to expand democracy and to destabilize itself. But as we will see shortly, despite his professed contrary commitment, Hayek too was drawn to authoritarian measures.

107. Hayek, *The Constitution of Liberty,* 148, 155.
108. Hayek, *Political Order,* 165.
109. Hayek, *The Mirage of Social Justice,* 147.
110. However, he was so troubled by what he perceived as the abuse of the term "democracy" that he suggested another name, "demarchy," for a majority rule that does not breach the rules of the market. Hayek, *Political Order,* 38–40.
111. Hayek, 98, 5.
112. Hayek, 151. Hayek outlines the institutional setup of his constitutional democracy on pp. 105–127.
113. Hayek, 109. See also Hayek, *The Constitution of Liberty,* 199–231.
114. Hayek, *Political Order,* 9.
115. Hayek, 11–13. Despite his critique of interest groups Hayek was remarkably cavalier about the problem of monopoly. According to him, monopoly power does not necessarily translate into political power, and even when it does, individual firms are much less likely to exercise political influence to interfere with the working of the market than other civil society groups (77–99).
116. Hayek, 150.
117. Hayek, 166.
118. Hayek, 75–76.
119. Hayek, 76.
120. Hayek, 77.
121. Hayek, 168; emphasis in original.
122. Hayek, 77.
123. Hayek, *Rules and Order,* 45.
124. Hayek, 47.
125. Arthur M. Schlesinger Jr., *The Vital Center: The Politics of Freedom* (1949; Boston: Houghton Mifflin, 1962), xii.
126. Hayek, 47.
127. Hayek, 153.
128. Daniel Bell, "Is There a Ruling Class in America?" in *The End of Ideology: On the Exhaustion of Political Ideas in the Fifties* (Cambridge, MA: Harvard University Press, 1960), 61.
129. Bell, "Is There a Ruling Class," 68, 69; emphasis in original.
130. Seymour Martin Lipset, *Political Man: The Social Bases of Politics* (Garden City, NY: Doubleday, 1960), 308.
131. Schlesinger, *The Vital Center,* 153–154.
132. Daniel Bell, "The End of Ideology in the West," in *The End of Ideology,* 405; emphasis in original.
133. Daniel Bell, "Status Politics and New Anxieties," in *The End of Ideology,* 121, 103.
134. All quotations in this paragraph come from Franklin D. Roosevelt, "State of the Union Address," January 6, 1941, Franklin D. Roosevelt Significant Documents, box 1, FDR 30, the FDR Library, http://www.fdrlibrary.marist.edu/archives /collections/franklin/?p = collections/findingaid&id = 510&rootcontentid = 1 44823&q = four + freedoms#id144856.

135. All quotations in this paragraph come from Harry S. Truman, "Address on Foreign Economic Policy, Delivered at Baylor University," March 6, 1947, Harry S. Truman Library and Museum, https://www.trumanlibrary.gov/library/public-papers/52 /address-foreign-economic-policy-delivered-baylor-university.

136. The distance between the perspectives expressed by FDR and Truman is significant but should not be overstated, especially in terms of policy. The totalitarianism-communism equation emerged as a potent political force in the mid- and late 1930s and exerted enormous pressure on the New Deal. Under that pressure, the New Deal veered from its earlier focus on direct regulation of the economy to the hitherto marginal Keynesian position approaching the government as a compensatory, not a regulatory, agency. Accompanied by the demise of a whole range of left economic visions, this change had effectively placed the Keynesian variant of the New Deal at the far left of the ideological spectrum. For a detailed account of the New Deal's internal transformation, see Alan Brinkley, *The End of Reform: New Deal Liberalism in Recession and War* (New York: Vintage, 1996).

137. For the debate over the Full Employment Act, see Brinkley, *The End of Reform,* 259–264. For antilabor provisions of the Taft-Hartley Act, see Elizabeth A. Fones-Wolf, *Selling Free Enterprise: The Business Assault on Labor and Liberalism* (Urbana: University of Illinois Press, 1994), 42–44; Howell John Harris, *The Right to Manage: Industrial Relations Policies of American Business in the 1940s* (Madison: University of Wisconsin Press, 1982), 105–158.

138. Nelson Lichtenstein, "From Corporatism to Collective Bargaining: Organized Labor and the Eclipse of Social Democracy in the Postwar Era," in *The Rise and Fall of the New Deal Order, 1930–1980,* ed. Steve Fraser and Gary Gerstle (Princeton, NJ: Princeton University Press, 1989), 144.

139. A massive literature identifies mass consumption as a defining feature of postwar America. A good place to start is Robert Griffith, "The Selling of America: The Advertising Council and American Politics, 1942–1960," *Business History Review* 57, no. 3 (1983): 388–412; Griffith, "Forging America's Postwar Order: Domestic Politics and Political Economy in the Age of Truman," in *The Truman Presidency,* ed. Michael J. Lacey (New York: Cambridge University Press, 1994); Elaine Tyler May, *Homeward Bound: American Families in the Cold War Era* (New York: Basic Books, 1998), chap. 7; Gary Cross, *An All-Consuming Century: Why Commercialism Won in Modern America* (New York: Columbia University Press, 2000), chaps. 3–4; Lizabeth Cohen, *A Consumer's Republic: The Politics of Mass Consumption in Postwar America* (New York: Knopf, 2003); Cynthia Lee Henthorn, *From Submarines to Suburbs: Selling a Better America, 1939–1959* (Athens: Ohio University Press, 2006). For a work that traces the construction of the consumer as a central figure of American liberalism from the 1880s to the 1940s, see Kathleen G. Donohue, *Freedom from Want: American Liberalism and the Idea of the Consumer* (Baltimore, MD: Johns Hopkins University Press, 2003).

140. Alan Wolfe makes a similar observation. Identifying the postwar formation of the political alliance around the promise of perpetual economic growth—which he calls the "growth coalition"—as an important turning point in American history, Wolfe suggests that it established a politics that is subservient to the demand of constant economic growth while unable to tackle fundamental

questions about the purpose of social life. Alan Wolfe, *America's Impasse: The Rise and Fall of the Politics of Growth* (New York: Pantheon, 1981).

141. David Potter, *People of Plenty: Economic Abundance and the American Character* (Chicago: University of Chicago Press, 1954), 112.

142. Potter, *People of Plenty,* 115.

143. Potter, 123.

144. Potter, 122, 118, 112–113.

145. Schlesinger, *The Vital Center,* 182.

146. Arthur Schlesinger Jr., "The New Mood in Politics" (1960), in *The Politics of Hope and The Bitter Heritage: American Liberalism in the 1960s* (1963; Princeton, NJ: Princeton University Press, 2007), 112.

147. Schlesinger, 113.

148. Schlesinger, 116–117.

149. Schlesinger, 118–119, 119.

150. Daniel Bell, "Work and Its Discontents: The Cult of Efficiency in America," in *The End of Ideology,* 252.

151. Bell, "Work and Its Discontents," 262, 263, 264.

152. Bell, 254, 255, 269.

153. Robert M. Collins, *More: The Politics of Economic Growth in Postwar America* (New York: Oxford University Press, 2000), 17–39.

154. Cohen, *A Consumer's Republic,* 122–165; Kenneth T. Jackson, *Crabgrass Frontier: The Suburbanization of the United States* (New York: Oxford University Press, 1985), 190–218.

155. Louis Roland Hyman, *Debtor Nation: The History of America in Red Ink* (Princeton, NJ: Princeton University Press, 2011), 132–172.

156. David Riesman, "Preface to the 1961 Edition," in *The Lonely Crowd: A Study of the Changing Social Character,* by David Riesman, with Nathan Glazer and Reuel Denny (1950; New Haven, CT: Yale University Press, 2001), lvii, lvi, lxvi. For Riesman's earlier arguments about these issues, see *The Lonely Crowd,* 213–224 (veto groups), 171 (apathy), 18 (economic abundance), 286–301 (leisure and play).

157. Riesman, "Preface to the 1961 Edition," lv.

158. Riesman, lx, lxi.

159. David Riesman, "Twenty Years After—a Second Preface," in Riesman, *The Lonely Crowd,* xxvi.

160. Riesman, "Twenty Years After," xxvii.

161. Riesman, xxvii, xxvii–xxviii.

162. Fred Hirsch, *Social Limits to Growth* (Cambridge, MA: Harvard University Press, 1976), 3.

163. Hirsch, *Social Limits to Growth,* 10.

164. Hirsch, 12.

165. Hirsch, 80.

166. With this question, I do not imply that there must be a single set of overarching principles for all social values. As Michael Walzer argues, there are—and should be—various value spheres, and it is desirable that the members of each sphere determine their own priorities. Michael Walzer, *Spheres of Justice: A Defense of Pluralism and Equality* (New York: Basic Books, 1983). I do mean that there must be continual public discussion about which social values

bear directly on citizenship, namely, political equality, and how those values ought to be organized.

167. Richard M. Nixon, "What Freedom Means to Us," *Vital Speeches of the Day* 25, no. 22 (1959): 677. For the widespread use of the same rhetoric in mass media, see Andrew L. Yarrow, "Selling a New Vision of America to the World: Changing Messages in Early U.S. Cold War Print Propaganda," *Journal of Cold War Studies* 11, no. 4 (2009): 3–45.

Chapter 6. The Erosion of Democratic Attunement and the Crisis of Democracy

1. In this respect, I agree with Margaret Canovan's assessment that "virtually the entire agenda of Arendt's political theory was set" by her reflections on totalitarianism, though we differ in our view as to the exact nature of that agenda. Margaret Canovan, *Hannah Arendt: A Reinterpretation of Her Political Thought* (Cambridge: Cambridge University Press, 1992), 7; hereafter cited as *Reinterpretation*. See also Mary Dietz, "Arendt and the Holocaust," in *The Cambridge Companion to Hannah Arendt*, ed. Dana Villa (Cambridge: Cambridge University Press, 2000), 86–109.

2. Susan Bickford, *The Dissonance of Democracy: Listening, Conflict, and Citizenship* (Ithaca, NY: Cornell University Press, 1996), 55–93; Patchen Markell, "The Rule of the People: Arendt, *Archê,* and Democracy," *American Political Science Review* 100, no. 1 (2006): 1–14; Leslie Paul Thiele, "The Ontology of Action: Arendt and the Role of Narrative," *Theory and Event* 12, no. 4 (2009); Ella Myers, *Worldly Ethics: Democratic Politics and Care for the World* (Durham, NC: Duke University Press, 2013), 85–138; Jade Larissa Schiff, *Burdens of Political Responsibility: Narrative and the Cultivation of Responsiveness* (New York: Cambridge University Press, 2014), 50–84.

3. Hannah Arendt, *On Revolution* (1965; New York: Penguin, 2006), 262.

4. Arthur M. Schlesinger Jr., *The Vital Center: The Politics of Freedom* (1949; Boston: Houghton Mifflin, 1962), 248.

5. Bernard Rosenberg, "Mass Culture in America," in *Mass Culture: Popular Arts in America,* ed. Bernard Rosenberg and David Manning White (Glencoe, IL: Free Press, 1957), 9.

6. Schlesinger, *The Vital Center,* 87.

7. Daniel Bell, "The Theory of Mass Society: A Critique," in *The End of Ideology: On the Exhaustion of Political Ideas in the Fifties* (Cambridge, MA: Harvard University Press, 1960), 25, 28.

8. Sheldon S. Wolin, "Hannah Arendt: Democracy and the Political," *Salmagundi* 60 (Spring–Summer 1983): 3, 4. For a good review of Wolin's political thought, see Antonio Y. Vázquez-Arroyo, "Sheldon S. Wolin and the Historicity of Political Thought," *Good Society* 24, no. 2 (2015): 146–163.

9. Wilfred M. McClay, *The Masterless: Self and Society in Modern America* (Chapel Hill: University of North Carolina Press, 1994), 217–218.

10. McClay, *The Masterless,* 217.

11. Hannah Arendt, "The Jew as Pariah" (1944); "Zionism Reconsidered" (1944); "Peace Armistice in the Near East?" (1950), in *The Jew as Pariah: Jewish Identity*

and Politics in the Modern Age, ed. Ron H. Feldman (New York: Grove Press, 1978), 76, 152, 214.

12. Hannah Arendt, *The Origins of Totalitarianism* (1951; New York: Harcourt Brace Jovanovich, 1973), 144; see also 156.
13. Arendt, *Origins,* 106–117, 155, 314–315.
14. Arendt, 155.
15. Arendt, 106–107.
16. Arendt, *On Revolution,* 262.
17. Arendt, *Origins,* 149.
18. Arendt, 126.
19. Arendt, 139.
20. Arendt, 140.
21. Arendt, 141.
22. Arendt, 137.
23. Arendt, 143; see also 145–146.
24. Arendt, 144, 146.
25. Arendt, 147–149, quote at 147.
26. Arendt, 151.
27. Arendt, 151, 156.
28. Arendt, 314–315.
29. Wolin, "Hannah Arendt," 6.
30. Arendt, *Origins,* 156.
31. Arendt, 316.
32. Arendt, 313.
33. Arendt, 317.
34. Arendt, 311.
35. Arendt, 352.
36. Arendt, 316, 307–308, 347–348.
37. Eric Voegelin, "The Origins of Totalitarianism," *Review of Politics* 15, no. 1 (1953): 68–76; David Riesman, "Some Observations on the Limits of Totalitarian Power" (1952), in *Individualism Reconsidered* (New York: Free Press, 1954), 414–425. For a discussion of Riesman's otherwise admiring critique of Arendt's theory of totalitarianism, see Peter Baehr, "Of Politics and Social Science: 'Totalitarianism' in the Debate of David Riesman and Hannah Arendt," *European Journal of Political Theory* 3, no. 2 (2004): 191–217. See also Richard H. Pells, *The Liberal Mind in a Conservative Age: American Intellectuals in the 1940s and 1950s* (New York: Harper & Row, 1985), 95; Richard H. King, *Arendt and America* (Chicago: University of Chicago Press, 2015), 60–63.
38. Arendt, *Origins,* 316, 317.
39. Arendt, 352.
40. Digitized Hannah Arendt Papers at the Library of Congress, Speeches and Writings File, 1923–1975, n.d., Outlines and Research Memoranda, 1946, n.d. (2 of 2 folders), http://memory.loc.gov/ammem/arendthtml/mharendtFolderP05.html, images 1–47, quote at image 42.
41. Arendt Papers, image 41.
42. Partly in response to the criticism that her portrayal of Soviet communism as a totalitarian regime akin to Nazism thoroughly lacked evidence, especially compared to her almost dizzyingly rich account of the German case, Arendt

set out to investigate "totalitarian elements in Marxism." (It was the title of her application for a Guggenheim Fellowship, which she was awarded in 1952.) Elisabeth Young-Bruehl, *Hannah Arendt: For Love of the World* (New Haven, CT: Yale University Press, 1982), 276–278.

43. Arendt, "Ideology and Terror," in *Origins,* 460.
44. Hannah Arendt, "Understanding and Politics" (1953), in *Essays in Understanding, 1930–1954,* ed. Jerome Kohn (New York: Schocken, 1977), 310.
45. See note 2 of this chapter.
46. Dana R. Villa, "Beyond Good and Evil: Arendt, Nietzsche, and the Aestheticization of Political Action," *Political Theory* 20, no. 2 (1992): 274–308.
47. Martin Jay, "Political Existentialism of Hannah Arendt" (1978), in *Permanent Exiles: Essays on the Intellectual Migration from Germany to America* (New York: Columbia University Press, 1986), 237–256; Ben Berger, *Attention Deficit Democracy: The Paradox of Civic Engagement* (Princeton, NJ: Princeton University Press, 2011), chap. 3; Hauke Brunkhorst, "Equality and Elitism in Arendt," in *The Cambridge Companion to Hannah Arendt,* ed. Dana R. Villa (Cambridge: Cambridge University Press, 2000), 178–198; George Kateb, *Hannah Arendt: Politics, Conscience, Evil* (Totowa, NJ: Rowman & Allanheld, 1984).
48. Jeffrey C. Isaac, *Arendt, Camus, and Modern Rebellion* (New Haven, CT: Yale University Press, 1992). On the influence of Sartre and Camus on postwar intellectuals, see George Cotkin, *Existential America* (Baltimore, MD: Johns Hopkins University Press, 2003), chaps. 5–7.
49. Hannah Arendt, *The Human Condition* (Chicago: University of Chicago Press, 1958), 41, 193–194.
50. Arendt, *The Human Condition,* 175–180. Arendt's use of the concept of disclosure is diametrically opposed to Heidegger's in that she situates it squarely in the public realm. Lewis P. Hinchman and Sandra K. Hinchman, "In Heidegger's Shadow: Hannah Arendt's Phenomenological Humanism," *Review of Politics* 46, no. 2 (1984): 202, 205–206; Canovan, *Reinterpretation,* 112–113; Dana R. Villa, *Arendt and Heidegger: The Fate of the Political* (Princeton, NJ: Princeton University Press, 1996), 140–142.
51. Arendt, *Origins,* 352.
52. Arendt, 451.
53. Deriving the concept of "home" from Arendt's account of refugees, Nicholas Xenos also recognizes that its main significance lies in providing the context for action: "Home here signifies a place in the world insofar as such a place makes acting in the world possible; that is, makes action meaningful through shared understandings and a shared interpretation of action." Nicholas Xenos, "Refugees: The Modern Political Condition," *Alternatives: Global, Local, Political* 18, no. 4 (1993): 419–430, quote at 427.
54. Arendt, *Origins,* 301.
55. Arendt, 180; emphasis in original.
56. Arendt, 179; see also 49.
57. Susan Bickford similarly observes that, in emphasizing the concept of appearance in her theory of action, Arendt "presupposes a particular kind of attention on the part of others." Self-disclosure is possible "only because of the active perceiving presence of others, who acknowledge, recognize, approve or disapprove." Bickford, *The Dissonance of Democracy,* 60, 62.

58. Arendt, *The Human Condition*, 184.
59. Arendt, 186.
60. Arendt, 190.
61. Arendt, *On Revolution*, 166.
62. Arendt, *The Human Condition*, 184; see also 173.
63. Arendt, 167.
64. Arendt, 172–173.
65. Arendt, 173.
66. Hannah Arendt, "Tradition and the Modern Age" (1954), in *Between Past and Future: Eight Exercises in Political Thought* (1961; New York: Penguin, 1968), 26; Canovan, *Reinterpretation*, 68–70, 255–264.
67. Roy T. Tsao, "Arendt against Athens: Rereading *The Human Condition*," *Political Theory* 30, no. 1 (2002): 103.
68. Tsao, "Arendt against Athens," 106; emphasis in original.
69. Tsao, 102, 102n13.
70. Canovan, *Reinterpretation*, 259–274. For a discussion of thoughtlessness, see Schiff, *Burdens of Political Responsibility*, 50–84.
71. Tsao points to Arendt's brief mention of Kant in her essay "What Is Freedom?" as evidence that she models her theory after Kant's transcendental schematism. Tsao's claim is curious, because in the passages he cites (144–145), Arendt *rebukes* Kant for dissolving freedom altogether in the *Critique of Pure Reason* and for failing to properly restore it in the *Critique of Practical Reason*. Arendt discusses Kant far more extensively in another essay, "The Crisis in Culture," which appears in the same book, but Arendt's sole subject in this essay is the *Critique of Judgment*. Hannah Arendt, "What Is Freedom?" and "The Crisis in Culture," both in Arendt, *Between Past and Future*.
72. Immanuel Kant, *Critique of Judgment*, trans. Werner S. Pluhar (Indianapolis: Hackett, 1987), §6, 54.
73. Arendt, "The Crisis in Culture," 222.
74. Kant, *Critique of Judgment*, §8, 59.
75. Arendt, *The Human Condition*, 50.
76. Arendt, "The Crisis in Culture," 222.
77. Arendt, 220.
78. Hannah Arendt, "Truth and Politics" (1967), in *Between Past and Future*, 241. Ronald Beiner associates enlarged mentality exclusively with actors, going so far as to suggest that Arendt advances two theories of judgment. "The emphasis shifts from the representative thought and enlarged mentality of political agents to the spectatorship and retrospective judgment of historians and storytellers." Ronald Beiner, "Interpretative Essay," in *Lectures on Kant's Political Philosophy*, by Hannah Arendt, ed. Ronald Beiner (Chicago: University of Chicago Press, 1982), 91. But judgment concerns not just the making of new claims but also the reception of claims made. Moreover, the distinction between the actor and the spectator is itself porous, insofar as both contribute to creating and maintaining the common world.
79. Kant, *Critique of Judgment*, §40, 160.
80. Hannah Arendt, *Lectures on Kant's Political Philosophy*, ed. Ronald Beiner (Chicago: University of Chicago Press, 1982), 70, 71; emphasis added.
81. Arendt, *The Human Condition*, 283.

82. The term "attunement" (*Stimmung*) appears in Kant's *Critique of Judgment*. Although Arendt never embraced the term, it is much closer in its meaning to what she refers to as community sense. Kant conceptualizes attunement, which can only be "determined by feeling (rather than by concepts)," as a motivating force of cognition. "By means of senses," he writes, attunement "induces" people to exercise their imagination; "without it cognition could not arise." Kant, *Critique of Judgment*, 88.
83. Arendt, "Understanding and Politics," 315–316.
84. Arendt, "Ideology and Terror," 465, 467.
85. Arendt, 467.
86. Hannah Arendt, "Karl Marx and the Tradition of Western Political Thought" (1953), partially reprinted as "Montesquieu's Revision of the Tradition," in *The Promise of Politics*, ed. Jerome Kohn (New York: Schocken, 2005), 65. For the significance of this lecture, delivered at Princeton University in 1953, to Arendt's later thought, see Canovan, *Reinterpretation*, 64.
87. Arendt, "Montesquieu's Revision," 65; see also Arendt, "What Is Freedom?," 152.
88. Arendt, "What Is Freedom?," 151; see also Arendt, *The Human Condition*, 192, 206.
89. Arendt argued that the "human heart" requires the "darkness" of privacy and is unsuitable for "the light of the public." More controversial was her claim that the attempt to bring private sentiments into politics "ends with the appearance of crime and criminality on the political scene." Arendt, *On Revolution*, 86, 88; see also Arendt, *The Human Condition*, 73–78. For a critique, see George Kateb, *Hannah Arendt*; cf. Dan Degerman, "Within the Heart's Darkness: The Role of Emotions in Arendt's Political Thought," *European Journal of Political Theory* 18, no. 2 (2019), first published online May 18, 2016, https://doi.org/10.1177/1474885116647850.
90. Arendt, *On Revolution*, 88.
91. Montesquieu, *The Spirit of the Laws*, trans. and ed. Anne M. Cohler, Basia Carolyn Miller, and Harold Samuel Stone (Cambridge: Cambridge University Press, 1989), book 3, chap. 1.
92. Arendt, "What Is Freedom?," 152.
93. Arendt, "Montesquieu's Revision," 67.
94. Arendt, *On Revolution*, 110.
95. Arendt, 114–115; emphasis added.
96. Patchen Markell, too, stresses the concept of attunement as a central element of Arendt's political theory. Patchen Markell, "The Rule of the People: Arendt, *Archê*, and Democracy," *American Political Science Review* 100, no. 1 (2006): 1–14. Suggesting that Arendtian beginning arises not out of a particular action's extraordinary qualities but "out of an agent's attunement to its character as an irrevocable event, and therefore also as a new point of departure," Markell concludes that "the most fundamental threat to democratic political activity lies in the loss of responsiveness to events: the erosion of the contexts in which action makes sense" (7, 12). While Markell and I share the emphasis on responsiveness as a central element of Arendt's political theory and an important concern of democratic theory, we seem to conceptualize the key concept of attunement differently. Markell seems to focus on practical activities, referring consistently to "practical engagement" or "practical attunement." The democratic attunement that I find in Arendt, however, works

before those activities are undertaken, inspiring, conditioning, and restraining them. In light of Arendt's emphasis on the boundlessness and unpredictability of action, the notion that it is conditioned and restrained in any way may sound strange. But her argument, as I interpret it, is that those qualities are only latent in action and can be realized only when certain conditions are met, including particular arrangements of subjectivities. What is important to Arendt's theory is less the vibrancy of practical engagement per se than the environment in which that vibrancy takes shape.

97. Arendt, *Origins,* 467; Arendt, "Montesquieu's Revision," 66; Arendt, "What Is Freedom?," 152.
98. In this respect, I depart from scholars who have emphasized the subjective, though shared, feeling of freedom as a central element of her theory of judgment. Linda M. G. Zerilli, "We Feel Our Freedom: Imagination and Judgment in the Thought of Hannah Arendt," *Political Theory* 33, no. 2 (2005): 158–188.
99. Arendt, *The Human Condition,* 9; see also 176, 247.
100. "The equality attending the public realm is necessarily an equality of unequals who stand in need of being 'equalized' in certain respects and for certain purposes." Arendt, *The Human Condition,* 215.
101. Arendt, *The Human Condition,* 57.
102. Arendt, 254.
103. Arendt, 6.
104. Arendt, 154.
105. Arendt, 309.
106. Arendt, 96–101.
107. Arendt, 151.
108. Arendt, 145.
109. Arendt, 322–323.
110. Arendt, "Ideology and Terror," 474.
111. Arendt, 475.
112. Arendt, 474, 475.
113. Arendt, *The Human Condition,* 212–214.
114. Arendt, 79–80.
115. Arendt, 215.
116. Arendt, 217.
117. Arendt, 218; emphasis in original.
118. Arendt, 217.
119. Arendt, 219, 218.
120. Arendt, 219.
121. For a critique of Arendt's historical account of modern revolutions, see Eric Hobsbawm, "Hannah Arendt on Revolution," in *Revolutionaries: Contemporary Essays* (London: Quartet Books, 1973), 201–208.
122. Hanna Pitkin, "Justice: On Relating Public and Private," *Political Theory* 9, no. 3 (1981): 335. See also Wolin, "Hannah Arendt," 14. For a more sympathetic interpretation, but one that still accepts the premise that Arendt treats issues concerning basic material needs as unpolitical, see Bickford, *The Dissonance of Democracy,* 72–73; Myers, *Worldly Ethics,* 116–117.
123. Arendt, *The Human Condition,* 38.
124. Arendt, 160.

125. Arendt, 160, 161.
126. Arendt, 162–167, quotes at 162, 165.
127. Arendt, *On Revolution,* 84.
128. Arendt, *The Human Condition,* 47.
129. Arendt specifically links labor's "unending" nature to the experience of "a hitherto unheard-of process of growing wealth, growing property, and growing acquisition," which became a central issue for "political theorists from the seventeenth century onward." Arendt, *The Human Condition,* 105–106.
130. Arendt, 133.
131. Arendt, *On Revolution,* 260.
132. Arendt, 261.
133. Arendt, *On Revolution,* 240–247, 263–271; *The Human Condition,* 215–216.
134. Arendt, *The Human Condition,* 200.
135. Arendt, 133–134.
136. Arendt's idiosyncratic, and at times simply bizarre, interpretation of Marx is noted by a number of her readers. W. A. Suchting, "Marx and Hannah Arendt's *The Human Condition,*" *Ethics* 73, no. 1 (1962): 47–55; Mildred Bakan, "Hannah Arendt's Concepts of Labor and Work," and Bhikhu Parekh, "Hannah Arendt's Critique of Marx," in *Hannah Arendt: The Recovery of the Public World,* ed. Melvyn A. Hill (New York: St. Martin's Press, 1979), 49–65, 67–100, respectively; Hanna Fenichel Pitkin, *The Attack of the Blob: Hannah Arendt's Concept of the Social* (Chicago: University of Chicago Press, 1996), 127–144.

Chapter 7. Conclusion

1. E.g., Colin Crouch, *Post-Democracy* (Malden, MA: Polity, 2004); Wolfgang Merkel, "Is Capitalism Compatible with Democracy?" *Zeitschrift für Vergleichende Politikwissenschaft* 8, no. 2 (2014): 109–128.
2. Thomas Ferguson and Joel Rogers, *Right Turn: The Decline of the Democrats and the Future of American Politics* (New York: Hill and Wang, 1986), 46–68.
3. Michel Crozier, Samuel P. Huntington, and Joji Watanuki, *The Crisis of Democracy* (New York: New York University Press, 1975).
4. For a detailed discussion of this process, see Greta R. Krippner, *Capitalizing on Crisis: The Political Origins of the Rise of Finance* (Cambridge, MA: Harvard University Press, 2011); Wolfgang Streeck, *Buying Time: The Delayed Crisis of Democratic Capitalism* (London: Verso, 2017).

BIBLIOGRAPHY

Ackerman, Bruce A., and James S. Fishkin. *Deliberation Day.* New Haven, CT: Yale University Press, 2004.

Addams, Jane. "A Modern Lear." In *The Jane Addams Reader,* ed. Jean Bethke Elshtain, 163–176. New York: Basic Books, 2002.

Adler, Les K., and Thomas G. Paterson. "Red Fascism: The Merger of Nazi Germany and Soviet Russia in the American Image of Totalitarianism, 1930s–1950s." *American Historical Review* 75, no. 4 (1970): 1046–1064.

Adorno, Theodor W., with Else Frenkel-Brunswik, Daniel J. Levinson, and R. Nevitt Sanford. *The Authoritarian Personality.* New York: Harper, 1950.

Ahmed, Sara. *The Cultural Politics of Emotion.* New York: Routledge, 2004.

Allen, Danielle S. *Talking to Strangers: Anxieties of Citizenship since Brown v. Board of Education.* Chicago: University of Chicago Press, 2004.

Almond, Gabriel, and Sidney Verba. *The Civic Culture: Political Attitudes and Democracy in Five Nations.* Princeton, NJ: Princeton University Press, 1963.

Alpers, Benjamin L. *Dictators, Democracy, and American Public Culture: Envisioning the Totalitarian Enemy, 1920s–1950s.* Chapel Hill: University of North Carolina Press, 2003.

Altieri, Charles. *The Particulars of Rapture: The Aesthetics of the Affects.* Ithaca, NY: Cornell University Press, 2003.

Amadae, S. M. *Rationalizing Capitalist Democracy: The Cold War Origins of Rational Choice Liberalism.* Chicago: University of Chicago Press, 2003.

Andersen, Esben Sloth. *Schumpeter's Evolutionary Economics: A Theoretical, Historical and Statistical Analysis of the Engine of Capitalism.* New York: Anthem, 2009.

Anderson, Perry. *Spectrum.* London: Verso, 2005.

Arendt, Hannah. *The Human Condition.* Chicago: University of Chicago Press, 1958.

——. *Between Past and Future: Eight Exercises in Political Thought.* New York: Penguin, 1968.

——. *The Origins of Totalitarianism.* New York: Harcourt Brace Jovanovich, 1973.

——. "Understanding and Politics." In *Essays in Understanding, 1930–1954,* ed. Jerome Kohn, 307–327. New York: Schocken, 1977.

——. *The Jew as Pariah: Jewish Identity and Politics in the Modern Age.* Ed. Ron H. Feldman. New York: Grove Press, 1978.

——. *Lectures on Kant's Political Philosophy.* Ed. Ronald Beiner. Chicago: University of Chicago Press, 1982.

——. "Montesquieu's Revision of the Tradition." In *The Promise of Politics,* ed. Jerome Kohn, 63–69. New York: Schocken, 2005.

——. *On Revolution.* New York: Penguin, 2006.

Ashby, W. Ross. *An Introduction to Cybernetics.* New York: John Wiley and Sons, 1956.

——. *Design for a Brain: The Origin of Adaptive Behaviour.* 2nd ed. New York: Wiley, 1960.

Astin, John D. "Easton I and Easton II." *Western Political Quarterly* 25, no. 4 (1972): 726–737.

Averill, James R. "A Constructivist View of Emotion." In *Theories of Emotion*, ed. Robert Plutchik and Henry Kellerman, 305–339. Vol. 1 of *Emotion: Theory, Research, and Experience*. New York: Academic Press, 1980.

Bachrach, Peter, and Morton Baratz. "Two Faces of Power." *American Political Science Review* 56, no. 4 (1962): 947–952.

———. "Decisions and Non-Decisions: An Analytical Framework." *American Political Science Review* 57, no. 3 (1963): 632–642.

Bachrach, Peter, and Aryeh Botwinick. *Power and Empowerment: A Radical Theory of Participatory Democracy*. Philadelphia: Temple University Press, 1992.

Baehr, Peter. "Of Politics and Social Science: 'Totalitarianism' in the Debate of David Riesman and Hannah Arendt." *European Journal of Political Theory* 3, no. 2 (2004): 191–217.

Bakan, Mildred. "Hannah Arendt's Concepts of Labor and Work." In *Hannah Arendt: The Recovery of the Public World*, ed. Melvyn A. Hill, 49–65. New York: St. Martin's Press, 1979.

Bang, Henrik P. "David Easton's Postmodern Images." *Political Theory* 26, no. 3 (1998): 281–316.

Barber, Benjamin. *Strong Democracy: Participatory Politics for a New Age*. Berkeley and Los Angeles: University of California Press, 2003.

Bay, Christian. "Politics and Pseudopolitics: A Critical Evaluation of Some Behavioral Literature." *American Political Science Review* 54, no. 1 (1965): 39–51.

Beard, Charles A. *An Economic Interpretation of the Constitution of the United States*. New York: Macmillan, 1935.

Beer, Stafford. *Platform for Change*. New York: Wiley, 1975.

———. *The Heart of the Enterprise*. New York: Wiley, 1979.

———. *Brain of the Firm*. 2nd ed. New York: Wiley, 1980.

Beiner, Ronald. "Interpretative Essay." In *Lectures on Kant's Political Philosophy*, by Hannah Arendt, 89–156. Chicago: University of Chicago Press, 1982.

Bell, Daniel. *The End of Ideology: On the Exhaustion of Political Ideas in the Fifties*. Cambridge, MA: Harvard University Press, 1960.

———. *Marxian Socialism in the United States*. Ithaca, NY: Cornell University Press, 1967.

Bellamy, Richard. "The Advent of the Masses." In *The Cambridge History of Twentieth-Century Political Thought*, ed. Terence Ball and Richard Bellamy, 70–103. Cambridge: Cambridge University Press, 2003.

Bennett, Stuart. "Norbert Wiener and Control of Anti-Aircraft Guns." *IEEE Control Systems* 14, no. 6 (1994): 58–62.

Berelson, Bernard R., Paul F. Lazarsfeld, and William N. McPhee. *Voting: A Study of Opinion Formation in a Presidential Campaign*. Chicago: University of Chicago Press, 1954.

Berger, Ben. *Attention Deficit Democracy: The Paradox of Civic Engagement*. Princeton, NJ: Princeton University Press, 2011.

Bettelheim, Bruno. "Individual and Mass Behavior in Extreme Situations." *Journal of Abnormal and Social Psychology* 38, no. 4 (1943): 417–452.

Bickford, Susan. *The Dissonance of Democracy: Listening, Conflict, and Citizenship*. Ithaca, NY: Cornell University Press, 1996.

Bogaards, Matthijs. "De-Democratization in Hungary: Diffusely Defective Democracy." *Democratization* 25, no. 8 (2018): 1481–1499.

Boorstin, Daniel. *The Genius of American Politics.* Chicago: University of Chicago Press, 1953.

Borch, Christian. *The Politics of Crowds: An Alternative History of Sociology.* Cambridge: Cambridge University Press, 2012.

Boulding, Kenneth. *The Organizational Revolution: A Study in the Ethics of Economic Organization.* New York: Harper, 1953.

———. *Conflict and Defense: A General Theory.* New York: Harper, 1962.

Bousquet, Antoine. "Cyberneticizing the American War Machine: Science and Computers in the Cold War." *Cold War History* 8, no. 1 (2008): 77–102.

Bracken, Paul. *The Command and Control of Nuclear Forces.* New Haven, CT: Yale University Press, 1984.

Brick, Howard. *Age of Contradiction: American Thought and Culture in the 1960s.* Ithaca, NY: Cornell University Press, 1998.

Brinkley, Alan. *The End of Reform: New Deal Liberalism in Recession and War.* New York: Vintage, 1996.

Brown, Wendy. "Moralism as Anti-Politics." In *Politics Out of History,* 18–44. Princeton, NJ: Princeton University Press, 2001.

———. "Neo-liberalism and the End of Liberalism." *Theory and Event* 7, no. 1 (2003). https://muse.jhu.edu/article/48659.

———. *Undoing the Demos: Neoliberalism's Stealth Revolution.* New York: Zone Books, 2015.

Brunkhorst, Hauke. "Equality and Elitism in Arendt." In *The Cambridge Companion to Hannah Arendt,* ed. Dana R.Villa, 178–198. Cambridge: Cambridge University Press, 2000.

Burgin, Angus. *The Great Persuasion: Reinventing Free Markets since the Great Depression.* Cambridge, MA: Harvard University Press, 2012.

Burnham, James. *The Managerial Revolution.* New York: John Day, 1941.

Butler, Judith. *Giving an Account of Oneself.* New York: Fordham University Press, 2005.

Caldwell, Bruce. "Hayek's Transformation." *History of Political Economy* 20, no. 4 (1988): 513–541.

———. "Hayek and Socialism." *Journal of Economic Literature* 35, no. 4 (1997): 1858–1866.

Campbell, Angus, Philip E. Converse, Warren E. Miller, and Donald E. Stokes. *The American Voter.* New York: Wiley, 1960.

Canovan, Margaret. *Hannah Arendt: A Reinterpretation of Her Political Thought.* Cambridge: Cambridge University Press, 1992.

Chase, Stuart. *A New Deal.* New York: Macmillan, 1933.

Churchman, C. West, Russell L. Ackoff, and E. Leonard Arnoff. *Introduction to Operations Research.* New York: John Wiley, 1957.

Ciepley, David. *Liberalism in the Shadow of Totalitarianism.* Cambridge, MA: Harvard University Press, 2006.

Cohen, Lizabeth. *A Consumer's Republic: The Politics of Mass Consumption in Postwar America.* New York: Knopf, 2003.

Cohen-Cole, Jamie. *The Open Mind: Cold War Politics and the Sciences of Human Nature.* Chicago: University of Chicago Press, 2014.

Coles, Romand. *Rethinking Generosity: Critical Theory and the Politics of Caritas.* Ithaca, NY: Cornell University Press, 1997.

Collins, Robert M. *More: The Politics of Economic Growth in Postwar America.* New York: Oxford University Press, 2000.

Connolly, William E. *Why I Am Not a Secularist.* Minneapolis: University of Minnesota Press, 1999.

——. *Neuropolitics: Thinking, Culture, Speed.* Minneapolis: University of Minnesota Press, 2002.

Cotkin, George. *Existential America.* Baltimore, MD: Johns Hopkins University Press, 2003.

Croly, Herbert. *Progressive Democracy.* New York: Macmillan, 1914.

Cross, Gary. *An All-Consuming Century: Why Commercialism Won in Modern America.* New York: Columbia University Press, 2000.

Crouch, Colin. *Post-Democracy.* Malden, MA: Polity, 2004.

Crowther-Heyck, Hunter. *Herbert A. Simon: The Bounds of Reason in Modern America.* Baltimore, MD: Johns Hopkins University Press, 2005.

Crozier, Michel, Samuel P. Huntington, and Joji Watanuki. *The Crisis of Democracy.* New York: New York University Press, 1975.

Daddis, Gregory A. *No Sure Victory: Measuring U.S. Army Effectiveness and Progress in the Vietnam War.* New York: Oxford University Press, 2011.

Dahl, Robert A. *A Preface to Democratic Theory.* Chicago: University of Chicago Press, 1956.

——. "The Behavioral Approach in Political Science: Epitaph for a Monument to a Successful Protest." *American Political Science Review* 55, no. 4 (1961): 763–772.

——. *Who Governs? Democracy and Power in an American City.* New Haven, CT: Yale University Press, 1961.

——. "Further Reflections on the 'Elitist Theory of Democracy.'" *American Political Science Review* 60, no. 2 (1966): 296–305.

Dahl, Robert A., and Charles Lindblom. *Politics, Economics, and Welfare.* New York: Harper, 1953.

Dalton, Russell J. "Political Support in Advanced Industrial Countries." In *Critical Citizens: Global Support for Democratic Government,* ed. Pippa Norris, 57–77. Oxford: Oxford University Press, 1999.

——. *The Good Citizen: How a Younger Generation Is Reshaping American Politics.* Thousand Oaks, CA: CQ Press, 2016.

Damasio, Antonio R. *Descartes' Error: Emotion, Reason, and the Human Brain.* New York: HarperCollins, 2000.

——. *The Feeling of What Happens: Body and Emotion in the Making of Consciousness.* New York: Harcourt, 2003.

Davis, Lane. "The Cost of Realism: Contemporary Restatements of Democracy." *Western Political Quarterly* 17, no. 1 (1964): 37–46.

Dean, Jodi. "The Politics of Avoidance: The Limits of Weak Ontology." *Hedgehog Review* 7, no. 2 (2005): 55–65.

Degerman, Dan. "Within the Heart's Darkness: The Role of Emotions in Arendt's Political Thought." *European Journal of Political Theory* 18, no. 2 (2019). First published online, May 18, 2016, https://doi.org/10.1177/1474885116647850.

della Porta, Donatella. *Can Democracy Be Saved?* Cambridge: Polity, 2013.

Desai, Meghnad. "Equilibrium, Expectations, and Knowledge." In *Hayek,*

Co-Ordination and Evolution: His Legacy in Philosophy, Politics, Economics and the History of Ideas, ed. Jack Birner and Rudy van Zijp, 32–43. London: Routledge, 1994.

de Sousa, Ronald. *The Rationality of Emotion.* Cambridge, MA: MIT Press, 1987.

Deutsch, Karl W. "Some Memories of Norbert Wiener: The Man and His Thought." *IEEE Transactions on Systems, Man, and Cybernetics* 5, no. 3 (1975): 368–372.

Dewey, John. "The Reflex Arc Concept in Psychology." *Psychological Review* 3, no. 4 (1896): 357–370.

——. *Human Nature and Conduct.* New York: Holt, 1922.

——. *The Public and Its Problems.* New York: Holt, 1927.

——. *Reconstruction in Philosophy.* New York: Beacon Press, 1948.

——. *Lectures in China, 1919–1920.* Honolulu: University of Hawaii Press, 1973.

——. *Freedom and Culture.* New York: Prometheus, 1989.

——. *Individualism Old and New.* New York: Prometheus, 1999.

Diamond, Larry. "Facing Up to the Democratic Recession." *Journal of Democracy* 26, no. 1 (2015): 141–155.

Dietz, Mary. "Arendt and the Holocaust." In *The Cambridge Companion to Hannah Arendt,* ed. Dana R.Villa, 86–109. Cambridge: Cambridge University Press, 2000.

Digby, James. "Operations Research and Systems Analysis at RAND, 1948–1967." Rand N-2936-RC (1988). http://www.rand.org/pubs/notes/N2936.html.

Diggins, John Patrick. "Pragmatism and Its Limits." In *The Revival of Pragmatism,* ed. Morris Dickstein, 207–234. Durham, NC: Duke University Press, 1999.

Disch, Lisa. "Toward a Mobilization Conception of Democratic Representation." *American Political Science Review* 105, no. 1 (2011): 100–114.

Donohue, Kathleen G. *Freedom from Want: American Liberalism and the Idea of the Consumer.* Baltimore, MD: Johns Hopkins University Press, 2003.

Duncan, Graeme, and Steven Lukes. "The New Democracy." *Political Studies* 11, no. 2 (1963): 156–177.

Eastman, Max. *Stalin's Russia and the Crisis of Socialism.* New York: W. W. Norton, 1940.

Easton, David. "Walter Bagehot and Liberal Realism." *American Political Science Review* 43, no. 1 (1949): 17–37.

——. *The Political System.* New York: Knopf, 1953.

——. *A Framework for Political Analysis.* Englewood Cliffs, NJ: Prentice Hall, 1965.

—— *A Systems Analysis of Political Life.* New York: Wiley, 1965

——. "The Relevance of Biopolitics to Political Theory." In *Biology and Politics: Recent Explorations,* ed. Albert Somit, 237–247. The Hague: Mouton, 1976.

Ebenstein, Alan. *Hayek's Journey: The Mind of Friedrich Hayek.* New York: Palgrave Macmillan, 2003.

Edwards, Paul N. *The Closed World: Computers and the Politics of Discourse in Cold War America.* Cambridge, MA: MIT Press, 1996.

Eisenach, Eldon J. *The Lost Promise of Progressivism.* Lawrence: University Press of Kansas, 1994.

Eisenberg, Avigail I. *Reconstructing Political Pluralism.* Albany: State University of New York Press, 1995.

Ekirch, Arthur A., Jr. *Ideologies and Utopias: The Impact of the New Deal on American Thought.* Chicago: Quadrangle, 1969.

Emery, Fred E., and Eric L. Trist. "Socio-Technical Systems." In *Management Science Models and Techniques,* vol. 2, ed. C. West Churchman and Michel M. Verhulst, 83–97. New York: Pergamon, 1960.

Engerman, David C. "Social Science in the Cold War." *Isis* 101, no. 2 (2010): 393–400.

Enthoven, Alain C., and K. Wayne Smith. *How Much Is Enough? Shaping the Defense Program, 1961–1969.* New York: Harper & Row, 1971.

Ercan, Selen, and Jean-Paul Gagnon. "The Crisis of Democracy: Why Crisis? Which Democracy?" *Democratic Theory* 1, no. 2 (2014): 1–10.

Erickson, Paul, Judy L. Klein, Lorraine Daston, Rebecca M. Lemov, Thomas Sturm, and Michael D. Gordin. *How Reason Almost Lost Its Mind: The Strange Career of Cold War Rationality.* Chicago: University of Chicago Press, 2013.

Esquith, Stephen L. *Intimacy and Spectacle: Liberal Theory as Political Education.* Ithaca, NY: Cornell University Press, 1994.

Eulau, Heinz. *The Behavioral Persuasion in Politics.* New York: Random House, 1963.

Femia, Joseph V. *Against the Masses: Varieties of Anti-Democratic Thought since the French Revolution.* Oxford: Oxford University Press, 2001.

Ferguson, Thomas, and Joel Rogers. *Right Turn: The Decline of the Democrats and the Future of American Politics.* New York: Hill and Wang, 1986.

Feser, Edward, ed. *The Cambridge Companion to Hayek.* Cambridge: Cambridge University Press, 2006.

Fishkin, James S. *The Voice of the People: Public Opinion and Democracy.* New Haven, CT: Yale University Press, 1995.

——. *When the People Speak: Deliberative Democracy and Public Consultation.* New York: Oxford University Press, 2011.

Flatley, Jonathan. *Affective Mapping: Melancholia and the Politics of Modernism.* Cambridge, MA: Harvard University Press, 2008.

Fones-Wolf, Elizabeth A. *Selling Free Enterprise: The Business Assault on Labor and Liberalism.* Urbana: University of Illinois Press, 1994.

Forrester, Katrina. "Hope and Memory in the Thought of Judith Shklar." *Modern Intellectual History* 8, no. 3 (2011): 591–602.

Fortun, M., and S. S. Schweber. "Scientists and the Legacy of World War II: The Case of Operations Research." *Social Studies of Science* 23, no. 4 (1993): 595–642.

Fowler, Robert Booth. *Believing Skeptics: American Political Intellectuals, 1945–1964.* Westport, CT: Greenwood Press, 1978.

Freedom House. *Democracy's Century: A Survey of the Global Political Change in the 20th Century.* New York: Freedom House, 2000.

Frezza, Daria. *The Leader and the Crowd: Democracy in American Public Discourse, 1880–1941.* Athens: University of Georgia Press, 2007.

Friedman, Milton. *Capitalism and Freedom.* Chicago: University of Chicago Press, 1962.

Friedrich, Carl J. "Review of *The Road to Serfdom.*" *American Political Science Review* 39, no. 3 (1945): 575–579.

Friedrich, Carl J., and Zbigniew K. Brzezinski. *Totalitarian Dictatorship and Democracy.* Cambridge, MA: Harvard University Press, 1956.

Fromm, Erich. *Escape from Freedom.* New York: Farrar & Rinehart, 1941.

——. *The Sane Society.* New York: Rinehart & Company, 1955.

Fukuyama, Francis. "The End of History?" *National Interest* 16 (Summer 1989): 1–18.

——. *The End of History and the Last Man.* New York: Free Press, 2006.

Fung, Archon. *Empowered Participation: Reinventing Urban Democracy.* Princeton, NJ: Princeton University Press, 2006.

Fung, Archon, Erik Olin Wright, and Rebecca Abers, eds. *Deepening Democracy: Institutional Innovations in Empowered Participatory Governance.* London: Verso, 2003.

Galison, Peter. "The Ontology of the Enemy: Norbert Wiener and the Cybernetic Vision." *Critical Inquiry* 21, no. 1 (1994): 228–266.

Gamble, Andrew. "Hayek on Knowledge, Economics, and Society." In *The Cambridge Companion to Hayek,* ed. Edward Feser, 111–131. Cambridge: Cambridge University Press, 2006.

Gilbert, James Burkhart. *Writers and Partisans: A History of Literary Radicalism in America.* New York: Wiley, 1968.

Gilligan, Carol. *In a Different Voice: Psychological Theory and Women's Development.* Cambridge, MA: Harvard University Press, 1982.

Gleason, Abbott. *Totalitarianism: The Inner History of the Cold War.* New York: Oxford University Press, 1995.

Golembiewski, Robert T., and Patrick Scott. "A Micropolitical Perspective on Rational Budgeting: A Conjectural Footnote on the Dissemination of PPBS." *Public Budgeting and Financial Management* 1, no. 3 (1989): 327–370.

Goluboff, Risa L. *The Lost Promise of Civil Rights.* Cambridge, MA: Harvard University Press, 2007.

Gordon, Peter E. "The Authoritarian Personality Revisited: Reading Adorno in the Age of Trump." *boundary 2* 44, no. 2 (2017): 31–56.

Green, Jeffrey E. *The Eyes of the People: Democracy in an Age of Spectatorship.* New York: Oxford University Press, 2010.

Greenberg, Udi. *The Weimar Century: German Émigrés and the Ideological Foundations of the Cold War.* Princeton, NJ: Princeton University Press, 2014.

Grief, Mark. *The Age of the Crisis of Man: Thought and Fiction in America, 1933–1973.* Princeton, NJ: Princeton University Press, 2015.

Griffith, Robert. "The Selling of America: The Advertising Council and American Politics, 1942–1960." *Business History Review* 57, no. 3 (1983): 388–412.

——. "Forging America's Postwar Order: Domestic Politics and Political Economy in the Age of Truman." In *The Truman Presidency,* ed. Michael J. Lacey, 57–88. New York: Cambridge University Press, 1994.

Guinier, Lani. "From Racial Liberalism to Racial Literacy: *Brown v. Board of Education* and the Interest-Divergence Dilemma." *Journal of American History* 91, no. 1 (2004): 92–118.

Gunnell, John G. *The Descent of Political Theory: A Genealogy of an American Vocation.* Chicago: University of Chicago Press, 1993.

——. *Imagining the American Polity.* University Park: Pennsylvania State University Press, 2004.

——. "Are We Losing Our Minds? Cognitive Science and the Study of Politics." *Political Theory* 35, no. 6 (2007): 704–731.

——. "The Reconstitution of Political Theory: David Easton, Behavioralism, and the Long Road to System." *Journal of the History of the Behavioral Sciences* 49, no. 2 (2013): 190–210.

Gurian, Waldemar. "Totalitarianism as Political Religion." In *Totalitarianism,* ed. Carl J. Friedrich, 119–138. New York: Grosset & Dunlap, 1964.

Gutmann, Amy, and Dennis Thompson. *Why Deliberative Democracy?* Princeton, NJ: Princeton University Press, 2004.

Habermas, Jürgen. "Reconciliation through the Public Use of Reason: Remarks on John Rawls's Political Liberalism." *Journal of Philosophy* 92, no. 3 (1995): 109–131.

———. *Between Facts and Norms.* Cambridge, MA: MIT Press, 1996.

Halberstam, David. *The Best and the Brightest.* New York: Ballantine Books, 1993.

Hallowell, John H. *The Decline of Liberalism as an Ideology.* Berkeley and Los Angeles: University of California Press, 1943.

Hammond, Debora. *The Science of Synthesis: Exploring the Social Implications of General Systems Theory.* Boulder: University Press of Colorado, 2003.

Hamowy, Ronald. "Law and the Liberal Society: F. A. Hayek's Constitution of Liberty." *Journal of Libertarian Studies* 2, no. 4 (1978): 287–297.

Hansen, Alvin H. "The New Crusade against Planning." *New Republic* 112 (January 1, 1945): 11–12.

Hanson, Russell L. *The Democratic Imagination in America: Conversations with Our Past.* Princeton, NJ: Princeton University Press, 1985.

Haraway, Donna J. "A Cyborg Manifesto: Science, Technology, and Socialist-Feminism in the Late Twentieth Century." In *Simians, Cyborgs, and Women: The Reinvention of Nature,* 149–181. New York: Routledge, 1991.

Harré, Rom, ed. *The Social Construction of Emotions.* Oxford: Blackwell, 1986.

Harris, Howell John. *The Right to Manage: Industrial Relations Policies of American Business in the 1940s.* Madison: University of Wisconsin Press, 1982.

Hartwell, R. M. *A History of the Mont Pelerin Society.* Indianapolis: Liberty Fund, 1995.

Hauptmann, Emily. *Putting Choice before Democracy: A Critique of Rational Choice Theory.* Albany: State University of New York Press, 1996.

———. "Can Less Be More? Leftist Deliberative Democrats' Critique of Participatory Democracy." *Polity* 33, no. 3 (2001): 397–421.

———. "From Opposition to Accommodation: How Rockefeller Foundation Grants Redefined Relations between Political Theory and Social Science in the 1950s." *American Political Science Review* 100, no. 4 (2006): 643–649.

———. "The Ford Foundation and the Rise of Behavioralism in Political Science." *Journal of the History of the Behavioral Sciences* 48, no. 2 (2012): 154–173.

Hay, Colin. "Re-Stating Politics, Re-Politicising the State: Neo-Liberalism, Economic Imperatives and the Rise of the Competition State." *Political Quarterly* 75, no. 1 (2004): 38–50.

———. *Why We Hate Politics.* Malden, MA: Polity, 2007.

Hayek, Friedrich A. "The Present State of the Debate." In *Collectivist Economic Planning,* ed. Friedrich A. Hayek, 201–243. London: Routledge, 1935.

———. *Individualism and Economic Order.* Chicago: University of Chicago Press, 1948.

———. "Freedom and Coercion: Some Comments on a Critique of Mr. Ronald Hamowy." In *Studies in Philosophy, Politics, and Economics,* 348–349. Chicago: University of Chicago Press, 1967.

———. *Law, Legislation, and Liberty.* Vol. 1, *Rules and Order.* Chicago: University of Chicago Press, 1973.

———. *Law, Legislation, and Liberty.* Vol. 2, *The Mirage of Social Justice.* Chicago: University of Chicago Press, 1976.

——. *Law, Legislation, and Liberty.* Vol. 3, *The Political Order of a Free People.* Chicago: University of Chicago Press, 1979.

——. *Hayek on Hayek: An Autobiographical Dialogue.* Ed. Stephen Kresge and Leif Wenar. Chicago: University of Chicago Press, 1994.

——. *The Road to Serfdom.* Chicago: University of Chicago Press, 1994.

——. *The Collected Works of F. A. Hayek.* Vol. 9, *Contra Keynes and Cambridge,* ed. Bruce Caldwell. Chicago: University of Chicago Press, 1995.

——. *The Constitution of Liberty.* Chicago: University of Chicago Press, 2011.

Hayles, N. Katherine. *How We Became Posthuman.* Chicago: University of Chicago Press, 1999.

Heims, Steve J. *Constructing a Social Science for Postwar America: The Cybernetics Group, 1946–1953.* Cambridge, MA: MIT Press, 1991.

Henthorn, Cynthia Lee. *From Submarines to Suburbs: Selling a Better America, 1939–1959.* Athens: Ohio University Press, 2006.

Herken, Gregg F. *Counsels of War.* New York: Knopf, 1985.

Herman, Ellen. *The Romance of American Psychology: Political Culture in the Age of Experts, 1940–1970.* Berkeley: University of California Press, 1995.

Heyck, Hunter. *Age of System: Understanding the Rise of Modern Social Science.* Baltimore, MD: Johns Hopkins University Press, 2015.

Higham, John. *Strangers in the Land: Patterns of American Nativism, 1860–1925.* 2nd ed. New Brunswick, NJ: Rutgers University Press, 1988.

Hill, Melvyn A., ed. *Hannah Arendt: The Recovery of the Public World.* New York: St. Martin's Press, 1979.

Hinchman, Lewis P., and Sandra K. Hinchman. "In Heidegger's Shadow: Hannah Arendt's Phenomenological Humanism." *Review of Politics* 46, no. 2 (1984): 183–211.

Hirsch, Fred. *Social Limits to Growth.* Cambridge, MA: Harvard University Press, 1976.

Hitch, Charles J., and Roland N. McKean. *The Economics of Defense in the Nuclear Age.* Cambridge, MA: Harvard University Press, 1960.

Hobsbawm, Eric. "Hannah Arendt on Revolution." In *Revolutionaries: Contemporary Essays,* 201–208. London: Quartet Books, 1973.

Hochschild, Arlie Russell. "Emotion Work, Feeling Rules, and Social Structures." *American Journal of Sociology* 85, no. 3 (1979): 551–575.

Hofstadter, Richard H. *The Age of Reform.* New York: Vintage, 1955.

Honig, Bonnie. "The Politics of Ethos." *European Journal of Political Theory* 10, no. 3 (2011): 422–429.

Hook, Sidney. *Political Power and Personal Freedom.* New York: Criterion, 1959.

Hoos, Ida. *Systems Analysis in Public Policy.* Berkeley: University of California Press, 1972.

Horkheimer, Max. *Eclipse of Reason.* London: Continuum, 2004.

Horkheimer, Max, and Theodor W. Adorno. *Dialectic of Enlightenment.* Stanford, CA: Stanford University Press, 2002.

Huntington, Samuel. *The Third Wave: Democratization in the Late Twentieth Century.* Norman: University of Oklahoma Press, 1993.

Hyman, Louis Roland. *Debtor Nation: The History of America in Red Ink.* Princeton, NJ: Princeton University Press, 2011.

Isaac, Jeffrey C. *Arendt, Camus, and Modern Rebellion.* New Haven, CT: Yale University Press, 1992.

Isaac, Joel. "The Human Sciences in Cold War America." *Historical Journal* 50, no. 3 (2007): 725–746.

Isaac, Joel, and Duncan Bell, eds. *Uncertain Empire: American History and the Idea of the Cold War.* New York: Oxford University Press, 2012.

Jackson, Ben. "At the Origins of Neoliberalism: The Free Economy and the Strong State, 1930–1947." *Historical Journal* 53, no. 1 (2010): 129–151.

Jackson, Kenneth T. *Crabgrass Frontier: The Suburbanization of the United States.* New York: Oxford University Press, 1985.

James, Michael R. *Deliberative Democracy and the Plural Polity.* Lawrence: University Press of Kansas, 2004.

Jardini, David R. "Out of the Blue Yonder: The Transfer of Systems Thinking from the Pentagon to the Great Society, 1961–1965." In *Systems, Experts, and Computers: The Systems Approach in Management and Engineering, World War II and After,* ed. Agatha C. Hughes and Thomas P. Hughes, 311–357. Cambridge, MA: MIT Press, 2000.

Jay, Martin. "Political Existentialism of Hannah Arendt." In *Permanent Exiles: Essays on the Intellectual Migration from Germany to America,* 237–256. New York: Columbia University Press, 1986.

Jones, Daniel Stedman. *Masters of the Universe: Hayek, Friedman, and the Birth of Neoliberal Politics.* Princeton, NJ: Princeton University Press, 2012.

Jones, William David. *The Lost Debate: German Socialist Intellectuals and Totalitarianism.* Urbana: University of Illinois Press, 1999.

Jonsson, Stefan. *Crowds and Democracy: The Idea and Image of the Masses from Revolution to Fascism.* New York: Columbia University Press, 2013.

Josephson, Matthew. *Infidel in the Temple.* New York, 1967.

Kant, Immanuel. *Critique of Judgment.* Trans. Werner S. Pluhar. Indianapolis: Hackett, 1987.

Kaplan, Fred M. *The Wizards of Armageddon.* New York: Simon & Schuster, 1983.

Kateb, George. *Hannah Arendt: Politics, Conscience, Evil.* Totowa, NJ: Rowman & Allanheld, 1984.

Kelley, John L. "The Revitalization of Market Liberalism." In *Bringing the Market Back In: The Political Revitalization of Market Liberalism,* 31–80. Basingstoke: Palgrave Macmillan, 1997.

Kennan, George F. "Totalitarianism in the Modern World." In *Totalitarianism: Proceedings of a Conference Held at the American Academy of Arts and Sciences, March 1953,* ed. Carl Friedrich, 17–31. Cambridge, MA: Harvard University Press, 1954.

——. "Overdue Changes in Our Foreign Policy." *Harper's,* August 1956, 27–33.

——. "The Sources of Soviet Conduct." In *Foreign Relations of the United States,* vol. 6, *1946: Eastern Europe; the Soviet Union,* 696–709. Washington, DC: Government Printing Office, 1969.

Key, V. O. *Public Opinion and American Democracy.* New York: Alfred A. Knopf, 1961.

King, Erica G. "Reconciling Democracy and the Crowd in Turn-of-the-Century American Social-Psychological Thought." *Journal of the History of the Behavioral Sciences* 26, no. 4 (1990): 334–344.

King, Richard H. *Arendt and America.* Chicago: University of Chicago Press, 2015.

Kirby, Maurice W. "Operations Research Trajectories: The Anglo-American Experience from the 1940s to the 1990s." *Operations Research* 48 (2000): 661–670.

Kline, Ronald R. *The Cybernetics Moment.* Baltimore, MD: Johns Hopkins University Press, 2015.

Kloppenberg, James T. *Uncertain Victory: Social Democracy and Progressivism in European and American Thought, 1870–1920.* New York: Oxford University Press, 1986.

Kohlberg, Lawrence. *The Psychology of Moral Development: Moral Stages and the Idea of Justice.* San Francisco: Harper & Row, 1981.

Kohn, Hans. *The Mind of Germany.* New York: Charles Scribner's Sons, 1960.

Krause, Sharon R. "Desiring Justice: Motivation and Justification in Rawls and Habermas." *Contemporary Political Theory* 4, no. 4 (2005): 365–385.

Krippner, Greta R. *Capitalizing on Crisis: The Political Origins of the Rise of Finance.* Cambridge, MA: Harvard University Press, 2011.

Kurlantzick, Joshua. *Democracy in Retreat: The Revolt of the Middle Class and the Worldwide Decline of Representative Government.* New Haven, CT: Yale University Press, 2013.

Lears, Jackson. "A Matter of Taste: Corporate Cultural Hegemony in a Mass-Consumption Society." In *Recasting America: Culture and Politics in the Age of Cold War,* ed. Lary May, 38–60. Chicago: University of Chicago Press, 1989.

Le Bon, Gustave. *The Crowd: A Study of the Popular Mind.* 2nd ed. London: T. F. Unwin, 1897.

LeDoux, Joseph. *The Emotional Brain: The Mysterious Underpinnings of Emotional Life.* New York: Simon and Schuster, 1996.

Leoni, Bruno. *Freedom and the Law.* Indianapolis: Liberty Fund, 1991.

Lichtenstein, Nelson. "From Corporatism to Collective Bargaining: Organized Labor and the Eclipse of Social Democracy in the Postwar Era." In *The Rise and Fall of the New Deal Order, 1930–1980,* ed. Steve Fraser and Gary Gerstle, 122–152. Princeton, NJ: Princeton University Press, 1980.

Lilienfeld, Robert. *The Rise of Systems Theory: An Ideological Analysis.* New York: Wiley, 1978.

Lippmann, Walter. *An Inquiry into the Principles of the Good Society.* Boston: Little, Brown, 1937.

Lipset, Seymour Martin. *Political Man: The Social Bases of Politics.* Garden City, NY: Doubleday, 1960.

Livingston, James. "The Strange Career of the 'Social Self.'" *Radical History Review* 76 (2000): 53–79.

Loewenstein, Karl. "Militant Democracy and Fundamental Right I." *American Political Science Review* 31, no. 3 (1937): 417–432.

Lowenthal, Leo. "Terror's Atomization of Man." *Commentary* 1 (January 1946): 1–8.

Lowi, Theodore J. *The End of Liberalism: The Second Republic of the United States.* New York: W. W. Norton, 1979.

Lührmann, Anna, Valeriya Mechkova, Sirianne Dahlum, Laura Maxwell, Moa Olin, Constanza Sanhueza Petrarca, Rachel Sigman, Matthew C. Wilson, and Staffan I. Lindberg. "State of the World 2017: Autocratization and Exclusion?" *Democratization* 25, no. 8 (2018): 1321–1340.

Lukes, Steven. *Power: A Radical View.* London: Macmillan, 1974.

Lustig, R. Jeffrey. *Corporate Liberalism: The Origins of Modern American Political Theory, 1890–1920.* Berkeley: University of California Press, 1982.

Lutz, Catherine. *Unnatural Emotions.* Chicago: University of Chicago Press, 1988.

Maddux, Thomas R. "Red Fascism, Brown Bolshevism: The American Image of Totalitarianism in the 1930s." *Historian* 40, no. 1 (1977): 85–103.

Madison, James, Alexander Hamilton, and John Jay. *The Federalist Papers.* Ed. Isaac Kramnick. New York: Penguin, 1987.

Mair, Peter. *Ruling the Void: The Hollowing of Western Democracy.* London: Verso, 2013.

Mancini, Matthew J. "Too Many Tocquevilles: The Fable of Tocqueville's American Reception." *Journal of the History of Ideas* 69, no. 2 (2008): 245–268.

Mandler, Peter. "Deconstructing 'Cold War Anthropology.'" In *Uncertain Empire: American History and the Idea of the Cold War,* ed. Joel Isaac and Duncan Bell, 245–266. New York: Oxford University Press, 2012.

Manin, Bernard. "On Legitimacy and Political Deliberation." *Political Theory* 15, no. 3 (1987): 338–368.

——. *The Principles of Representative Government.* New York: Cambridge University Press, 1997.

Mannheim, Karl. "The Crisis of Culture in the Era of Mass-Democracies and Autarchies." *Sociological Review* 26, no. 2 (1934): 105–129.

——. "The Democratization of Culture." In *Essays on the Sociology of Culture,* 171–246. London: Routledge, 1992.

Marcus, George, W. Russell Neuman, and Michael Mackuen. *The Affective Intelligence and Political Judgment.* Chicago: University of Chicago Press, 2000.

——. *The Affect Effect: Dynamics of Emotion in Political Thinking and Behavior.* Chicago: University of Chicago Press, 2007.

Markell, Patchen. "The Rule of the People: Arendt, *Archê,* and Democracy." *American Political Science Review* 100, no. 1 (2006): 1–14.

Masani, Pesi R. *Norbert Wiener, 1894–1964.* Basel: Birkhaþuser, 1990.

Masani, Pesi R., and R. S. Phillips. "Antiaircraft Fire Control and the Emergence of Cybernetics." In *Norbert Wiener: Collected Works, with Commentaries,* vol. 4, ed. Pesi R. Masani, 141–179. Cambridge, MA: MIT Press, 1976.

Massumi, Brian. *Parables of the Virtual.* Durham, NC: Duke University Press, 2002.

Mattson, Kevin. *Creating a Democratic Public: The Struggle for Urban Participatory Democracy during the Progressive Era.* University Park: Pennsylvania State University Press, 1998.

May, Elaine Tyler. *Homeward Bound: American Families in the Cold War Era.* New York: Basic Books, 1998.

Mayo, Henry. *An Introduction to Democratic Theory.* New York: Oxford University Press, 1960.

McClay, Wilfred M. *The Masterless: Self and Society in Modern America.* Chapel Hill: University of North Carolina Press, 1994.

McClelland, J. S. *The Crowd and the Mob: From Plato to Canetti.* London: Routledge, 2011.

McClosky, Herbert. "Consensus and Ideology in American Politics." *American Political Science Review* 58, no. 2 (1964): 361–382.

McCoy, Charles A., and John Playford, eds. *Apolitical Politics: A Critique of Behavioralism.* New York: Thomas Y. Crowell, 1967.

Medearis, John. *Joseph Schumpeter's Two Theories of Democracy.* Cambridge, MA: Harvard University Press, 2001.

Menze, Ernest A., ed. *Totalitarianism Reconsidered.* Port Washington, NY: Kennikat Press, 1981.

Merkel, Wolfgang. "Embedded and Defective Democracies." *Democratization* 11, no. 5 (2004): 33–58.

———. "Is Capitalism Compatible with Democracy?" *Zeitschrift für Vergleichende Politikwissenschaft* 8, no. 2 (2014): 109–128.

Merriam, Charles E., and Harold F. Gosnell. *Non-Voting: Causes and Methods of Control.* Chicago: University of Chicago Press, 1924.

Milkins, Sidney M., and Jerome M. Mileur, eds. *Progressivism and the New Democracy.* Amherst: University of Massachusetts Press, 1999.

Mill, John Stuart. *On Liberty and Other Essays.* New York: Oxford University Press, 2008.

Mills, C. Wright. *Sociology and Pragmatism: The Higher Learning in America.* New York: Paine-Whitman, 1964.

Mindell, David A. *Between Human and Machine: Feedback, Control, and Computing before Cybernetics.* Baltimore, MD: Johns Hopkins University Press, 2002.

Mirowski, Philip. *Machine Dreams: Economics Becomes a Cyborg Science.* New York: Cambridge University Press, 2002.

———. "A History Best Served Cold." In *Uncertain Empire: American History and the Idea of the Cold War,* ed. Joel Isaac and Duncan Bell, 61–74. New York: Oxford University Press, 2012.

Mirowski, Philip, and Dieter Plehwe, eds. *The Road from Mont Pèlerin: The Making of the Neoliberal Thought Collective.* Cambridge, MA: Harvard University Press, 2009.

Mitchell, William C. "Politics as the Allocation of Values: A Critique." *Ethics* 71, no. 2 (1961): 79–89.

Montesquieu. *The Spirit of the Laws.* Ed. and trans. Anne M. Cohler, Basia Carolyn Miller, and Harold Samuel Stone. Cambridge: Cambridge University Press, 1989.

Mosse, George L. *The Crisis of German Ideology: Intellectual Origins of the Third Reich.* New York: Grosset & Dunlap, 1964.

Müller, Jan-Werner. *Contesting Democracy: Political Thought in Twentieth-Century Europe.* New Haven, CT: Yale University Press, 2011.

Mumford, Lewis. *The Golden Day.* New York: Boni and Liveright, 1926.

Myers, Ella. *Worldly Ethics: Democratic Politics and Care for the World.* Durham, NC: Duke University Press, 2013.

Nagel, Thomas. "Moral Conflict and Political Legitimacy." *Philosophy and Public Affairs* 16, no. 3 (1987): 215–240.

Nash, George H. *The Conservative Intellectual Movement in America, since 1945.* New York: Basic Books, 1976.

Neu, Jerome. *A Tear Is an Intelligent Thing: The Meaning of Emotion.* New York: Oxford University Press, 2000.

Neuchterlein, James. "The Dream of Scientific Liberalism: The New Republic and American Progressive Thought, 1914–1920." *Review of Politics* 42, no. 2 (1980): 167–190.

Neumann, Franz. *Behemoth: The Structure and Practice of National Socialism.* New York: Oxford University Press, 1942.

Newman, Louise Michele. *White Women's Rights: The Racial Origins of Feminism in the United States.* New York: Oxford University Press, 1999.

Ngai, Sianne. *Ugly Feelings.* Cambridge, MA: Harvard University Press, 2005.

Niebuhr, Reinhold. *The Children of Light and the Children of Darkness: A Vindication of Democracy and a Critique of Its Traditional Defenders.* New York: Charles Scribner's Sons, 1944.

———. *The Irony of American History.* New York: Scribner's Sons, 1952.

———. *Moral Man and Immoral Society.* Louisville, KY: Westminster John Knox Press, 2001.

Nisbet, Robert. "Many Tocquevilles." *American Scholar* 46 (1976–1977): 59–75.

Noble, David F. *America by Design: Science, Technology, and the Rise of Corporate Capitalism.* New York: Alfred A. Knopf, 1977.

Norris, Pippa. *Democratic Phoenix: Reinventing Democratic Activism.* New York: Cambridge University Press, 2002.

Novick, David. "The Department of Defense." In *Program Budgeting: Program Analysis and the Federal Budget,* ed. David Novick, 81–117. Cambridge, MA: Harvard University Press, 1965.

Nussbaum, Martha. *Love's Knowledge.* Oxford: Oxford University Press, 1990.

———. *Upheavals of Thought: The Intelligence of Emotions.* Cambridge: Cambridge University Press, 2000.

Nye, Joseph S., Jr., Philip D. Zelikow, and David C. King, eds. *Why People Don't Trust the Government.* Cambridge, MA: Harvard University Press, 1997.

Nye, Robert A. *The Origins of Crowd Psychology: Gustave Le Bon and the Crisis of Mass Democracy in the Third Republic.* London: Sage, 1975.

Ortega y Gasset, José. *The Revolt of the Masses.* New York: W. W. Norton, 1932.

Palmer, Gregory. *The McNamara Strategy and the Vietnam War: Program Budgeting in the Pentagon, 1960–1968.* Westport, CT: Greenwood Press, 1978.

Parekh, Bhikhu. "Hannah Arendt's Critique of Marx." In *Hannah Arendt: The Recovery of the Public World,* ed. Melvyn A. Hill, 67–100. New York: St. Martin's Press, 1979.

Parsons, Talcott. "On Building Social System Theory: A Personal History." *Daedalus* 99 (1970): 826–881.

Pateman, Carole. *Participation and Democratic Theory.* Cambridge: Cambridge University Press, 1970.

Patterson, Thomas E. *The Vanishing Voter: Public Involvement in an Age of Uncertainty.* New York: Vintage, 2003.

Pells, Richard H. *Radical Visions and American Dreams: Culture and Social Thought in the Depression Years.* New York: Harper & Row, 1973.

———. *The Liberal Mind in a Conservative Age: American Intellectuals in the 1940s and 1950s.* New York: Harper & Row, 1985.

Pharr, Susan J., and Robert D. Putnam, eds. *Disaffected Democracies: What's Troubling the Trilateral Countries?* Princeton, NJ: Princeton University Press, 2000.

Phillips, Anne. *The Politics of Presence.* Oxford: Oxford University Press, 1995.

Pickering, Andrew. "Cyborg History and the World War II Regime." *Perspectives on Science* 3 (1995): 1–45.

———. *The Cybernetic Brain.* Chicago: University of Chicago Press, 2010.

Pitkin, Hanna. "Justice: On Relating Public and Private." *Political Theory* 9, no. 3 (1981): 327–352.

———. *The Attack of the Blob: Hannah Arendt's Concept of the Social.* Chicago: University of Chicago Press, 1996.

Plamenatz, John P. *Democracy and Illusion.* London: Longman, 1973.

Plehwe, Dieter, and Bernhard Walpen. "Between Network and Complex Organization: The Making of Neoliberal Knowledge and Hegemony." In *Neoliberal Hegemony: A Global Critique,* ed. Dieter Plehwe, Bernhard Walpen, and Gisela Neunhöffer, 27–50. New York: Routledge, 2006.

Plotke, David. "Representation Is Democracy." *Constellations* 4, no. 1 (1997): 19–34.

Pollock, Friedrich. "State Capitalism: Its Possibilities and Limitations." *Studies in Philosophy and Social Science* 9, no. 2 (1941): 200–225.

Potter, David. *People of Plenty: Economic Abundance and the American Character.* Chicago: University of Chicago Press, 1954.

Protevi, John. *Political Affect: Connecting the Social and the Somatic.* Minneapolis: University of Minnesota Press, 2009.

Przeworski, Adam. "Minimalist Conception of Democracy: A Defense." In *Democracy's Values,* ed. Ian Shapiro and Casiano Hacker-Cordón, 23–55. New York: Cambridge University Press, 1999.

Purcell, Edward A., Jr. *The Crisis of Democratic Theory.* Lexington: University Press of Kentucky, 1973.

Rana, Aziz. "Progressivism and the Constitution." In *The Progressives' Century,* ed. Stephen Skowronek, Stephen M. Engel, and Bruce Ackerman, 41–64. New Haven, CT: Yale University Press, 2016.

Rancière, Jacques. *Disagreement: Politics and Philosophy.* Minneapolis: University of Minnesota Press, 2008.

Ranney, Austin, ed. *Essays on the Behavioral Study of Politics.* Urbana: University of Illinois Press, 1962.

Rawls, John. *A Theory of Justice.* Cambridge, MA: Harvard University Press, 1971.

———. "Justice as Fairness: Political, Not Metaphysical." *Philosophy and Public Affairs* 14, no. 3 (1985): 223–251.

———. "Political Liberalism: Reply to Habermas." *Journal of Philosophy* 92, no. 3 (1995): 132–180.

———. *Justice as Fairness: A Restatement.* Ed. Erin Kelly. Cambridge, MA: Harvard University Press, 2001.

———. *Political Liberalism.* New York: Columbia University Press, 2007.

Reddy, William. *The Navigation of Feeling: A Framework for the History of Emotions.* Cambridge: Cambridge University Press, 2001.

Reisch, George A. *How the Cold War Transformed Philosophy of Science.* New York: Cambridge University Press, 2005.

Ricci, David M. "Democracy Attenuated: Schumpeter, the Process Theory, and American Democratic Thought." *Journal of Politics* 32, no. 2 (1970): 239–267.

———. *The Tragedy of American Political Science: Politics, Scholarship, and Democracy.* New Haven, CT: Yale University Press, 1984.

Richardson, George P. *Feedback Thought in Social Science and Systems Theory.* Philadelphia: University of Pennsylvania Press, 1991.

Riesman, David. "Some Observations on the Limits of Totalitarian Power." In *Individualism Reconsidered,* 414–425. New York: Free Press, 1954.

Riesman, David, with Nathan Glazer and Reuel Denny. *The Lonely Crowd: A Study of the Changing Social Character.* New Haven, CT: Yale University Press, 2001.

Riker, William H. *Liberalism against Populism: A Confrontation between the Theory of Democracy and the Theory of Social Choice.* Prospect Heights, IL: Waveland Press, 1982.

Rochlin, Gene I. *Trapped in the Net: The Unanticipated Consequences of Computerization.* Princeton, NJ: Princeton University Press, 1998.

Rodgers, Daniel T. "In Search of Progressivism." *Reviews in American History* 10, no. 4 (1982): 113–132.

——. *Atlantic Crossings: Social Politics in a Progressive Age.* Cambridge, MA: Harvard University Press, 1998.

Rorty, Amélie. "Explaining Emotions." In *Explaining Emotions,* ed. Amélie Rorty, 139–161. Berkeley: University of California Press, 1980.

Rosanvallon, Pierre. *Counter-Democracy: Politics in an Age of Distrust.* New York: Cambridge University Press, 2008.

Rosenberg, Bernard. "Mass Culture in America." In *Mass Culture: Popular Arts in America,* ed. Bernard Rosenberg and David Manning White, 3–12. Glencoe, IL: Free Press, 1957.

Rosenblueth, Arturo, Norbert Wiener, and Julian Bigelow. "Behavior, Purpose and Teleology." *Philosophy of Science* 10, no. 1 (1943): 18–24.

Ross, Dorothy. *The Origins of American Social Science.* New York: Cambridge University Press, 1991.

Rousseau, Jean-Jacques. *The Social Contract and Discourses.* Trans. G. D. H. Cole. London: Everyman Library, 1993.

Schattschneider, E. E. *The Semi-Sovereign People: A Realist's View of Democracy in America.* New York: Holt, Rinehart and Winston, 1960.

Scherer, Klaus R., and Paul Ekman, eds. *Approaches to Emotion.* Hillsdale, NJ: L. Erlbaum Associates, 1984.

Schick, Allen. "The Road to PPB: The Stages of Budget Reform." *Public Administration Review* 26, no. 4 (1966): 243–258.

——. "A Death in the Bureaucracy: The Demise of Federal PPB." *Public Administration Review* 33, no. 2 (1973): 146–156.

Schiff, Jade Larissa. *Burdens of Political Responsibility: Narrative and the Cultivation of Responsiveness.* New York: Cambridge University Press, 2014.

Schlesinger, Arthur M., Jr. "Reinhold Niebuhr's Role in American Political Thought and Life." In *Reinhold Niebuhr: His Religious, Social, and Political Thought,* ed. Charles W. Kegley and Robert W. Bretall, 126–150. New York: Macmillan, 1956.

——. *The Vital Center: The Politics of Freedom.* Boston: Houghton Mifflin, 1962.

——. "The New Mood in Politics." In *The Politics of Hope and The Bitter Heritage: American Liberalism in the 1960s,* 105–120. Princeton, NJ: Princeton University Press, 2007.

Schumpeter, Joseph A. *Capitalism, Socialism and Democracy.* New York: Harper, 1942.

——. "Review of *The Road to Serfdom.*" *Journal of Political Economy* 54, no. 3 (1946): 269–270.

Seidelman, Raymond, with the assistance of Edward J. Harpham. *Disenchanted Realists: Political Science and the American Crisis, 1884–1984.* Albany: State University of New York Press, 1985.

Shapley, Deborah. *Promise and Power: The Life and Times of Robert McNamara.* Boston: Little, Brown, 1993.

Shearmur, Jeremy. "Hayek, Keynes, and the State." *History of Economics Review* 26, no. 1 (1997): 68–82.

———. "Hayek's Politics." In *The Cambridge Companion to Hayek,* ed. Edward Feser, 148–170. Cambridge: Cambridge University Press, 2006.

Shils, Edward. "Authoritarianism: 'Right' and 'Left.'" In *Studies in the Scope and Method of "The Authoritarian Personality,"* ed. Richard Christie and Marie Jahoda, 24–49. Glencoe, IL: Free Press, 1954.

———. "Ideology and Civility: On the Politics of the Intellectual." *Sewanee Review* 66, no. 3 (1958): 450–480.

Shklar, Judith N. *After Utopia: The Decline of Political Faith.* Princeton, NJ: Princeton University Press, 1957.

Shweder, Richard A., and Robert Alan LeVine, eds. *Culture Theory: Essays on Mind, Self, and Emotion.* New York: Cambridge University Press, 1984.

Simon, Herbert A. "On the Application of Servomechanism Theory in the Study of Production Control." *Econometrica* 20, no. 2 (1952): 247–268.

———. "Notes on the Observation and Measurement of Political Power." *Journal of Politics* 15, no. 4 (1953): 500–516.

———. "A Behavioral Model of Rational Choice." *Quarterly Journal of Economics* 69, no. 1 (1955): 99–118.

———. *Administrative Behavior: A Study of Decision-Making Processes in Administrative Organizations.* 4th ed. New York: Free Press, 1997.

Simpson, Christopher. *Science of Coercion: Communication Research and Psychological Warfare, 1945–1960.* New York: Oxford University Press, 1996.

———. ed. *Universities and Empire: Money and Politics in the Social Sciences during the Cold War.* New York: New Press, 1998.

Skinner, Quentin. "The Empirical Theorists of Democracy and Their Critics: A Plague on Both Their Houses." *Political Theory* 1, no. 3 (1973): 287–306.

Smith, T. V. "Review of *The Road to Serfdom.*" *Ethics* 55, no. 3 (1945): 224–226.

Solevey, Mark. *Shaky Foundations: The Politics-Patronage-Social Science Nexus in Cold War America.* New Brunswick, NJ: Rutgers University Press, 2013.

Solomon, Robert C. *The Passions: The Myth and Nature of Human Emotion.* Garden City, NY: Anchor Press, 1976.

Son, Kyong-Min. "A Discordant Universe of Pluralisms: Response to Wenman." *Political Theory* 43, no. 4 (2015): 533–540.

Sorzano, J. S. "David Easton and the Invisible Hand." *American Political Science Review* 69, no. 1 (1975): 91–106.

Soule, George. "How Long Prosperity?" *New Republic* 45 (February 3, 1926): 289–291.

———. "The Boon of Falling Prices." *New Republic* 50 (May 11, 1927): 328–330.

———. "Are Depressions Avoidable?" *New Republic* 65 (February 11, 1931): 342–344.

———. "Gold and the Industrial Depression." *New Republic* 64 (November 12, 1931): 339–343.

Spiro, Herbert, and Benjamin R. Barber. "Counter-Ideological Uses of 'Totalitarianism.'" *Political Society* 1, no. 1 (1970): 3–21.

Stears, Marc. *Demanding Democracy: American Radicals in Search of a New Politics.* Princeton, NJ: Princeton University Press, 2010.

Streeck, Wolfgang. *Buying Time: The Delayed Crisis of Democratic Capitalism.* London: Verso, 2014.

Suchting, W. A. "Marx and Hannah Arendt's *The Human Condition.*" *Ethics* 73, no. 1 (1962): 47–55.

Swedberg, Richard. *Schumpeter: A Biography.* Princeton, NJ: Princeton University Press, 1991.

Terada, Rei. *Feeling in Theory.* Cambridge, MA: Harvard University Press, 2001.

Thiele, Leslie Paul. *The Heart of Judgment: Practical Wisdom, Neuroscience, and Narrative.* New York: Cambridge University Press, 2006.

——. "The Ontology of Action: Arendt and the Role of Narrative." *Theory and Event* 12, no. 4 (2009). https://muse.jhu.edu/article/368584.

Thomas, William. *Rational Action: The Sciences of Policy in Britain and America, 1940–1960.* Cambridge, MA: MIT Press, 2015.

Tomkins, Silvan S. "Affect Theory." In *Approaches to Emotion,* ed. Klaus R. Scherer and Paul Ekman, 163–195. Hillsdale, NJ: L. Erlbaum Associates, 1984.

——. "The Socialization of Affect and the Resultant Ideo-Affective Postures Which Evoke Resonance to the Ideological Polarity." In *Exploring Affect: The Selected Writings of Silvan S. Tomkins,* ed. E. Virginia Demos, 168–195. Cambridge: Cambridge University Press, 1995.

——. "What Are Affects?" In *Shame and Its Sisters: A Silvan Tomkins Reader,* ed. Eve Kosofsky Sedgwick and Adam Frank, 33–74. Durham, NC: Duke University Press, 1995.

Torcal, Mariano, and José R. Montero, *Political Disaffection in Contemporary Democracies: Social Capital, Institutions and Politics.* London: Routledge, 2006.

Truman, David. *The Governmental Process: Political Interests and Public Opinion.* New York: Knopf, 1951.

Tsao, Roy T. "Arendt against Athens: Rereading *The Human Condition.*" *Political Theory* 30, no. 1 (2002): 97–123.

Ulrich, Werner. "A Critique of Pure Cybernetic Reason: The Chilean Experience with Cybernetics." *Journal of Applied Systems Analysis* 8 (1981): 33–59.

Umpleby, Stuart A., and Eric B. Dent. "The Origins and Purposes of Several Traditions in Systems Theory and Cybernetics." *Cybernetics and Systems* 30, no. 2 (1999): 79–103.

Urbinati, Nadia. "Representation as Advocacy: A Study of Democratic Deliberation." *Political Theory* 28, no. 6 (2000): 758–786.

——. "Continuity and Rupture: The Power of Judgment in Democratic Representation." *Constellations* 12, no. 2 (2005): 194–222.

——. *Democracy Disfigured: Opinion, Truth, and the People.* Cambridge, MA: Harvard University Press, 2014.

——. "Reflections on the Meaning of the 'Crisis of Democracy.'" *Democratic Theory* 3, no. 1 (2016): 6–31.

Urbinati, Nadia, and Mark E. Warren. "The Concept of Representation in Contemporary Democratic Theory." *Annual Review of Political Science* 11, no. 1 (2008): 387–412.

Vázquez-Arroyo, Antonio Y. "Liberal Democracy and Neoliberalism: A Critical Juxtaposition." *New Political Science* 30, no. 2 (2008): 127–159.

——. "Sheldon S. Wolin and the Historicity of Political Thought." *Good Society* 24, no. 2 (2015): 146–163.

——. *Political Responsibility.* New York: Columbia University Press, 2016.

Verba, Sidney. "Organizational Membership and Democratic Consensus." *Journal of Politics* 27, no. 3 (1965): 467–497.

Villa, Dana R. "Beyond Good and Evil: Arendt, Nietzsche, and the Aestheticization of Political Action." *Political Theory* 20, no. 2 (1992): 274–308.

——. *Arendt and Heidegger: The Fate of the Political.* Princeton, NJ: Princeton University Press, 1996.

——, ed. *The Cambridge Companion to Hannah Arendt.* Cambridge: Cambridge University Press, 2000.

Voegelin, Eric. "The Origins of Totalitarianism." *Review of Politics* 15, no. 1 (1953): 68–76.

——. "The New Science of Politics." In *Modernity without Restraint,* 75–242. Columbia: University of Missouri Press, 2000.

von Bertalanffy, Ludwig. *General Systems Theory.* New York: Braziller, 1968.

Waldner, David, and Ellen Lust. "Unwelcome Change: Coming to Terms with Democratic Backsliding." *Annual Review of Political Science* 21, no. 1 (2018): 93–113.

Walker, Jack L. "A Critique of Elitist Theory of Democracy." *American Political Science Review* 60, no. 2 (1966): 285–295.

Walzer, Michael. *Spheres of Justice: A Defense of Pluralism and Equality.* New York: Basic Books, 1983.

Waring, Stephen P. "Cold Calculus: The Cold War and Operations Research." *Radical History Review* 63 (1995): 29–51.

Warren, Mark E., and Hilary Pearse, eds. *Designing Deliberative Democracy: The British Columbia Citizens Assembly.* New York: Cambridge University Press, 2008.

Weintraub, E. Roy. *How Economics Became a Mathematical Science.* Durham, NC: Duke University Press, 2002.

Wenman, Mark. "William E. Connolly: Resuming the Pluralist Tradition in American Political Science." *Political Theory* 43, no. 1 (2015): 54–79.

Westbrook, Robert B. *John Dewey and American Democracy.* Ithaca, NY: Cornell University Press, 1999.

White, Morton G. *Social Thought in America: Revolt against Formalism.* New York: Viking, 1949.

White, Stephen K. *Sustaining Affirmation: The Strengths of Weak Ontology in Political Theory.* Princeton, NJ: Princeton University Press, 2000.

Wiebe, Robert H. *The Search for Order, 1877–1920.* New York: Hill and Wang, 1967.

Wiener, Norbert. *I Am a Mathematician.* Garden City, NY: Doubleday, 1956.

Wildavsky, Aaron. "The Political Economy of Efficiency: Cost-Benefit Analysis, Systems Analysis, and Program Budgeting." *Public Administration Review* 26, no. 4 (1966): 292–310.

Wohlstetter, Albert. "Analysis and Design of Conflict Systems." In *Analysis for Military Decisions,* ed. E. S. Quade, 103–148. Santa Monica, CA: RAND, 1964.

Wolfe, Alan. *America's Impasse: The Rise and Fall of the Politics of Growth.* New York: Pantheon, 1981.

Wolff, Robert Paul. "Beyond Tolerance." In *A Critique of Pure Tolerance,* by Robert Paul Wolff, Barrington Moore Jr., and Herbert Marcuse, 3–52. Boston: Beacon Press, 1965.

Wolin, Sheldon S. "Hannah Arendt: Democracy and the Political." *Salmagundi* 60 (Spring–Summer 1983): 3–19.

——. "Fugitive Democracy." *Constellations* 1, no. 1 (1994): 11–25.

——. "Norm and Form: The Constitutionalizing of Democracy." In *Athenian Political Thought and the Reconstruction of American Democracy*, ed. J. Peter Euben, Josiah Ober, and John R. Wallach, 29–58. Ithaca, NY: Cornell University Press, 1994.

——. *Democracy Incorporated: Managed Democracy and the Specter of Inverted Totalitarianism.* Princeton, NJ: Princeton University Press, 2008.

Xenos, Nicholas. "Refugees: The Modern Political Condition." *Alternatives: Global, Local, Political* 18, no. 4 (1993): 419–430.

Yarrow, Andrew L. "Selling a New Vision of America to the World: Changing Messages in Early U.S. Cold War Print Propaganda." *Journal of Cold War Studies* 11, no. 4 (2009): 3–45.

Young, Iris Marion. *Inclusion and Democracy.* Oxford: Oxford University Press, 2000.

Young, Stephanie Caroline. "Power and the Purse: Defense Budgeting and American Politics, 1947–1972." PhD diss., University of California, Berkeley, 2010.

Young-Bruehl, Elisabeth. *Hannah Arendt: For Love of the World.* New Haven, CT: Yale University Press, 1982.

Zajonc, Robert. "On the Primacy of Affect." In *Approaches to Emotion,* ed. Klaus R. Scherer and Paul Ekman, 259–270. Hillsdale, NJ: L. Erlbaum Associates.

Zerilli, Linda M. G. "We Feel Our Freedom: Imagination and Judgment in the Thought of Hannah Arendt." *Political Theory* 33, no. 2 (2005): 158–188.

INDEX